RABINDRASANGEET VICHITRA
(Rabindrasangeet Miscellany)

About the author

Santidev Ghosh, the son of Kalimohan, a close associate of Rabindranath Tagore in the setting up the Rural Reconstruction Unit at Visva-Bharati, and Monorama Devi, was born on 24 Baisakh 1317 (May 07, 1910) in Chandpur in the erstwhile East Pakistan.

Santidev had his school education at the Santiniketan Ashrama Vidyalaya which Tagore had founded in 1901. This is where he acquired proficiency in music, dance and acting under the direct guidance of the Poet himself and Dinendranath. As Tagore's emissary, he visited Sri Lanka, Burma and Indonesia to learn music and dance of neighbouring countries.

Santidev joined Visva-Bharati in 1930 as a teacher. He married Smt. Ila Ghosh in 1946. Later he became Professor and Head of the Department of Rabindra Music and Dance at Sangit-Bhavana, Visva-Bharati. He also served as the Principal of the institute between 1964-68 and 1971-73.

Santidev was appointed a member of the Advisory Board of Akashvani, Calcutta in 1948 and served as a member of the Publication Committee of the Sangeet-Natak Academy, New Delhi (1956-60). He was the President of the Music Section of Prabasi Bango Sahitya Sammelan and Assam Sahitya Sammelan (1964). The prolific singer widely travelled in India and abroad. He visited the United Kingdom, Japan, Bangladesh, Sri Lanka and the former USSR in order to acquaint himself with the culture and traditions of those countries and also propagating ideals of Rabindranath.

Santidev has to his credit quite a few authentic publications on the subject Music and Dance. They include *Rabindra Sangeet* (Tagore Music). *Java O Balir Nrityageet* (Music and Dance of Java and Bali), *Rupakar Nandalal* (Artist Nandalal), *Bharatiya Gramin Sanskriti* (Folk Culture in India), *Rabindranather Sikshadarshe Sangit O Nritya (Music and Dance in Rabindranath's Educational Philosophy), Gurudev Rabindranath O Adhunik Bharatiya Nritya* (Gurudev Rabindranath and Dances of Modern India), Rabindra Sangeet, Vichitra (Rabindra Sangeet Miscellany), *Nrityakala O Rabindranath* (The Art of Dance in the Eyes of Rabindranath) and *Jiboner Dhrubatara* (The Polestar of Life), his autobiography.

Santidev's proficiency in the fields of Music and Dance has been richly rewarded. He was awarded the Padma Bhushan by the Government of India in 1985, Deshikottama by Visva-Bharati in the same year. He also received Honorary D. Litt. from Burdwan and Rabindra Bharati Universities in 1991 and 1990 respectively. West Bengal Government honoured him with the Allauddin Puraskar (1997) and Tamraphalak (1981). He was also a recipient of the Ananda Puraskar and Rathindra Puraskar. He was honoured with a Special Medal from Russia on Tagore's Birth Centenary in 1961. He also served as a Fellow, Sangeet Natak Academy, New Delhi and Rabindra Tattvacharya at the Tagore Research Institute, Kolkata.

Santidev died on 1 December 1999.

RABINDRASANGEET VICHITRA
(Rabindra Sangeet Miscellany)

Santidev Ghosh

Translated by
Mohit Chakrabarti

CONCEPT PUBLISHING COMPANY, NEW DELHI-110059

Cataloging in Publication Data—DK
Courtesy: D.K. Agencies (P) Ltd. <docinfo@dkagencies.com>

Ghosh, Santidev, 1910-1999.
[Rabīndrasaṅgīta bicitra. English] Rabindrasangeet vichitra = Rabindra sangeet miscellany / Santidev Ghosh ; translated by Mohit Chakrabarti.
p. cm.
Translated from Bengali.
Includes index.
ISBN 8180693058

1. Tagore, Rabindranath, 1861-1941.—Criticism and interpretation. I. Chakrabarti, Mohit, 1941- II. Title. III. Title: Rabindra sangeet miscellany.

DDC 891.447 109 22

ISBN : 81-8069-305-8 (HB)

First Published 2006

Published and Printed by
Ashok Kumar Mittal
Concept Publishing Company
A/15-16, Commercial Block, Mohan Garden,
New Delhi-110059 (India)

Phones : 25351460, 25351794
Fax : 091-11-25357103
Email : publishing@conceptpub.com

DEDICATED

TO

THE AFFECTIONATE LATE SUBHAMOY GHOSH (BHULU)

— *Dada*

PREFACE

To sit at the feet of a great master is in itself a rare chance. To sit at the feet of a great scholar in Rabindrasangeet like Santidev Ghosh is, indeed, more than good fortune and a blessing.

Notwithstanding the unusual ukase in the arena of Rabindrasangeet that even now runs riot and, more often than not, tarnishes the image of Rabindranath Tagore as a incomparable contributor to the world of music, Santidev, like a lone but uncompromising crusader, has taken up the arduous task of shattering a lot of vicissitudes and disillusions about Rabindranath and his songs.

Santi-Da, as we endearingly and respectfully call him, is an enkindling institution by himself. Prior to his visit to Japan on an invitation to participate in the *Bharat Utsav* (Festival of India) as an exponent of Rabindrasangeet, he assigned to the present translator the task of translating his "*Rabindra Pravartita Nritya*" (*Desh,* Vinodan : 1987)- "Dance as introduced by Rabindranath"— which he read out in the *Bharat Utsav* in Japan. In fact, it is the everflowing fountain of inspiration of Santi-Da with which the present translator is abundantly blessed.

Words fail to express my endless gratitude to Santi-Da who has from time to time inspired me with suggestions and criticisms to improve the work.

I do not want to belittle by mere mentioning the generosity of Sri Prabhat Kumar Pal, my friend and colleague, who has always inspired me to complete my work.

I am grateful to my student, Smt. Subhra Seal, a former employee of the Rabindra-Bhavana, Visva-Bharati, Santiniketan, who has taken all the interest in supplying me with *The Visva-Bharati Quarterly* for the English rendering of Tagore's "*Amar Sonar Bangla, Ami tomay bhalobasi*" by Amiya Chakraborty, which is quoted in the Appendix.

I cannot but recall and owe my endless indebtedness and inspiration that Pranati Chakrabarti, my wife, has always provided me, leaving aside her personal interest for my excellence in the work. Now that she is my inmost endearing partner in tears of bereavement for life beyond life, I serenely listen to her soft-spoken loving and living words within myself : 'Beside you am I forever, march on!'

How can I repay her, and where?

Mohit Chakrabarti

Seemantika
Seemanto Palli
Santiniketan-731235
India

Photo for Rabindranath Tagore

A LETTER OF GURUDEV RABINDRANATH TO THE AUTHOR

Santiniketan
21.1.41

Affectionate Santi,

I have two points of advice only. You are brought up in this very Ashram. If you made yourself unholy even by any serious temptation through association with the cinema and the like, you will show dishonour to the Ashram and to me.

Second, the treasure of my songs is within you. It will be your duty to disseminate these songs correctly. I am in the position of your grandfather. Hope, you will keep my advice in mind.

With good wishes,

Rabindranath

CONTENTS

INTRODUCTION

The book *Rabindrasangeet* that I published in 1349 B.E. (1942) may be called an introduction to the revered Gurudev Rabindranath's life of music, dance and histrionics. For this very reason, being not satisfied, the interested readers time and again requested me to write on this part of the life of Gurudev in greater detail. I did not get time to comply with that request under heavy pressure in my life as a teacher in Santiniketan. In spite of that, it was due to the eagerness and enthusiasm for the editors of a few journals that I did not discontinue writing *in toto* but even under constraints I have been compelled to write now again. These very writings have been arranged and published in this *Rabindrasangeet Vichitra (Rabindrasangeet Miscellany).*

Music, dance and drama have a very respectful position in the manifestation of the diverse avenues of the life of the revered Gurudev. Just as he had a deep devotion to the Indian heritage, so also had he that same towards the European culture. He also accepted that in his creative work. But at the time of expression, the synchronized Indian form was revealed.

I firmly believe that there is the necessity of a lot of time to complete writing about this life of the revered Gurudev because first, one will have to sincerely find out like a real historian and researcher many important news about his life as a musician, that has still remained unpublished. In addition to this, there will be the need for direct contact between the history of the Bengali music and culture of the nineteenth century and all the songs composed in the Bengali language. Just after collecting historical facts of Gurudev's life as a musician and of those of the Bengali music and after advancing a bit necessary to be acquainted with the diverse trends of the music of Bengal, I have been able to distinctly feel its importance. It is possible for me alone to complete this vast span of work. Many persons should come forward to undertake this responsibility enthusiastically. And through this conjoint endeavour, it will be possible to know Gurudev especially as a creator- inheritor of the Bengali music and culture of the last century and the significance of his creation by developing the trend of music of the last century in conformity with the new age.

I had the opportunity to go through many books on music in the Bengali language published in the nineteenth and the twentieth centuries and a pretty few books and essays on historical research bearing expensive ideas of the cultural trend of Bengal of the last century. I have been profusely assisted by these books and essays at the time of writing the essays of the book *Rabindrasangeet Vichitra (Rabindrasangeet Miscellany).* I gratefully acknowledge this. I am also grateful to Sri Sagarmoy Ghosh and Sri Amitabha Choudhury whose encouragement and assistance quickened the publication of this book *Rabindrasangeet Vichitra (Rabindrasangeet Miscellany).*

Vaisakh 1379
April 1972

Santidev Ghosh

1 RABINDRANATH'S THOUGHTS ON MUSIC

The revered Gurudev Rabindranath was a composer of songs and a very fine singer. Besides these, the quality that is manifested in him as an interpreter of music is not to be found in any of his contemporary music composer or singer. The analytical discussions on the nature of all music—Indian or European—that he has left behind in written form are uparalleled in Bengal's literature on music. He has been able to marvellously introduce each of those with dexterity. Apart from these, if one is attuned to his thoughts on the role of music in human life, one would be able to eliminate the narrowness nursed in the so-called educated mind. From a study of those writings, it is clearly understood that he never saw music as an object of apparent luxury but, like the vision of a meditator, looked by entering very intensely into the inner world of music. To clarify this point, I am quoting a few extracts from his writings. The theme of the first one is our song. Gurudev writes :

> "Although in childhood, I did not naturally learn how to sing as usual, fortunately my mind was flooded with the inherent permanent effect of music. At that time, there was no end to pursuit of songs in our house. Vishnu Chakrabarti was the Acharya of music. He was an expert in Hindusthani music. In my boyhood, as a consequence, the songs I was habituated to hear all the time were not ones of the amateur group. That was why the pose of the *Kaloati* songs instinctively accumulated within me. Those who are very fastidious about the purity of *raga-ragini* are hardly to be compared with me. That is to say : in spite of having some ideal on the finer intricacies of tuning, my mind did not encounter impediments in practice, but an orientation in general on the nature and 'rasa' of *Kaloati* songs was firmly established in my inner mind".

However, when I think over the natural trends and different dimensions of expression of the treasures of the permanent effect inherent in songs that filled in my mind in boyhood, I can understand the nature of the country of ours about songs.

In accordance with the words of Gurudev, "The tune that treasured up in my mind appeared in unison with words at the time of its expression. From boyhood, when my intense love for songs wanted to manifest itself, it did not create the unmixed form of music. With the marriage of music and poetry, it was rather difficult to apprehend which one was greater.

The water that is stored in the cloud in the form of vapour in the sky manifests itself in the very shower of rains. The juice that is secretly accumulated in a tree is expressed in mingled forms through leaves and flowers. In case of music also, there are manifestations of these forms. One is in the form of pure music and the other through a mixed form with poetry. There are differences in nature in man. The twofold form of expression of music takes place in accordance with these differences. This is evident in Hindusthan and Bengal. Undeniably, music in Bengal is a companion to poetry, if not a follower. But, in the Western Hindustan, it is established by itself. Its words 'follow like a shadow'. Leaving aside *Bhajan*-music, we will see that music, in the West, which takes the help of sentences makes the latter very insignificant. Music there is totally independent; it expresses itself alone".

"In Bengal, the natural manifestation of the emotions of the heart is in literature. The public will drink joyfully out of it for time immemorial— this is evident from the honey-comb of literature. It is words alone for which the Bengalees feel an attraction from the heart. For this very reason, in India, the meditation for words was the most revealing one in this very province. But the fullness of expression of human being cannot be had in words alone, for this music, as an independent entity, is extinct in Bengal. It has its seat beside the very words."

Gurudev has got its evidence in *Kirtan.* According to him, "The music of the *Kirtan* is exquisite, but its significance lies in unison between the music and the built-in rhymed lines of poetry. Its *raslila* is, as it were, with the *padavalis.* It will not at all tolerate uniqueness. The uniqueness of music is best revealed in instruments. Bengal has no instrument of her own. .... Our flute of the cowboy or the *ektara* of the *Vairagi* is nothing in comparison to *Vina, Ravav, Sarod,*

Sitar, Esraz, Sarangi etc. Besides this, it is a shame on our part to tolerate the introduction of a musical instrument named concert in Bengal as a terrible mockery to public percussion instrument, and it is a crime on our part to derive 'joy' out of this.

"By observing these symptoms I believe, the development of music in association with poetry in Bengal would be a peculiar thing. There would be no customary unity of *raga-raginis* in it, as the same is not to be found in *Kirtan.* In other words, songs would lose their distinctive features; there would be pitfalls of rules because it would have to negotiate the claim of words. But, in such a marriage between music and words, if reciprocal peculiarities are not mutually consolidated in synchronization, union becomes *sans* loveliness. For this, in a song, words are to compromise with it for the sake of the lyric; they are to become purposeful of the tune. However, poetry and fine arts of this type would, as I think, gradually become extensive. At least, in the history of my own poetics, I see that to compose songs that is to unify words with music only has now become my prime meditation."

Gurudev knew : "Where music excels in its own uniqueness, the purity of its rules and regulations revealed cannot be sustained as a song in association with words but if one is capable of acquiring the reciprocal musical patterns, one gets the appropriate right to make an exception to the rule. In poetry, too, there are rhyme patterns. A great poet does not endeavour to cautiously maintain that pattern pin-pointedly. That is, he rules over rules even, but even to administer those rules, he cannot but admit the rules. Where uniqueness stands for indiscipline, fine arts enjoy holidays there. For this, if one wants to allow freedom of one's power of creativity, one necessitates education and the ability to control more.

"We have two kinds of food. One is for necessity and the other sans necessity. One is rice and the other *amrita* (nectar). We are equal to all beasts and creatures of the earth in our hunger for food, but in our hunger for the nectar, we are in the group of gods in heaven. Music is one of the manifold trends of the nectar.

"It is to be remembered that whatever is *amrita*, that which surmounts the necessity and expresses itself upholds the highest glory of humanity. The nation which is a glutton is only meeting her daily demands; in death alone she receives her extinction. Greece has remained immortal even today not in her wealth, affluence and national solidarity but essentially because of her creation as the joy of the soul, whatsoever. There is a responsibility to each nation and this is to create one's own heavenly world on earth. Greece is living in her own created world of heaven. Music is the expression of joy of the human being; it is beyond eliminating the wants of his own of a human being, and so, it is for all mankind and for all times. The grandeur of a kingdom or an empire is destroyed, but the manifestation of this joy is endless.

"Those terrible old persons who evaluated the price of a thing as it weighs, consider the essence to be equivalent to excess, and look down upon performing fine arts like music as a luxury. They do not know that beauty heralds the hero. The force that expresses itself merely as a force is bare wrestling, but the true expression of force is beauty".

The total energy of a tree is revealed in its flower. It alone exists in its broad trunk, but the fruit that it brings forth in its flower, foretells the forest of the future in its seeds, and this is its immortality. In literature, music and in fine arts of different kinds, the very life-force makes immortality a reality—not in the office or in the courts, nor again, in mills and factories. The *Upanishad* says, none by birth becomes immortal; those who have understood the infinite, become immortal—*"Amritaste bhavanti"*. In the understanding of wants follow the cloth mill, the factories for jute sacks, in the understanding of the infinite is the birth of music, we are creators. The creator who reigns by sitting on the throne of the sun and the moon heralds the learned with the crown and says, "Bravo! your tune is synonymous with me. How glorified that learned man is and how does he complete his life on earth! His soul becomes a permanent one beside His assembly of the Immortal."

It is by specially feeling this need for music in human life that Gurudev stood against the educational policies of the educationists indifferent to contemporary fine arts and music like a revolutionary and categorically states at the time of establishing Santiniketan, and, later on, Visva-Bharati : "In the midst of this narrowness in education, our life has gradually become maimed. So it would not be appropriate to allow this. Music and fine arts will have be honoured in the proposal that we have made for setting up this centre of education.

In the different periods and in different provinces of India, the different procedures that are strewn in distorted forms in case of music and fine arts will have to be revived from the different stratas of the society and will have to be integrated.

"In this way the models for our sense of appreciation and taste will be correctly developed. Our music and fine arts will, then, manifest in beauty and realty. Then we will be able to truly and cautiously evaluate foreign arts, and even though we will accept ideas and concepts from these, we will not be blamed with the offence of stealing."

Prior to setting up Visva-Bharati, Gurudev said, "If Visva-Bharati is established, the study of Indian music and painting will be her main part : let this be our resolution."

We have come to know through Gurudev's thoughts on music how he looked at the music of the different stratas of India or how he felt the same and why he gave an honourable place to music in the education of Santiniketan. But he was a traveller trotting the avenues of the world. So by establishing Visva-Bharati he said that there the world makes its home in a single nest. It is, therefore, not possible for the music-interested Gurudev to remain aside with the music of his own country only. In his thoughts on music, we also see the reflection of the music of the different countries of the world. Specially, we come across his numerous writings on the European music. He has studied, heard and pondered over that music. He has tried to understand and draw the attention of everyone to the points of differences and unity with the Indian music.

In analysing the nature of the European music, Gurudev has said, "By paying attention to the English music that was previously laughed at to be enjoyed, one receives greater enjoyment. At present, some sort of taste has been developed, through practice, on the European music, and it is understood that if practised, one can have a total essence out of the European music. It is needless to specially refer to my likings for our indigenous music. But there is no doubt about a great deal of difference between them.

"To me, the main point of difference between the English songs and our songs is that the English music is one of the human world, while our music is one of Nature vast and lonely, that is not definite, unspeakable, serene and sombre. The gravity and sombreness among the vast *raginis* like *Kanada, Tori*, etc., are as if, not of a particular person. They are, as it were, of this companionless universe on the edge of the shoreless infinite".

"This characteristic feature of the music of our country greatly appeals me. Different *raginis* related to the morning, noon, afternoon, evening, mid-night, the rains or the spring have been composed in our country. The new *raginis* that are going on in the secret *nahabatkhana* (musical entry gate) of the *khasmahal* (main apartment) of the Lord of the Universe have appealed the inward ears of our learned persons. That there is a braver expression of the mind at the backdrop of outward expression is informed by the *Tori kanada.*

"Harmony or assonance of voice is the main factor in the European music whereas the grammar of *raga-raginis* is the sine qua non of our music. I have felt it again and again that our songs surpass our happiness or sorrow. On our marriage occasions, *sahana* goes on in the *rasanchowki* (a platform for music at the entrance). But where do the waves of amusement play in the tune of that *sahana*? There is not a least of the restlessness of youth in it. That is sombre empathy in every fold of its *meed.* In our country, playing on the foreign band along with *shahnai* in the modern marriage is a part of affluent barbarities. The difference between the two is very clear. The earth is trembled with the assembly of joy and merriments derived out of the tunes of the foreign band. The overflow of the tune of the band is also the same as the crowd, their laughing conversations, dress and constumes, exaggerated exhibitionism in flowers, leaves and light. But the dark night that remains silent by encompassing the assembly of amusement of the wedding ceremony where the unending function of people beyond people is enkindled with the serene halo of the silent meeting of the stars, the tune of *sahana* enters with the message of that place, our music slowly opens the main gateway to the amusement hall of mankind and welcomes the endless amidst the crowd. Our music is of a singer's solo music. But it is not one for a single corner, it is one throughout the world."

"The European music is as if entangled with the realistic world of man. So we see, the tune of the European song can be applied by considering incidents and descriptions of all kinds. The songs of Europe greatly attracted my heart from one end. It seemed to me that this song is romantic. It is very difficult to say through analysis what actually romantic is. But to speak in general, the romantic aspect is one of varieties, affluence. It is an aspect that embraces the eternal play of waves in the sea of life, an aspect of the criss-cross of light and shadow on the unending restlessness of speed. It is expressing the diversities of human life in the translated form through the tunes of the song."

"In the European music, the master is restrained with far greater hard and fast rules. The composer of the song signals the boundaries of the music in his own hands, the master strictly conforms to it. That he should remain very squeezed is not the fact, but, again the avenues of his unusual thumping are also closed. In every song of Europe, there is a characteristic feature. The master is to maintain it cautiously and proceed accordingly. In this music, in accordance with the wishes of the composer himself, slackness in beats takes place in the middle, and each time the song is not allowed to heave a sigh of relief in front of the *sam* (middle) by making an account of its beats. This is because, the composer studies the needs of the music in full and delimits its boundaries. Consequently, the quarrel between the tune and the beat is arrested. The *bol* (wordings in music) of the European music is not to be obtained in *mridanga.* It takes the same seat in the songs of harmony in an endearing form".

"In our country, to strive for music is fundamental; our all complexities are concerned with that music. In Europe, practice of voice is fundamental, they win over the impossible with that voice. Those who are genuine audience in our country remain satisfied only with hearing the song sung, the audience of Europe hear the song."

Notwithstanding Gurudev's observation on basic differences between the music of two countries, he did not say that the union between the two is not at all possible. According to him, "In music, we are in need of an external association. If we are well introduced with the European music, we will be able to learn how we can truly use our music greatly".

In almost every country of Asia today there is a unison of ideas between the East and the West. There is a possibility of new creation with this unison. In the first stage of this unison the differences in colour between the two trends sustain, the emphasis on imitation does not die down. But sincere union gradually takes place if there is life force in that union. Like a grafted tree, the difference between the new and the old is eliminated and the speciality of juice grows in the fruit. This has happened in our modern literature.

I don't understand why it will not take place in music, too. We are waiting for the mind through which this union is possible. If the study of the European music would be the same as that of the European literature that was spread among the educated oriental society, there would undoubtedly have been a new avenue of expression of *rasa* (appreciation) in the Eastern music.

" ..... who can emphatically say that even though it admits the assonance of voice, our *raga-raginis* do not at all safeguard themselves? We cannot ascertain beforehand, through hard and fast rules, what performance the force of creation can accomplish. But the introduction of new aspects in creation is possible only by the powerfully talented; it is not an act of the novice or the mediocre. Like the European literature, our music has also a very great wealth. If we do not understand it, that would indicate our poverty in the power of sensibilities. If it is at all not possible to accept that, aristocracy is not justified through that."

"But, then, it is also certain that, if we want to introduce harmony in our songs, its pattern would be different. At least, if it wants to go ahead by passing the main tune, it would be an adamant affair on its part."

"If our vast *tan kartal* is transferred to the department of harmony, the original nature and poignancy of the original song are saved and its course of efflorescence remains wide open."

2 THE INFLUENCE OF FOREIGN CULTURE ON BENGALEE LIFE

In the city of Calcutta the English got the opportunity to live comfortably and peacefully after the Battle of Plassey (1757). To speak frankly, from then onwards, they truly became the king of Bengal. Afterwards, the Nawabs who remained in power, were simply at the whims of the English, having practically no power of their own. Naturally, the style of the way of life of the English in Calcutta was changed. Everyone had enough money. At the same time they were greatly desirous of entertaining their minds with dance, music, theatre and so on in their society. Amateur music clubs and theatre groups were established at a great cost. In Calcutta, the first theatre on the European model was set up in 1779. The practice of the European instrumental music and vocal music, the European dance, opera, ball dance, military band etc. continued well. The singers, percussioners, dancers and danceuses and actors were also brought from England. In the beginning, the amateur group was the principal one for many years. In 1783, in an amateur theatre like this, famous dramas like Shakespeare's *Hamlet, King Lear, Othello, Richard III* etc. had been well acted. Before that, there was no place for women in the European theatre. In the role of women, men played their parts in the costumes and dresses of women. In 1783, the women of Europe were first permitted to play in the theatre with men. In those days, the chief source of entertainment of the Europeans was to attend the concert and songs in the club or witness acting in the theatre.

Very often the dance of professional dancers took place. Manifold instrumental music like symphony, sonneta etc. of famous composers received very great appreciation.

1795-96 is a memorable year in the history of the theatre of Bengal. Herasim Levadev, a Russsian musician and bandmaster, came to Calcutta and by making translation of two English dramas, made arrangements for acting by the Bengalee actors and actresses. A

Bengalee named Golaknath Das who was the chief assistant of Levadev helped with this translation of the drama by instilling it with the lyrics of the poems of Bharatchandra. To witness the acting of this drama, many people of the Bengalee Society came along with the English.

Towards the very beginning of the nineteenth century, in and around Calcutta, that is the Europeans of the towns like Chandannagar, Kidderpore, Dum Dum etc. formed groups of the amateur concert and the theatre and made good arrangements for the entertainments of their mind. Among the men and women of the European Society, one knows from a study of their numerous letters how strong their aspirations were for spending the time by attending music and acting of dramas. An English lady states in a letter from Calcutta to her own country :

> "In winter, concerts and ball dances take place. One is to attend these performances through ticket. We are enjoying music conferences of diverse types. There is no other better avenue of spending time than attending the theatre in the evening".

That the English alone took main role in acting and music in Calcutta is not true. In that group, there were the Italians and the Germans. They had also enough influence on the European society of Calcutta.

In this era, great pomp and grandeur of music, ball dance of the female dancers, theatre, fancy dress, band etc. were associated with dining and drinks of the festive days of the English. By imitating them, the Indian rich society of Calcutta arranged foreign entertainments for the foreign princes on special occasions or in the feast at a great cost. Outside Calcutta, the rich Zamindar communities also did not lag behind in this affair, as it is known from the history of the Zamindar of Krishnanagar. "Formerly, among the people of this country the English band was known to the English who lived near Calcutta. It was not possible for people of distant places to bring them unless they could spend much. Girishchandra (1802-1841) of the royal family brought a group of English percussionists to Krishanagar and made arrangements of training for a few belonging to the cobbler families by them."

In those days, the Bengalees had no particular connection with the theatres founded by the English or the music club. Everything was totally an affair of the English. But, in 1813, when the English formed an amateur dramatic association named "The Chowringhee Theatre," Dwarakanath Tagore was found to be a member of the governing body. From this point of view, he is perhaps the only Bengalee member. We see him as its member upto 1835. When the theatre was about to be closed on account of debt, then Dwarakanath made an auction bid for more than Rupees thirty thousand and saved the theatre. A few years afterwards (1879), the theatre house was totally turned into ashes by fire. Prior to his first tour in England, Dwarakanath was associated with the "Louis"—another theatrical association.

In the first half of the nineteenth century, the influence of the English theatre was there among the other rich Bengalees of Calcutta. Prasannakumar Tagore of the Tagore house of Pathuriaghata was the chief of these enthusiasists. He formed an amateur theatre group, "The Hindu Theatre." Acting of English dramas only was performed. The Hindu Theatre continued well from 1831 upto 1835. Besides this, a group of Bengalees made arrangements, in 1805, for the acting of a Bengali drama named "Vidyasundar" on the model of the European theatre. The news item, on this acting, by the newpapers of that era is remarkable.

"Vidyasundar in Bengali, after the English fashion; it commences with music of orchestra which was very pleasing. The native musical instruments, such as the Sitar, the Sarangi, the Pakhawaj and others, were played by the Hindus, almost all the Brahmins, and among them, the violin was managed by Brajanath Goswami".

From the last half of the nineteenth century to the first half of the twentieth century, the introduction of Orchestra music that is greatly in vogue in the Bengalee theatre of Calcutta and is heard by us in the acting in *Jatra* performance even now, was, I presume, made at the very time of acting the drama named "Vidyasundar" in 1835. Another remarkable point of the news was the play on the violin by Brajanath Goswami. Prior to this, there is never any news item with regard to the play on a violin by a Bengalee. We do not get any information how Brajanath learnt playing on a violin. But this much has been known that in 1824, one could learn European songs and music from renowned teachers, at Rupees eight to sixteen per month, in an English club of Calcutta. Moreover, the rich Bengalees, too, of that era appointed separate teachers with a view to learning European music.

In those days, there was no scope for the Bengalees to act with the English. The English selected people from their own community and made them to act. The first exception to this was recorded in 1849. At that very time, a handsome Bengalee youth first participated in acting with the English. He acted a remarkable character of Shakespeare's famous drama *Othelio* and charmed every audience indigenous or foreign. The acting of the drama was held in *San-Suchi,* a theatre governed by the English. Just after this historical incident, great enthusiasm ushered forth among the Bengalees towards the Bengali drama in the English system. The new dramas in the Bengali language began to be acted on a new model by the amateur groups of the rich society. On July 31, 1857, a drama named "Ratnavali" was staged in the rest house of Jatindramohan Tagore at Belgachia. Jatindramohan Tagore himself was its main source of inspiration. Iswarchandra and Pratapchandra Sinha, the rich zamindars of Paikpara, were his assistants.

Jatindramohan gave assignments to Kshetramohan Goswami, the music teacher of his family and Jadunath Pal to organize an indigenous group of orchestra on the model of the European theatre. They also composed *gat* (tune-patterns) on the basis of indigenous *raga-raginis* effective to a chorus. In this concert, side by side with indigenous musical instruments, European instruments were also used. The instrumentalists wrote the *gats* (tune-patterns) on the paper in the newly introduced Bengali notations, placed it in front of them, and played on the instruments by seeing these as done in the European system. In Bengali, the first Bengali notations came out of this concert alone. Jatindramohan Tagore always participated in the theatre, operas and other musical performances of the English of Calcutta. He saw and heard all these and at the time of the acting of "Ratnavali" he was enthusiastic in using the indigenous concert in the drama. After the orchestra of the drama "Vidyasundar" in 1835, it was in this very drama "Ratnavali" where the enthusiasm for the music of the orchestra was seen anew. In 1859, when Jatindramohan Tagore formed an ameteur theatre and concert group at his own residence, foreign instruments were also used side by side with the indigenous ones, e.g. 2 violins, 2 tenors, 2 flutes, 1 violin cello, 1 clareonet and 1 double bass. Moreover, it is also known that Sourindramohan Tagore, the brother of Jatindramohan, appointed a German musician as a teacher at his own residence in order to know the European music thoroughly and studied European scriptures on music. Not only did he learn music himself, but he also taught the boys of the house and it was at his own encouragement that gave Krishnadhan Bandyopadhyay and Dakshinacharan Sen, the earlier students of music group, the opportunity to learn well. That Sourindramohan Tagore studied the European music very well can be known from his numerous publications of books, in English and Bengali, on music written by him. Those who have read "Geet-Sutradhar" by Krishnadhan Bandyopadhyay would easily feel how, after much poignant practice and study of the European music, it was possible for him to compose the book. The Indian orchestra group formed by Dakshinacharan Sen was known as the best group towards the latter half of the nineteenth century. In would not have been possible without a sound knowledge of the European music to achieve glory by him in that era by organising a chorus group of indigenous instruments.

The era of the ameteur theatre backed by the rich Bengalees of Calcutta ended in 1872 with the efforts of Girish Ghosh, Amritalal Bose and others. The origin of the professional theatre started from then onwards. They gave the name of this theatre as the "National Theatre". Amritalal had said that by attending the acting and hearing the song of the professional theatre and opera groups coming from abroad, he and many young persons like him were greatly encouraged to form a professional theatre group of that type. As a consequence, the "National Theatre" was set-up. A few years afterwards, with the initiative of this theatre, an acting performance of a musical drama in Bengali language was first made in Bengal in total imitation of the Italian opera. This drama, acted in 1879, is another significant incident in the history of the drama of Bengal.

One of its reasons was that a musical drama of this type was the first in the stage of Bengal. And the second reason was that this very drama saved easy avenues for revered Gurudev Rabindranath to write the musical drama "Valmiki Pratibha". I quote a few extracts published in contemporary newspapers on this musical drama acted in the National Theatre.

"For the last few years 'Sanskrit Jatra' has been acted in the National Theatre in the name of the opera. Instead, the directors have now advanced to show real acting through music.

"Just as there are one or two words and songs immediately following these in the professional *Jatra,* the directors are now showing real acting with music from the beginning to the end as done in the Italian opera with replies and counter replies and wailing soliloquies, Needless to say, this system is totally new in the dramatic society of Bengal and for that reason, it is difficult to play one's role.

"Last saturday a drama named "Kaminikunja" of the aforesaid musical drama type was staged at Rajani. As this type of drama was first acted, the theatre hall was filled with hundreds of audience".

".... The heroine. Srimati Kadamvini.... Her voice as high, beautiful as charming. She enamoured every audience by her dance and music."

After successful acting of the drama, a letter published in the column of letters in the newspaper is worth reference here. In the letter, the audience write :

> " We were, in the meantime, present in the auditorium for dramas in the acting of many persons interested in dramas, but such type of new incidence never came across us.... We hope, the directors of the auditorium for dramatic performances of this type would win the hearts of the public by introducing decent and best matters of this type".
>
> "If there was a play upon words between the pause of each music among persons interested in the drama "Kaminikunja", a revolution could have appeared in the acting of dramas on that day".

The editor himself protested against this letter. In reply, he has written :

> "It appears that the audience has a different taste. If there is a play upon words in between music, it cannot be called acting along with music. That is only a *Sanskrit Jatra*. The directors of the dramatic institutions give advertisements that 'Kaminikunja' is composed in accordance with the Italian opera. In fact, that alone is appropriate."

From this incident it is more or less understood that a totally music-drama which in the English language is called the opera, is, for the very first time, composed and acted in Bengal.

From the very beginning of the amateur theatre in Calcutta, the concert of the indigenous *gat* (tune-pattern) composed on the basis of the European drama was a compulsory part of the drama. For that, the rich had to appoint the groups of instrumentalists and bandmasters at a great cost of money. To eliminate the want of instrumentalists of foreign musical instruments , separate educational institutions also grew up. There the only assignment was to prepare the choric group and for the need of the group, train the youth. In the period of professional theatre, we come across a news through an advertisement published in the "Amrita Bazar Patrika", Janurary 1873. In it, the following matter is stated :

> "The Bowbazar Choric Society has been playing on the English instruments for the last four to five years by exerting serious labour. Five persons are required. Piano, Harmonium, Concertina, Flute, Flat-Flute. The Principal (Bandmaster), Parvaticharan Das, will teach".

From all these accounts, it is pretty understood that, in correspondence with the European Society, the Bengalees were first introduced with altogether a new trend of foreign dance, musical instruments and acting towards the end of the eighteenth century. Afterwards, it is seen towards the beginning of the nineteenth century that there was a great deal of interest for the study of this trend and it is seen towards the second half of this century that there is a great deal of endeavour to bring about harmony between the European and the Indian trends. Consequently, the orchestra of the indigenous *gat* (tune-pattern) in the indigenous and the foreign instruments, songs in the Bengali language and tragedies profusely rich in dance, national songs, in the Bengali language, the origin of the Bengali notations, the Indian books on music in the European notations, the extensive use of various European musical instruments with vocal songs in the *Jatra* and in the theatre and Bengali musical dramas in the model of the Italian Opera—all these were seen. Music academies and colleges and schools for learning music were established. The English government arranged for teaching the Indian music in the primary schools of the district of Bankura. Maharaj Sourindramohan Tagore himself composed books on songs for the covenience of teaching.

The Tagore family of Jarasanko was one of the educated rich of Calcutta. In this family, the first who was able to receive the right to be honoured in both the European and the Bengali societies of Calcutta was Dwarakanath Tagore, the grand-father of Gurudev Rabindranath. He was born in 1794. In his very youth, he was well established and well-known in Calcutta in education, wealth and esteem. He had a strong love for European education and culture. It is clearly known from his biography how deep his attraction was for European music and acting of dramas.

Towards the first half of the nineteenth century, an Englishman has left a description of Prince Dwarakanath Tagore, in his memoirs, after the latter's death, how he had seen and known the latter when he was staying in Calcutta. In it, we find :

> "Dwarakanath had the good taste to appreciate European music and theatricals and so quickly became enamoured of Italian opera, when in his own country, that he engaged one of the travelling artists to give him lesson in singing. No wonder, therefore, that he yielded to the intoxication of similar delight on a large scale when he arrived in England".

By constructing the residence at Jorasanko, in 1823, Dwarakanath invited many Indian and foreign distinguished persons in *Grihapravesh* (Entrance in the residence) ceremony at night. He arranged English music and dance to entertain them. That the guests were happy to participate in this occasion and returned in joy was expressed in the newspaper of those days. Dwarakanath Tagore had a rest house named "Belgachhia Villa" at Belgachhia, Calcutta. It was the property of the Tagore house of Jorasanko upto July 1, 1857. That house was afterwards made an auction bid by Raja Pratapchandra Sinha Bahadur of Paikpara. In this villa, the Viceroy with his companions was invited by Dwarakanath in November, 1836. The best European groups of singers and instrumentalists—Liston, Miss Harvey, Siemony—were appointed to entertain everyone with music on that day. The actors and actresses of the French Opera—Flobby, Madame la Marie, Walete, Ton—also came. The invitation ceremony for the Viceroy started with songs and music, in the middle, after dinner; foreign dance like Waltz, Coyodril, Gallop began.

When Lord Aucland came as Viceroy, he was also invited by Dwarakanath in the same way.

On February 25, 1841, too, in honour of Miss Emily Eden, Dwarakanath arranged dance and evening dinner at this villa. The dance continued upto midnight.

Maharshi Devendranath Tagore, his son, wrote in his autobiography on this : " In the garden of Belgacchia, a feast was held with unusual grandeur for the ladies like Miss Eden, the sister of the Governor General, and the Sahibs. The garden was absolutely turned into a heavenly residence with appearance, quality, status, beauty, dance, drinks and light." Moreover, we have already come to know from our discussion about the close intimacy between Dwarakanath and the English as a sponseror of the English Ameteur theatre group.

When Dwarakanath first went to England for the first time (1842), he took a few persons to look after him. In a letter of Satyendranath Tagore, the elder brother of Gurudev Rabindranath and Dwarakanath's grandson, we get a list of those persons. Satyendranath has written :

> "He (Dwarakanath) had 17 servants with him, among whom were two native servants. He had with him, besides a secretary, one interpreter, a German musician, and another gentleman, who, with his physician. Dr. Martin, would make a party of five. These were his constant companions."

It is also interesting to note here that in this troupe of Dwarakanath, there was also a German musician who was for all times appointed. While he was living in England, Dwarakanath came in close intimacy with Maxmueller, the indologist. Maxmueller has left behind a description of a day's incident of the life of Dwarakanath as a lover of music, in his memoirs. He has written :

> "Dwarakanath was greatly devoted to music, and he loved Italian and French music much. He sang and I played on the piano with that song. In this way, our days passed in joy. He had a very good voice. One day I told him to sing a purely Indian song. The song that he sang first was not exactly Indian. It was a Persian *Gajal* and I also did not get special flavour out of that. As I began to request him again and again to sing a purely Indian song, he smilingly said, 'You will not be able to enjoy that'. Then, in order to keep my request, he played on himself and sang a song. Truly speaking, I could not, in fact, enjoy anything. It seemed to me that in the song, there was neither any tune nor any rhythm nor even any harmony. When told about this, Dwarakanath said, 'You are all of the same type. If anything appears new to you or fails to win your heart, you immediately turn a deaf ear to that. When I first heard Italian musical song, I also did not find any interest, but, even then, I did not remain indifferent. I went on practising once again till I was able to enter deep into it. This happens in every subject'."

In 1844, during his tour in England for the second time, he bought an organ, sent it to his own country and wrote in a letter :

> "Prior to fixing the barrels of the organ, it is better to check the same through by Babbing Young. In it, some are set in the indigenous tune, the rest are with the Opera."

From this biography of Dwarakanath Tagore, it is clearly revealed that in this family he himself was the first inspirer in the practice of European music.

He practised with great sincerity. That trend continued in his family in the later period also and we come across that trend in Gurudev Rabindranath and his later descendents. Dwarakanath died in England in 1846.

We know very well about the love for national songs of Maharshi Devendranath Tagore, the son of Dwarakanath. But it is also known that in his early youth he sometimes practised in learning from an English teacher how to play on a European piano. As he was in favour of foreign instruments, in 1845, when the method of prayer was newly introduced in the *Brahmo Samaj* (society), the foreign instrument 'Accordian' was once used with *Brahma Sangeet*. When the harmonium was introduced in Calcutta, the use of this insturment came to a close.

Dwijendranath Tagore, the eldest son of Devendranath, also knew how to play on a piano, but he had no musical voice. He had a piano for his own use. Later on, Dwijendranth and his brother, Satyendranath, learnt how to play on a harmonium and accompanied with the music in the *Brahmo Samaj.* Gurudev has said about Dwijendranath : "He could not know how to sing a song. He could play on a foreign flute but that was not meant for the song it was simply for measuring the tune in different *raga-raginis* mathematically."

There is a significance in the expression 'measuring the tune'. The scientists in accoustics of Europe discovered that the sound derived from vibrations of equal distance that we hear is the musical sound.

In every second, vibration-oriented sounds from sixteen to forty-eight thousand in number reach our ears. No sound of more or less vibrations than the above can be heard. In the male and the female voice, 190-678 and 572-1606 sounds of vibration are expressed respectively. The lowest tune *sa* of the *Udara gram* or pitch that comes out the voice of a person, has 256 vibrations. The following analysis of vibrations of sounds may be mentioned :

Tunes		Number of Vibrations
Re	"	288
Ga	"	320
Ma	"	341
Pa	"	384
Dha	"	426
Ni	"	480

In the above way, if we double vibrations of the tune of *Udara,* we will get *Mudara* and if we make vibrations four times, we will encounter the tune of the pitch of "Tara". By reading the phonetics of foreign music, Dwijendranath experimented on the vibrations of the Indian *Suddh, Kadi* and *Komal raga-raginis* through playing on the flute.

Jyotirindranath Tagore was able to play on the piano, violin, harmonium, organ and other instruments very well. He tried to make an indigenous tune follow a moving ideal like a poem by taking a *gat* (tune-pattern) on the piano and trying to remodel it in the European rhyme, pause and maximization and minimization of sounds.

Hemendranath, Gurudev's third elder brother, was also greatly devoted to music. He made good arrangements for his sons and daughters to learn the European instrumental and vocal music along with the Indian music. Gurudev has said about Pratibha Devi, the daughter of Hemendranath :

> "In boyhood, Pratibha and I were brought up together. The third elder brother made Pratibha an expert in foreign music. With that we know that she was not allowed to forget the way to national song".
> "The quality of foreign songs is that tunes are very purely practised there. The ears become attuned and with the restraint of the piano, no slackness in beats is also allowed".

To explain how Pratibha Devi was expert in the practice of the European music, Pramatha Choudhury remarks : "She (Pratibha Devi) played clsssical foreign music on the piano. I have heard 'Funeral March' and 'Moonlight Sonata' at least a thousand times."

Indira Devi has said : " The twin stream of indigenous and foreign music endlessly flowed in his (Hemendranath's) room. He wanted to make his eldest daughter, Pratibhadidi, an expert in all arts".

Manisha, his fourth daughter, set the tunes of the piano in the Vedic chanting '*Tamiswaranang*' and in some of the songs of Rabikaka (uncle Rabi) e.g. 'Padaprante rakha sevake' (Keep thy serviceman on the edge of thy feet) etc.

Both Surendranath and Indira Devi, the son and the daughter of Satyendranath Tagore, received lessons on the European music very well. Indira Devi has written in her own memoir on this :

> "From the very childhood, we were brought up in the climate of both indigenous and foreign song and music. We see in the Tagore family that these two trends are more or less going on. Those who are inquisitive about the history of the music of Bengal in those days would naturally remember the name of Sourindramohan Tagore of Pathuriaghata in this connection. I am still in possession of some indigenous *gats* (tune-patterns) with foreign harmony and written in foreign notations by his son, Promod Kumar Tagore. Gurudas, a grandson of Sourindramohan or the little king, had also experimented upon introducing a song through harmonization of a certain Vedic *stotra* (lines) on the stage of Calcutta in those days".
>
> "My love for foreign music is, of course, due to my education in the Loreto Convent. I had the good opportunity there to learn playing on a piano from Ms. Slater, the organist of St. Paul's Cathedral and violin from Manjato, the Italian violinist. Theoretical question papers in music were sent to our country from the Trinity College of Music, Cambridge. I passed upto its intermediate course".
>
> "I remember, Rabikaka once asked my elder sister, Sarala Devi, Suren, my elder brother, and myself to compose a *gat* (tune-pattern) of a piano with harmony on the poem "Nirjharer Swapnabhanga" (The Awakening of the Waterfall). It was stated that the best composer would be rewarded by him. Amongst us, it was only Suren who encouragingly and laboriously complied with his request".
>
> Sarala Devi was the daughter of Swarnakumari Devi, Gurudev's elder sister. To teach the daughter European music

and piano, a European lady teacher was appointed. That teacher made Sarala Devi to practise in the European music for an hour regularly.

In later periods, many of the sons and daughters of this house have practised in the European music. Some of them made cord and harmony of many songs of Gurudev and published in journals also. In the era of the ameteur theatre introduced by the rich of Calcutta, an inclination for constituting an amateur theatre with orchestra was seen among the youths of the Tagore house of Jorasanko. Gurudev's senior brothers and their friends framed a theatrical community in the residence. Krishnabehari Sen, the brother of Keshav Sen, was their teacher in histrionics. After the acting of the two dramas "Krishnakumari" and "Ekei Bale Ki Sabhyata" here, they acted, in January, 1867, "Navanatak" composed by Ramnarayan Tarkaratna after many months' rehearsal. The drama was acted for nine nights in a row, The tune-pattern of the concert of the drama was composed by Vishnu Chakrabarti, the house tutor. At night, rehearsals on musical instruments took place. Of the instruments were a harmonium, two or three violins, 'Karatal', 'Dhol', 'Vayatabla', 'Clarionet', 'Pecklo', 'Bass Violin'. It is not known whether any drama was acted after the acting of "Navanatak".

It seems that as the young persons of this family were entangled with the movement of the Hindu Mela, they did not get scope to be engaged in the acting of dramas. In this period it is not known if there were amateur theatres among the other rich also. After the closure of the acting of dramas in the Tagore family of Jorasanko for a pretty few years, we come to know that in 1877, prior to Gurudev's first tour in England, a drama written by Jyotirindranath was acted. Gurudev has said in this memoir that it was for the first time that he participated in the acting of the drama. The name of the drama was "Emon karma aar karbo na" ("I won't do an act like this"). Gurudev acted in the role of Aleek Prakash. This was for the first time that the ladies of the house were allowed to act in a drama. After this incident, in 1879, at the encouragement of Jyotirindranath, a musical drama "Vasanta Utsava" (The Spring Festival) written by Swarnakumari Devi was acted.

Then Gurudev was in England with the family of his elder brother,

Satyendranath. "Vasanta Utsava" was fully composed in the pattern of musical drama of the opera type. It was acted to entertain the assembled hosts in the "Assembly of learned persons" in the house. The acting of a musical drama of the opera type was for the first time made in the Tagore house of Jorasanko. But I think that there is a necessity of finding out the reasons how Jyotindranath was encouraged in composing a drama of the opera type and making it acted.

Meanwhile, the discussion that we have made on the drama-based replies and counter-replies through music from the beginning to the end as seen in the Italian Opera like "Kaminikunja" acted towards the end of January 1879 in the National Theatre, I think that the same influence was behind the opera of Swarnakumari's "Vasanta Utsava". As a drama of the new type, "Kaminikunja" attracted the mind of the then Bengalee society of Calcutta and was also appreciated everywhere. I assume that the young persons of the Tagore house were also certainly pleased at seeing this new type of opera in the Bengali language and consequential to their pleasure, the opera or the musical drama named "Vasanta Utsava" was born. Sarala Devi, the daughter of Swarnakumari Devi, wrote on the drama "Vasanta Utsava" in her memoir :

> "At the very time of Rabindranath's living in England, the acting of the musical drama "Vasanta Utasava" written by my mother was held under the direction of Jyotirindranath. The house was then moved with the great resonance of music."

Hiranmoyee Devi also informs in this connection :

> "The creation of the poetic drama from Jorasanko started from this very "*Vasanta Utsava*". It is a matter of great regret that my mother did not preserve the hilarious latter any more that Rabimama (Uncle Rabi) had written after going through the book in England. After his return from England, the acting of "*Vasanta Utsava*" was made in the interior courtyard of the house."

Gurudev returned from England in February, 1880. After his arrival, he saw that arrangements had been going on for the acting of the drama "Manmoyee" written by Jyotirindranath. Gurudev, too, acted in it. The drama was not fully a musical drama. As Jyotirindranath could not forget the dramas of the pure opera type of 1879, he made Gurudev to write the two musical dramas viz., *"Valmiki Pratibha"* and *"Kalmrigaya"* for two years consecutively, and he himself helped in adding lyrics to the words. Everyone of the family showed his acting before the invited learned audience. A few years afterwards, Gurudev, out of his own initiatives, composed the musical drama *"Mayar Khela"*.

Of the Bengalees of the nineteenth century, those who were trying to acquire European music and histrionics and who were encouraged to find out new avenues with their influences, the Tagore family of Jorasanko was one of the best among them. And Gurudev Rabindranath was the pioneer in creative activities.

3 THE INFLUENCE OF FOREIGN MUSIC ON RABINDRANATH'S SONGS

Before making any discussion on the influence of European music on the songs of Gurudev Rabindranath, we will have to see well how far he had studied this music, how much direct knowledge he had about it and how he had achieved it. His own statements and the memoirs of his relatives about the same are our only guide. About his first knowledge of the European music, he informs :

> "At seventeen, when I first came to Europe, I came to know it intimately, but even before that time I had heard European music in our own household. I had heard the music of Chopin and others at an early age."

Elsewhere, he has said :

> "As a young boy, I heard European music being played on the piano; much of it I found attractive, but I could not enter fully into the spirit of the thing."

From the above two statements, it is understood that at the time when Rabindranath was born, there was the persuit of European music in his family and that musical environment attracted him enough in his boyhood. On his first hearing a song, he has written :

> "I first heard European songs when I was 17 years old during my first visit to London. The artiste was Madame Nilsson, who had a great reputation in those days."

He (Rabindranath) first went to England, at the age of 17, in September 1878. The tenure of his living there is altogether one year and five months. During this period, he not only studied but also heard

European music on different occasions and practised vocal music with enthusiasm. From his letters of those days, it is known that he had often danced 'Gallop' and 'Lancers' in association with instruments like piano, violin etc. at the invitation of Evening Party, fancy ball and other dance and song. If there was any programme of amusement at Brighton, Miss K informed everyone of Gurudev, escorted them, told them strories while in leisure and taught the boys singing songs. In "*Jeevansmriti*" (Autobiography), he has written :

> "When I was in Brighton, I once went to hear the song of a famous singer in the institution for music there. I am failing to recollect her name. She might be either Madam Nilsson or Madam Albani. I have never before heard such wonderful power of the voice."

Here, in the house of Dr. M, Gurudev Rabindranath went to attend music and entertainment at the invitation scheduled in the evening. At the request of many of them, he sang two Bengali songs in addition to the one '*Permer Katha aar bolona*' ('Don't say about love any more'). That evening was passed in joy in songs and music and dinner. Afterwards, he lived with the K family of Mr. K in London. There he saw that his third daughter, Miss A. practised song and music almost everyday and she had also studied on songs. Gurudev Rabindranath writes about the family :

> "I am pretty happy in this family. The evening is joyfully spent in study and music."

Elsewhere, he has written :

> "Sometimes we enjoy songs and music. Meanwhile, I have learnt a lot of English songs. I do not want to exaggerate but, truly speaking, people now very well praise my voice. I sing. Miss A plays on. Miss. A has taught me many songs."

In "*Jeevansmriti*" (Autobiography), we encounter a few more descriptions of his musical life in those days :

> "A got my shelter in the residence of a lady Dr. Scott (Mrs. Scott). She finished all her housedhold duties and in the evening she fully participated in our studies, songs and music."

I had a great intention that I would hear, in tune, the Irish Meldiz, learn it and present the same to Aukshay Babu..... In England, I heard and learnt some Irish Meldiz, but I had not the desire to complete all the songs any more...."

Returning home I sang these and other foreign songs before the relatives. Everyone asked why the voice of Rabi was so changed; it appeared to be foreign of interesting type.

The revered Indira Devi, in her recollection of Gurudev's life as a musician at the time of his first stay in London, writes :

> "We reached (London) probably in 1877 with mother. Later on, in 1878, Rabikaka and fathter came. From that very time, he (Rabindranath) was introduced with foreign music, and I have heard that the foreign audience were pleased at his tuning and forceful voice of *tarsaptak's* high pitch which is called 'tenor' there. I remember that he sang the famous songs of those days like
> "Won't you tell me, Molly darling"
> "Darling, you are growing old"
> "Good-bye, sweet heart, good-bye".

Intensely influenced by foreign music, Rabindranath returned from London in 1880. Shortly after his return to the country, he had to compose the musical drama "*Valmiki Pratibha*" at the encouragement of his elder brother Jyotirindranath. He composed this drama to entertain the invited guests who were eminent litterateurs, through acting in a normally held annual function at the residence named "Vidvajjan Samagam Sabha" (The place of the Assembly of Scholars). "*Valmiki-Pratibha*" was first acted in February, 1881. Remembering this occasion, he writes :

> "........ "*Valmiki-Pratibha*" was born in the midst of the practice of national and foreign music. Most of its tunes are national but in this musical drama it has to be extracted elsewhere from the dignity in seated assemblies; one who is habituated to fly has been pulled down on the ground to be utilized for the purpose of running.

To employ music in the service of the drama in this way has not become inconsistent of fruitless. This is the speciality of the musical drama, "*Valmiki-Pratibha*". My mind was specially arrested with the joy of this freedom of music to unhesitatingly utilize it for every possible way ....Merely three songs were taken from the foreign music... Of the foreign music, two were utilized in the intoxication of the dacoits and I have set one Irish tune in the wailful song of the goddess of the forest. In fact, "*Valmiki-Pratibha*" is not a book of poetry for study; it is a new experiment on music. One would fail to appreciate it if one does not hear it at the time of acting. "*Valmiki-Pratibha*" is not the same as what is called opera in the European language; it is a playlet in music.... The subject-matter is only acted in tunes, it has very little beauty of music separately".

One cannot but admit that in the Indian music, "*Valmiki-Pratibha*" is a new experiment. In our country, many full-fleged musical dramas of ancient trends are in vogue even tody. The acting of "*Kaminikunja*" on the model of the Italian opera in the National Theatre of Calcutta and of the musical drama "*Vasanta-Utsava*" in the house of Rabindranath were made. The conversation of the characters in these dramas were faultlessly arrested in the tune, rhyme and pause of songs, and so, the actors did not sing in the pattern of acting. It was sung in the pattern of customary songs by keeping a cautious eye to *ragini* and *tal* (beat)—their *sam* (pause), *fank* (gap), and *matra* (accent).

For "*Valmiki-Pratibha*", Gurudev composed songs of the pattern of Hindi and Bengali ones in vogue, but in the rules of their singing, he fully ignored the practice, in vogue, of singing through elaboration of *raga-raginis* without disobeying the *sam* (pause) or *tal* (beat) or the rules of *fank* (gap). At the time of the acting of this drama, he expressed the different characters in the rhythm of ordinary talks or the songs with *raga-raginis* in the pattern of speech. One might ask in this connection : How did the method of this type of music come to Gurudev's mind? We will get the anwer from his own writing. He has written in "*Jeevansmriti*", (Autobiography) :

> "I read in an article of Herbert Spencer that normally where there is a flow of emotion of the mind, some tune appears by itself. In fact, we do not express anger, sorrow or joy or surprise only through words, there are tunes with words. Man has derived music out of this subsequent tune, through excellence in conversation. This statement of Spencer attracted my mind. I thought why it would not be feasable to go on acting, in accordance with this, by attuning from the

> beginning to the end and by expressing different ideas in the midst of songs. There is some sort of this endeavour in *kathakata* (Presentation of stories/episodes through histrionics) in our country. Sentences in it sometimes take help of tune but that is not purely music in harmony with standardised *tal.* Just as blank verse rhyme is as a rhyme, this is also the same as a song. It has no strict regimentation of *tal;* a *matra* of *lay* is there. Its only purpose is not to express a specific *ragini* or *tal* in a purified form but to unfold the inherent emotions of ideas in words. The string of songs in "*Valmiki-Pratibha*" was not fully eliminated, yet in order to follow ideas, the *tal* has been dwarfed. As acting is the primary one, the exception to this *tal* does not bring forth sorrow in the audience."

Of the two songs of the intoxicated band of the burglars that he composed in 1881 for "*Valmiki-Pratibha*" by applying foreign tune, one is "Kali Kali bolo re aaz" (Speak out Kali Kali today) and the other, "Tave aay save aay" (Then come, come ye all). The wailful song of *Vanadevi* (The goddess of the forest) composed in the Irish tune is "Mari o kahar vachha (Ah, whose darling she is !). This song was not there at first. It is composed in 1815 at the time of the re-acting of the drama.

We think that the appropriate avenue of evaluating Rabindrasangeet in total prerspectives can be had out of the thought that came in the mind of Rabindranath on composing songs as a consequence to his experience in the practice of indigenous and foreign tune in "*Valmiki-Pratibha*". He extensively expressed his the-then thoughts on music in his three essays published in three years consecutively. We have neither given attention to nor discussed significatly these three essays. But in these three essays the original mystery related to the manifold creations of music in the music career of Gurudev is concealed. Bearing this in mind, I would quote a bit extensively the subject-matter of these essays for the convenience of readers.

Nearly two months after the acting of "*Valmiki-Pratibha*" that is, in the month of April, Gurudev delivered a lecture on music in a conference of the Bethune Society, Calcutta. The lecture was published in the issue of Jaistha 1288 B.C. (May 1881) in the journal " *Bharati*" under the title "*Sangit O Bhav*" (Music and Idea). Vide *Sangit Chinta* (Thoughts on Music), Vaishakh 1373 B.C. (April 1966). I quote extracts from the lecture along with the example of songs that he said :

"The slumber of the society of Bengal had just been broken a few days ago. At present, a new vigour is started in its body...... In our society of Bengal, a new movement has appeared, even the waves of that movement are reaching the shores of Europe. Now, in spite of innumerable endeavour whatsoever, who dares arrest these waves? Simultaneously, with this movement, a new awakening of music has taken place in our country. Music has just now arisen, the work for the same has not yet started well. Discussions on music in various ways are still a far cry. A lively waveful current in the stagnent water of the science of music in our country through criss-cross of new opinions is not yet created".

"Our science of music .... a dead science.... we do not see the countenance—manifold, diverse, mysterious, shadowy, changeable.

My intention is : let there be a union between poetry and music, the companion of poems, by emancipating the latter from the iron prison of the science of music.....

What was the aim of *raga-ragini?* Certainly, it was nothing but to express ideas. When we speak, even then there are tonal variations and diverse mysteries of ether in the voice..... Those tonal variations and mysteries of ether are heightened in excellence in music. Music is, therefore, only the best medium of mental expression........ Music is nothing but reading out poems in the best way. The idea that we incompletely express through speed is expressed more completely in *raga-raginis.* So the purpose of *raga-ragini* is to express ideas only..... Now *raga-ragini* itself has turned to be the aim.... Now by simply hearing a song everyone wants to see if *Jayjayanti, Vehag* or *Kanada* are maintained.... Just as there are differences between a grammarian and a poet, so are the same between an *Ostad* (Expert) and a thoughtful singer.

Now if persons versed in music begin to discover, with special attention, the different ideas in different *raginis,* music is then really benefitted. Tell me where the idea contained in the *raga-ragini* of ours will go........

The experts in music draw everyone's attention to that idea. Please find out why a special idea occurs in a special *raga-ragini.* Take, for instance, why in *Puravi* alone we remember the evening and in *Bhairavi* only, the morning........

Let us see which tunes should be joyful, and which ones, sorrowful...... When we cry, then there is very little difference between two side-by-side tunes, the voice of weeping rolls over each soft tune, the tune becomes very strained. When we laugh—ha, ha, ha, ha — there is not a single soft tune, nor even is there a strained tune; a gulf of difference is there between two side-by-side tunes, and with the tilt of *tal* (beat), tune comes out. The *ragini* (tune) of sorrow slowly moves like the sorrowful night, it is to go through every soft tune. The *ragini* of happiness, on the other hand, moves very speedily like happy days and topples over tunes in twos or threes. In our *raga-ragini*, there is no tune representing boistrous temperament. There is no sudden rise (climax) or fall (anticlimax). The tune of exaggerated hilariousness is very casual. In English tunes, there are terrible hilarious ones but there is hardly any such one in our *raginis.* But, in the music of our country, there is no want of tunes representing weeping. It is possible to cry in almost all *raginis.* Every type of idea from a scream to calm sorrow can be expressed in our tunes.

Whatever happy tunes we have are ones full of luxury and emotional sentimentalism. ... Many a time, if we want to compose songs of hilariousness, we set the tune in swift beats, whatever idea it expresses. The swift beat is of course a part of expression of happy ideas.....

Tal, too is a part of expression of ideas....... With the change of ideas, it is necessary to quicken and prolong beats, too. It is not proper that everywhere tuning should be equally maintained. It is better that one makes expression of ideas as the main objective and tuning and beat, as the secondary one... It is better to do away with the rule that exists in our music that one should reach *sam* by any means. It is enough if there is an equal accent of beats : it seems that there should be no further regimentation. It, then, affects normalcy.... Let there be beats as it is; let, again, there be accent as it is, I am feeling any incovenience in an absence of such a regimentation that one must return to a certain sphere in *Sam.* Even in a musical drama that is to be acted in tune from beginning to end it is specially necessary not to have any beat in certain spheres. Otherwise, it is impossible to have real enjoyment out of a drama.....

> *Raga-ragini-aalap* are non-verbal music.... in *aalap,* too, it is not only to throw tunes from the vocal cord, it is necessary to have tune-patterns that express ideas. I place music in a higher position than the singers... They want to establish the tune on the words of the song, while I want to place the words of the song upon the tune. They go on setting words to extract tunes. I go on setting tunes to extract words ..... Ordinary poetry is meant for reading, the poetry of music is meant for hearing..... The poetry of songs cannot be read; it can only be heard.
>
> ...... My submission to the experts in music is this : Please enquire into the science that explains how and why ideas are expressed through different tune-patterns....... Please involve yourselves in the discovery of the favourable and unfavourable tunes related to the *raginis* of happiness, sorrow, anger or astonishment...... Let there be separate names of our *raga-raginis* in accordance with those of different ideas. There are classes of learning practising tunes and *raga-raginis* in our schools of music. Let there be classes for learning ideas of *raga-raginis* also."

This essay is, in fact, an analysis of the nature of "*Valmiki-Pratibha*". The characteristics of experiments anew of "*Valmiki-Pratibha*" are that almost all its songs cannot be sung apart by dissociating these from the drama and as a poetry the songs are not such as to enjoy them through reading. For these reasons, he (Gurudev) has said : "This drama is a garland of drama in the thread of songs". He sang in the pattern of conversation by binding various realistic conversations based on joy and sorrow, laughter and tears, fear, joke, excitement, surprise etc. easily in the different Indian tunes and *raga-raginis* in the drama. For this, there were transformations in *raga-raginis.* They did not conform to the pattern in vogue. He accepted foreign tune and pattern in case of tunes of terrible excitement because, in our songs, there was no song of excitement or intoxication that is appropriate to the band of burglars. As almost all the songs were sung in the rhythm of conversation there was no restraint of *tal* of either the *tabla* or the *pankhoaaz.* This is the reason why it is seen from the first edition of the musical drama "*Valmiki-Pratibha*" in book form that there is no reference to *tal* except that of *raga-raginis* in his song. But in those days and even upto many years afterwards, references to *raga* and *tal* were made along with songs in all books on music by Rabindranath. If one minutely observes, one would assert that the fundamental topics to be discussed in this essay were the above.

As Gurudev Rabindranath had to keep himself a great deal off from the customary previous avenue of musical drama at the time of his new experimentations with "*Valmiki-Pratibha*", he wanted to explain by the lecture and essay "*Sangeet O Bhav*" (Music and Idea) in support of this novelty that, in those days, that type of novelty was seen to be very necessary in the Indian music.

In continuation of the lecture and essay entitled "*Sangeet O Bhav*", Gurudev published another essay titled "Sangeeter Utpatti O Upojogita" ("The origin and necessity of Music") in the *Bharati, Asad* (September) issue next, vide "*Sangeet Chinta*" (Thoughts on Music). The essay was, in fact, an explanation of Herbert Spencer's essay, "The Origin and Function of Music". He says in the essay "*Sangeet O Bhav*" : "When we speak, even then there are upwardness and downwardness of tunes and diverse mysteries of ether in the voice. In spite of these, expressions of ideas remain incomplete to a great extent. That upwardness and downwardness of tunes and mystery of ether become excellent in music". He wanted to establish, with the opinions of Herbert Spencer, this statement in the second essay through exhaustive analysis. The principal subject-matter of the essay "Sangeeter Utpatti O Upojogita" is :

> "Symptoms of excitments are expressed in the muscles and feeling nerves of all animals with the awakening of joy or sorrow or other mental attitudes. In accordance with the speciality and extent of attitude, the muscles of the throat are contracted. Our vocal cords take different shapes according to their contractions of different magnitudes, and differences of sounds occur according to those different shapes. So it is clear that the different sounds coming out of our voice are a physical manifestation of different attitudes.
>
> If there is a special excitement of attitude, we come above or go down to our normal medium tune.... We go beyond the tune of normal coversation with the influence of forceful attitude.
>
> The trend of the attitude related to daily conversations is different from that of the conversation in excitement. Conversation in excitement bears the same symtom as music

does. The changes that take place in our voice with the excitement of joy, sorrow etc. reach the apex in music only.... The tune of music is also high, everything in a song is tune. The tune of a song is far higher or lower than that of normal conversation, and in the tune of a song, the high and the low tunes play on and on. The tune of excited attitude receives its fulness in music as far as those of expressions of intense happiness or sadness through the voice......

In all conversations, there are two components : speech and how that speech is pronounced. Words are signs of ideas and the procedures of speech uttered are signs of feeling. Some special words express our ideas outwardly and the tune expresses the joy and sorrow of our mind that awakens simultaneously with these ideas...... We simultaneously speak twofold words of ideas and feelings.

The language of emotions in us can achieve clarity with the immedieate pleasure that music affords us. The language of emotion alone is the origin of music."

"....... The day is coming when we will speak in music only.....

" The music of our country.... has so far gone away from normalcy as separation between feeling and music has taken place, only a lump of quagmire of tunes and remnants in the forms of the patterns and structures of *raga-raginis* are left. Music has turned into muddy image—lifeless, heartless.....

"Our indigenous feelingless music is of the worst type. So long as we will not be able to bring forth feeling in it, we will fail to identify ourselves as musicians of the high order."

Gurudev took the help of feeling even at the time of speaking, in the tune of songs, the various dialogues of the blend of laughter and tears, anger and surprise used in "*Valmiki-Pratibha*". In other words, the words of joy and sorrow, anger etc. that the actors normally express in their voice, that very normalcy of the voice was maintained in this drama at the time of acting with songs mixed with *raginis.* In those days, Gurudev considered our Indian music to be of the worst type in absence of this type of the method of music with feeling.

"Sangeet O Kavita" (Music and Poetry), the third essay of Gurudev, was published in the journal *Bharati* in the month of *Magh* (January) next. In this essay he says :

"Two components—words and tunes—are there to express

> our ideas. The tune expresses almost the same extent of ideas as our words do. Even the idea of words depends on the tune. The same word expresses many meanings in different tunes. Both words and tunes can be considered to be existent side by side within expression of ideas. Our languages of feeling are built by a unison of the language of tune and that of words. In a poem, we give importance to the language of words, while in music, to the laguage of feelings..... The tunes that we use in coversations in accordance with some rules are not used by us in music in the same way. We select tunes and nicely arrange them. Just as a peom expresses its ideas in selected beautiful words, a song also expresses ideas through nicely selected tunes".

In the language of arguments, nothing is required besides conventional tunes of conversation, but music necessitates tunes of the language of emotions that go beyond agruments. In this matter also, music is exactly the same as poetry. In music, too, there are rhythms. The mysteries of its tunes are continually going on through beats. There is no disciplined beat in the tune of conversations, there are beats in music. Music and poetry have divided these two parts of expression of ideas within themselves. But music has not achieved so much progress in expression of ideas as poetry. There is a reason for this. Empty words have no attraction. They have neither any meaning nor do they sound pleasing in ears. But a tune bereft of ideas has an attraction; it sounds sweet in ears. For this, even though there is an absence of ideas, one derives sensual happiness out of it. Much attention has not, therefore, been adhered to ideas in music. The tune has become a rebel through this gradual indulgence and has dominated over feelings..... This hopeless condition of music is due to the fact that its land is fertile. A sweet tune appears as soon as it is heard; for this, the music has not to till ideas laboriously. But as only correct words have no sweetness enough, poetry has to cultivate ideas for the cause of life. For this alone, poetry has achieved such a glory, and music, such a downfall.......

Poetry has ascended to a high order, and music has fallen down to a low level. In poetry, all ideas fine like the air or blunt like a stone can be expressed but in music that cannot be done.

Matthew Arnold says, "The function of music is to select only a single, permanent idea of the mind and to stay on a single part of a chain of ideas..... The function of poetry is more extensive. The external beauty of the moment, too, should be described by her like an artist and the transitory overflow of ideas should also be sung by her like a singer. Moreover, the stream of life is a subject for her that should be narrated. She is to travel from ideas to ideas and from situations to situations. She does not create a picture of a fixed standing posture nor does she describe only a permament idea of a certain period of time. The subject of poetry is moving, flowing, changeable ideas. Every shadowy land of a moving idea cannot be reflected in music. Music only explains a permanent fixed idea. But we say that it is not correct that a moving idea is not at all inimitable for music but even now music has not reached this age. In music and poetry, we do not see any more point of difference except those of progress."

The above is practically an elaborate explanation of that portion of the essay "Sangeet O Bhav" where he has said that the Indian Science of Music is fixed, motionless and no mysterious, shadowy, changeable beauty of countenance of miscellaneous, diverse ideas can be seen. Here he says that music has not that advantage to express all ideas as fine as the air and as blunt as a stone, like poetry. It has not yet become possible for music to express moving ideas like poetry. Music has not yet achieved so much progress as made by poetry in expressing ideas.

From these three essays it is at least understood that Gurudev had before him the model of the European thoughts on music and launched new experiments on music in "*Valmiki-Pratibha*", and, in this period, he had also this belief that the Indian music is less advanced to a great extent than the European music.

On the eve of youth, Gurudev was deeply attracted by the European culture as a whole and this is known from a study of the various letters in his book "*Europe Pravasir Patra*" (Letters from a foreigner in Europe) published in those days. In the preface to this book, he unhesitatingly said :

> "What has appeared in mind from a first sight of the foreign society has been expressed. But whatever benefit does one receive out of this or not, it gives an account of the formation and changes of the opinions of a Bengalee when he goes to England."

We have already been introduced with the opinions of

Rabindranath, that were, to a great deal, formed and changed in the European trend of ideas in music, too.

After the acting of "*Valmiki Pratibha*" and publication of these essays, the second musical drama, "*Kalmrigaya*" was acted on December 23, 1882. Remembering this musical drama, Gurudev writes in "*Jeevansmriti*" : "Being encouraged by this new technique about the songs of "*Valmiki-Pratibha*", I wrote another musical drama of this class."

In "*Kalmrigaya*", only six songs composed in the foreign song and rhythm or which are called break away songs are incorporated, These are :

1. Phoole Phoole dhale dhale (Drowsing on every flower)
2. Sakali Phooralo (Everything is over)
3. Mana na manili (Ye did not obey forbiddance)
4. Tui aay re kachhe aaay (O bhai dekhe ja) (Come ye nearer, come) (O brother come and see)
5. O dekhbi re bhai (O brother, you will see)
6. Enechhi mora, enechi mora (Brought we have, we have brought)

The subsequent songs were composed with the help of the Indian songs of different patterns.

Not many Bengali songs not meant for musical drama, of this broken ones of the foreign type are found in large numbers in this era. It is known that he composed only three Bengali songs of this broken type, one within the period from his first stay in London upto six years next, that is, within 1885. The *Brahmasangeet* beginning with 'Ohe dayamoy nikhil aasroy' (O one full of charity and the refuge of the world) and the two songs of the miscellaneous section—'Poorano shei diner katha' ('Tales of bygone days') and 'Kotavar behevechhinu (How may times did I think)— can be stated as examples to the above. From an observation of the number of break away songs it is seen that although Gurudev had a deep attraction for foreign songs, he had no significant eagerness for composing break away songs.

During the reacting of "*Valmiki-Pratibha*" in 1886, the song 'Mari O Kahar bachha (Ah, whose darling he is) was added anew as one of wailings of *Vanadevi.* Its tune is that of "*Kalmrigaya's*" song 'Mana na Manili' (Forbiddence ye did not obey). "*Valmiki-Pratibha*" was greatly extended in the acting of this time. So he said in the preface to the reprinted second edition of this musical drama :

> "Many names are taken from the musical drama "*Kalmrigaya*" in changed or corrected forms".

In "*Jeevansmriti*", he writes :

> "I mixed a great deal of the portions of the musical drama ("*Kalmrigaya*") along with "*Valmiki-Pratibha*"......"

In the acting of this musical drama this time, he retained only four songs of the tune of foreign ones :

1. Kali Kali bol re aaz (Speak Kali Kali today)
2. Tave aay save aay (Come, then, ye all come)
3. Enechhi mora, enechhi mora (Brought we have, we have brought)
4. Mari O Kahar bachha (Ah, whose darling he is)

He composed nearly twenty songs anew of the indigenous pattern and with these, nine songs in all of "*Kalmrigaya*" were added.

In narrating the enthusiasm that arose in his mind on new experimentations at the time of composing these two musical dramas consequtively, he writes in "*Jeevansmriti*".

> "I have not composed anything in the same enthusiasm with which I wrote "*Valmiki-Pratibha*" and "*Kalmrigaya*". Then Jyotidada was everyday engaged almost all the day in drilling the *Ostadi* songs, in accordance with his desires, by setting them on the piano. Consequently, some of the *raginis* at times flashed with unique image and resonance of ideas. When the tunes that slowly move with their gutts in the hard and fast rules, were non-customarily made to run to and fro, new unthinkable power was seen in their nature in that revolution and these purturbed our mind all the time. The tunes are, as it were, speaking on different aspects, thus we could distinctly hear.

These two dramas were written in the joy of devastation in such a gutt as to bring forth revolution of music. This is why there are dances of *tal-betal* (tunes and non-tunes) and no selection or evaluation of English or Bengali.... Surprisingly, nobody expressed any resentment for the adventure revealed on music in the aforementioned two musical dramas and everyone has returned home with a happy mind."

These statements of "*Jeevansmriti*" remind us of his lectures and essays of 1881.

The third musical drama "*Mayar Khela*" was acted in December 1888. He started composing the songs of this drama nearly a year ago. The ladies acted in the Bethune College, the audience were also women only. Gurudev writes on this drama : "Long after composing "*Valmiki-Pratibha*" and "*Kalmrigaya*", I wrote a musical drama entitled "*Mayar Khela*" but that was of a different type. In that, music, and not drama, is fundamental. As "*Valmiki-Pratibha*" and "Kalmrigaya" are garlands in the thread of songs, "*Mayar Khela*" is a garland in the thread of drama. It does not depend on the current of incidents; its main component is the very emotion of the heart. In fact, when I wrote "*Mayar Khela*", the whole mind was drenched with the flow of music".

The main point of difference between this musical drama and the previous two musical dramas is that most of its songs can be detached from the drama and can be enjoyed as songs by singing these separately. Besides this, the rhythm of the *tal* of *tabla* is also maintained in its many songs. This is why we see reference to *tal* also along with that of the *raginis* of the songs of this drama. In spite of this, it is fully a musical drama and during its acting, most of its songs were sung fully in the rhythm of conversation by disobeying the rules of stipulated rhythm of *tal*. There is one broken-song of the foreign tune in this musical drama. The song is 'Aha aajie Vasante' (Aha today in this spring). It is composed in the tune of the previous song 'Mana na manili' (Forbiddence ye did not obey). It may be noticed that, it was the inclination of all the members of his family and himself to compose musical dramas and to act them by singing their songs in the same system in the seven years from 1881 to 1888. In addition to this, all the Bengali songs of the model of foreign break away songs traced out so long were composed by him at this time. After composing "*Mayar Khela*", he neither showed his enthusiasm for writing musical dramas any more nor did he show interest in composing Bengali songs of the break-away European pattern.

In 1890, Rabindranath went to England for the second time. He was then 29 years old. He started with great enthusiasm, reached there in the month of September, but as he was feeling home-sick, he stayed there for a month only and returned to his country in November. The purpose for which he went to England did not succeed, but we get a beautiful account of how he had passed this one month in the study of music of that country from his book "*Oorop-Yatrir Diary*". Referring to his one month's stay in London and returning by sea, in the diary of music, he informs :

> "In the evening, we made another session of music. Walter Mall plays on the piano fairly well. Miss Mall and I have sung many songs together. They are praising a lot of my voice. Mall was suggesting that if I made a practice of my voice, I could sing in the St. James Hall concert. I have a voice of a fairly high standard......
>
> .... The whole day has almost passed in music..... Miss Mall taught singing...... I have brought new songs (notations of songs)....... They were tasted through singing.
>
> Have played tennis, sang songs at Oswalds, heard music, had my meal after returning home, and have come to the bed-room after practising music again.
>
> .... Miss Mall made me sing all the songs. After the song 'Remember me,' she slowly said to me after the song, "Mr. T, I shall remember you".
>
> "I learnt a bit of singing from Miss Mall....... She made me sing in the concert. Much applause was received.... A very fat girl sang excellently. It was she who played on the song's accompaniment. I sang Gounod's *Serenade* and *if.* At present I sing in a louder voice by making a great deal of courage....
>
> "So much of taste for the European music has been attained now through practice as it is at least understood out of this that if practised, the total cadence of the European music may be achieved.
>
> "I had to sing many songs tonight also. Afterwards when I was repeating an indigenous *ragini* along with a musing sound looking at the sea in darkness by catching hold of the railing of the ship, it seemed to me very sweet. I was tired of singing English songs. All on a sudden, the heart was soaked with the emotion of indigenous songs.

(The beautiful girl) : "Last night you came and said to me : Aren't you going to sing ? I said, yes. Saying this, I went to sing .....

"She (The Australian girl)........ said to me, 'Let's go to Music Saloon and play on songs and music.' Reaching there, I started singing. Today they have made me sing again and again till late at night. I sang Ave Maria and one or two songs more reasonably well. The much unknown girl, by extending her face through the window, thanked me a lot. Today, at dawn, it seemsed to me that my song had really appealed them—it was not only a surprise because it was the song of an Indian. Just now Connolly came and said to me, 'I say Tagore, you sang awfully well this evening. The thwarted voice with which I had formerly sung is erroneous as I am feeling now. I sang a song 'Then (You'll) remember me'. It has greatly appealed my new friend.. (The Austrilian sister) plays on the piano pretty well. She was playing on a tune very much known to me that day. When I was at Park Street, I often made a parody to it. Probably, it was a Cavatina or Estudiantina or Dance de Seville or anything unusual. But as it was known to me, it greatly appealed me. I had to sing tonight also.

"Mrs. Moeller requested me to sing; she played on a piano. Mrs. Moeller said : 'It is a treat to hear you sing'. Webb came and said : 'What would we do without you, Tagore? There's nobody on board who sings so well!' However, as I came on board the ship, my songs are being fairly appreciated. The main point is : none of the English songs that I sang before this was in the tenor pitch and so voice did not spread. This time I have bought all music of the high pitch, and so, profuse appreciation is pouring forth.

"Schiller (a German co-passenger) said to me, 'If you regularly practise your voice, miraculous improvement might take place. You have a mine of wealth in your voice'."

From the quotations, it is clearly understood that even after an elapse of nearly ten years, Gurudev did not forget the practice of vocal music of the western country made at the age of seventeen or eighteen when he first went to England. Much improvement of his power of singing has, therefore, been made with the practice for a few days, and, as a singer, he is also winning appreciation. But this time, after returning home for the second time, we do not get any news of excitement for foreign music like the first time. Also, there are no news about composing any new musical drama or Bengali songs based on foreign break-away song. But this much is known that, in any period of 1893, he once more made the acting of "*Valmiki-Pratibha*" with great pomp and grandeur. He himself acted in the role of Valmiki this time also. Many of the Tagore house like Gaganendranath, Abanindranath etc. were in the band of burglars. Indira Devi played the role of Saraswati and Abhigna Devi did that of the girl. Arrangements for this acting were made on the occasion of the invitation accorded to the wife of the-then Governor General of India, Lord Lansdown at the house of Jorasanko. In her book "*Rabindra-Smriti*" (Reminiscence of Rabindranath), Indira Devi has given a brief account of this :

> "While coming from London, my father (Satyendranath Tagore) invited Lady Lansdown, wife of the-then Governor General and his co-passenger to come to the house of Jorasanko....... When the wife of the Governor-General expressed her desire to attend the invitation after her arrival in Calcutta, a special arrangement for acting of the drama "*Valmiki-Pratibha*" was made. A few more distinguished English personalities like Lady Eliot, wife of the-then Lieutenant Governor-General etc. were with Lady Lansdown."

The picture of Rabindranath in the role of Valmiki, with which we are today familiar, was taken this time, in 1893. It is heard that, the gown that Gurudev stretched behind from shoulder to leg in the dress of Valmiki was for the first time used and it was formerly not worn. Thinking over the wife of the Governor-General and other distinguished English guests, this was added to the dresses of this time as a token of the king of the band of burglars. The bodies of the band of burglars were covered with shirt, *pyjamas* and *pagris* (headgears) as far as possible in imitation of the Kabulis (the people of Kabul) so that no part of their body attracts the eyes of the distinguished lady guests.

Another item is to be specially mentioned in connection with this musical drama. There was no exception to the decoration of the stage, as it was attempted to decorate the stage in the realistic pattern by following the foreign model in portraying scenes and in other procedures in the theatres of Calcutta in those days. The description that Shilpacharya Abanindranath (Abanindranath, the artist-principal) has left behind on the stage-craft of the "*Valmiki-Pratibha*" of 1893 is to be found in his book "*Gharoa*" (Homely). Two cotton storks, a dead deer dumped with straw, boars in the bush of aram were portrayed in the scene and banyan branches were adjusted on the stage. With scenes like pouring water on the stage through pipes of tinplates at the time of songs of rains, lightning through the mirror, the sound of lightning through beating tin plates, rolling two dumbels from the roof of the first floor to and fro, entering the stage with the booty by riding a pony, and feeding the pony with grass on the stage, the invited ladies and sahibs were greatly pleased. From this, it is understood how strong the influence of London in acting, music and decoration on Gurudev was till he was 32 years. How intense his love was for foreign music is known from the letters written by him in those days. From a letter written in 1894, it is known :

> "Prior to my return this time, when 'S' came at noon in the Park Street, you sat on the piano, I was preparing for singing songs....."

In another letter he writes : If Beli (his first daughter) becomes pretty expert in indigenous and foreign music, then my intention will, to a great extent, be fulfilled.

"I was intensely willing that I would lie thus and somebody would go on playing music on the piano one after the other from the adjacent room. Among those, my that very Chopin would also be there. If the desire that grows in the mind remains unsatisfied, even then there is some sort of happiness within it."

Referring to Gurudev's devotion to foreign music, Indira Devi writes :

"Of course, I have played on the piano along with many foreign songs of Rabikaka. Those have still remained silent spectators in my bound excercise book of songs. For instance :

> 'In the glooming'
> 'Then you will remember me'
> 'Good night, good night, beloved !'

The 'If' of Swinburne etc. Moreover, the famous song of Ben Jonson, 'Drink to me only with thine eyes' was oriented in 'Katavar Bhevechhinu' (How many times did I think'). Rabikaka sang with the twin music of the piano and the violin another song—Ave Maria, the famous chant of the Roman Catholics—which greatly appeals me .... He would also sing, out of fun, the tune of English songs like 'Darling, you are growing old' etc. in a strained way." (*Rabindra-Smriti*).

In this way, we get a distinct account of the successful practice of the foreign vocal music in Rabindranath from seventeen/eighteen years till he was 39 years old. There is no doubt that he has no amateurish knowledge of European music like the other educated Indians coming from Europe. So I think that there is enough value of his opinions on European music.

In his early youth, he published his adverse criticism on the Indian music in full support of the European music. But it is seen that towards the time nearer to his thirty years, he first felt that the nature of music of the two countries are not the same. There is a great deal of difference between the two. We know this from his "*Europe Yatrir Diary*" published in 1890. From then onwards, he began to think about the real nature of the music of the two countries and the difference between them, if any or not. In the diary on October, 10, he writes :

> " .... Now, through practice, so much taste for the European music has been achieved as to be understood at least this : If one practises, one would receive the full cadence out of the European music. It is needless to say in particular that I like our indigenous music. But that there are differences between the two is undeniable."

Six days after this, he writes :

> "To me, the main difference between the indigenous and the foreign music is that the English song is one of the human habitation while our song is the indefinite, unspeakable one of boundless lonely nature."

Nearly four years afterwards, in a letter written in 1894, this comparative thought of the music of the two countries on the part of Gurudev was more extensively expressed. He wrote :

> "I think the world of the day is the European music, it is a melee of a moving great harmony in tunes or without tunes, in bits or parts, while the world at night is our Indian music, a pure pathetic sombre unmixed *ragini.* Both perturb us but both are antagonistic... What can be done?.... We the Indians, live in the reign of that night. We are enamoured with the

> indivisible, *sans* beginning. Ours is the lonely individual's song, the song of Europe is one of the groups of the human habitation. Our song draws the audience out of the limit of day-to day joys and sorrows of mankind and takes him to the companionless and of deliverance that is at the root of the universe. The European song, on the other hand, goes on in diversity dancing with the endless ups and downs of human joy and sorrow."

This thought of Rabindranath in analysing the nature of the Indian and the European music has flown in the same pattern from now onwards till the end of his life. In the chapter 'Vilati Sangit' (Foreign Music) of his autobiography "*Jeevan-smriti*" published in 1911, he rediscussed on the difference between the two types of music of the two countries and said :

> "The European music is, as it were, diversely associated with the realistic life of man. So we see, in Europe, musical tune can be applied depending on every type of incident and description. If we want to do so in our indigenous tune, then it becomes peculiar, as there is no cadence consequential to this. Our song, as it were, crosses the day-to-day barriers of life, and, for this, there are so much of pathos and deliverance in it;....
> "....... The songs of Europe greatly attracted my mind from more than one aspect. It seems to me, these songs are romantic; those are expressing the diversities of human life by translation in the tune of a song. It is not proper that in our music there is no such effort anywhere, but that effort has not become forceful and successful.

Moreover, in his early youth, he said in his lecture : the singers "want to establish the tune of the words in songs, I want to establish the words of song on the tune. They go on setting words in order to bring out the tune, I go on setting the tune in order to bring out the words." This time he is unhesitatingly admitting the erroneousness of the statement and is saying :

> "I unhasitatingly confess today (the lecture of 1881) the statement that I had expressed with so much gutts to be false.

> The art of music has itself a special nature and a special assignment. When there are words in a song, it is not proper that words should surpass the tune of a song, taking this opportunity. They are only carriers of the song. A song is great by its own grandeur. Why will it undergo slavery of words? The song begins where words end. The song dominates over the very unspeakable. It speaks the very same as the words cannot do. For this, the less the disturbance of words are, the better. In Hindustani songs, words are so few that the tune can easily spread its appeal by surpassing them. In this way, the excellence of music lies where the *ragini* can awaken our mind exquisitely as a pure sound. But in Bengal there is, for a long time, much dominance of words alone that pure music here has not achieved its independent power. For this, in this country, she is to live under the unbrella of her sister, the art of poetry. She has tried to manifest her excellence by depending on everyone beginning from the *Padavali* of the Vaishnav poets to the songs of Nidhubabu.... This has again and again been felt at the time of composing songs."

Gurudev has repeated the same opinion in different ways in the rest of his later life in many writings on music, and at the time of discussions on music of both the countries. This opinion is fully well formulated. So no further change of this opinion occurred.

The fundamental informations derived out of this discussion on the influence of foreign music on the songs of Rabindranath are the following :

> A very great deal of eagerness for composing musical dramas and acting is a result of the influence of thoughts of the European music from 1881 to 1886.

About the songs of the musical dramas the methods adopted to sing these at the time of acting were not in accordance with any ideal of the Indian musical drama, ancient or in force.

We would call the process of composing and singing the songs of the Indian tunes of the musical dramas through the influence of the European thoughts on music, the results of a co-ordinated influence.

All Bengali songs on the European break-away ones were

composed in the era of the musical drama. Most of the songs were composed encompassing musical dramas.

Many persons think that the Bengali songs were oriented on the English ones as the only mark of influence. According to us, it is not correct. Due to paucity of this song in number and in the absence of composition of break-away songs after Gurudev was 20 years old, it can, of course, be said that he did not, in the meanwhile, find out splendour of music to inspire him throughout his life. Moreover, as the break-away songs were born out of exact imitations from the point of view of tune, there was no further enthusiasm in Gurudev's mind to compose songs in this way. The real influence of the European music will, therefore, have to be found out elsewhere. Its beginning at the time of composing the musical drama and its influence till the last day of life have been expressed in different dimensions in Rabindra Sangeet. It may be called the coordinated influence of both of the trends.

I am quoting a list of English songs that Gurudev learnt well in England during the period 1878-1890, so long available :

1. 'Won't you tell me, Molly darling'.
2. 'Darling, you are growing old'.
3. 'Good-bye, sweet heart, good-bye'.
4. 'Then you will remember me!'
5. 'In the glooming'.
6. 'Good night, good night, beloved'.
7. 'Go where glory waits thee'.
8. 'The Vicar of Bray'.
9. 'Of all the wives as e'er (Nancy Lee)'.
10. 'The British Grenadiers.'
11. 'Ye bank and braes'.
12. 'Robin Adair'.
13. 'If' (By Swinburne)
14. 'Drink to me only with thine eyes', (by Ben Jonson)
15. 'Ave Maria' (Roman Catholic Chant)
16. 'Serenade' (By Gounod)

That Gurudev was well acquainted with Messe Solennelle of Gounod and Faust, Funeral March and Galops of Chopin and the Parsifal Opera of Wagner can be assumed from his writings.

4 SONGS OF MOVING EMOTIONS

After the first acting of the musical drama "*Valmiki-Pratibha*" in 1287 B.C. (1880). Gurudev Rabindranath said in his two essays "*Sangit O Bhav*" ("Music and Ideas") and "*Sangit O Kavita*" ("Muisc and Poetry") published in 1288 B.C. (1881) : In Indian music, no such mysterious, shadowy and changeable forms of diverse ideas of poetry are seen. Unlike music, it has been possible to express ideas as fine as air and as blunt as a stone. Songs of ideas full of motion like poetry are not composed with the help of *raga-raginis* in our country. The Indian music expresses a permanent idea only.

After his practice of the European vocal music during his visit to England in his first youth, Gurudev thought of the above lackings in the Indian music and, to solve the same, he composed the musical drama "*Valmiki-Pratibha*" and launched experimentations with it through acting.

Gurudev returned from England in the month of *Magh* 1286 B.E. (February 1880). Next year, towards the middle of the month *Falgun* (March), "*Valmiki-Pratibha*" was acted. He started composing the drama and rehearsing it a few months ago. How the work of co-ordiation between the indigenous and the foreign songs went on through the piano of Jyotirindranath Tagore, the elder brother, at the time of composing the songs of the drama is narrated by Gurudev in his "*Jeevansmriti*" (Reminiscence of life) :

> "I did not compose anything more in the same enthusiasm as I did "*Valmiki-Pratibha*" and "*Kalmrigaya*". Then Jyotidada was ready almost everyday in placing the *Ostadi* songs in the piano and in drilling them. As a consequence, a unique image and resonance of ideas of the *raga-raginis* were expressed. As soon as the tunes that maintain their gutts in hard and fast rules were made to run in a haphazard manner, a new unthinkable power was seen in their revolution and these

> always purturbed our mind. We could hear distinctly that the tunes were as if speaking. Often Aukshay Babu and I tried to add words in tunes simultaneously with that resonance of music of Jyotidada."

From the above description it is is known that after his return from abroad, Gurudev tried to express, along with Jyotidada and Aukshay Babu, the various songs of indigenous tunes anew in the model of European ones. There is no such account of an attempt like this before.

Almost all the songs of "*Valmiki-Pratibha*" are of *raga-raginis* or two-lined or four-lined tuned song. But when the characters of the drama speak in replies or counter-replies among themselves in the tune of songs, then, through changes of *raginis* one after the other or of *lay* in accordance with ideas, the marks of movement in association with different ideas fine or blunt in the song of a complete scene are easily felt. But the marks of this type have been separately expressed in a special song in the first scene of this drama. The reason is : this song is exactly composed in imitation of the English songs, which we would call the English-oriented Bengali song. The song is "Kali kali bolo re aaz" ('Speak Kali kali today'). In the song, prior to their going ahunting, the band of burglars are conveying their prayer to their worshipped goddess *Shyama-ma* (Mother Shyama) in an intoxicated language. In the first four-lines of the song, there is a broken rhyme of slow *lay* (movement), but the *lay* from the fifth line "oi ghor matta kare nritya" (Yonder the dancng does deeply intoxicate) to "Ha ha ha" is *drut* (quick); one will have to sing in *madhya lay* (mid-movement) and by breaking the rhyme from "Aare bal re Shyama mayer joy (say, victory to mother Shyama) to the rest of the song. To express the idea of thrilling, one necessitates varieties in the pronunciation of words and in the pattern of expression of voice of the song.

Broken rhyme of slow movement

Kali kali bal re aaz,
Balho, ho, ho, bolho, ho, ho, balho!
Namer jore sadhiba kaaz,
Balho, ho, balho, balho!
(Speak Kali Kali today,
Say ho ho ho, say ho ho ho, say ho!

We would meditate today by the strength of the name,
Say ho, ho, say ho, say ho!)

Drut (The Quick Rhyme)

Oai ghor matta kare nritya, rangamajhare
Oai laksha laksha yaksha raksha gheri Shymare
Oai lattapattakesh, atta atta hashe re,
Hahaha, hahaha, hahaha!
(With that intense intoxication the dance goes on in the midst of the stage
Lakhs of yaksha saviours are encircling Shyama,
Yonder is the one with dishavelled hair bursting out with laughter/Hahaha, hahaha, hahaha!).

Broken Rhyme of the Mid-movement

Aare bal re Shyama maayer joy joy,
Joy joy, joy joy, joy joy, joy joy,
Aare bal re Shyama maayer joy, joy joy,
Aare bal re Shyama maayer joy.
(Speak out the victory of mother Shyama, victory, victory,
victory, victory victory, victory victory, victory victory,
Speak out the victory of mother Shyama, victory, victory,
speak out the victory of mother Shyama).

In this way, at the time of composing songs of "*Valmiki-Pratibha*", a new avenue of adding tunes to songs opened out to Gurudev. In other words, he was inspired with composing songs worth singing from beginning to end by considering the ideas of lines one after another at a stretch without setting the tunes through the system of division of lines as done in the Indian music. He also understood that it is also necessary to change *lay* at places, keeping an eye to the idea of words at the time of singing.

This new endeavour of Gurudev to compose songs was not only limited to "*Valmiki-Pratibha*" but we also notice its manifestation in his one or two songs of lyrical emotion in those days. Prior to his first sojurn to England, Gurudev composed the song "Bali, O aamar Golap bala" ("I say, O my girl of roses") in one idea, at Ahmedabad. After his return from abroad, he revised the song. The form in which we get the song at present was made in the period of experimentation of composing songs with the influence of the European thoughts on music.

Behag Ektala

Bali, o aamar golap-bala,
Tolo mu' khani, tolo mu' khani,
Kusuma kunja karo aala!
Bali, keeser sharam eto!
Sakhi, keeser sharam eto!
Sakhi, patar majhare lookaye mu'khani
Keesher sharam eto!
Bala, ghumaye parechhe dhara,
Sakhi, ghumay chandra tara,
Priye, ghoomay dikbalara,
Priye, ghumay jagat jata.
Sakhi, balite maner katha,
Bala, emon samay katha!
Priye, tolo 'mu' khani aachhego aamar
Praner katha kata!
Aami emon sudhir sware,
Sakhi, kahiba tomar kane,
Priye, swapaner mata se katha aasiye
Pashibe tomar prane.
Tabe, mu khani tulia chaao
Sudhire mu' khani tulia chaao!
Sakhi, ekti chumban daao
Gopane ekti chumban daao!

(I say, O my girl like roses, raise your face, raise, enlighten the garden of flowers!
I say, why so ashamed!
Friend, why so ashamed!
Friend, hiding the face amidst leaves,
Why so ashamed!
Girl, asleep is the earth,
Friend, asleep are the moon and the stars,
Dear, asleep are the girls of the horizon,
Dear, asleep all the world.

Friend, to tell the words of the mind
Say, where that time is!
Dear, raise your face, what a sea of words
there is in my mind!
I, with voice very cool,
Friend, in your ears would speak,
Dear, dreamlike that would come
and speak in your heart
Then, look holding up your face,
Slowly look holding up your face,
Friend, only a kiss allow,
Only a kiss allow!)

In the very same period, and in the same model, Gurudev composed the song 'Sakhi, bhabona kahare bale' in the *Vehag-Khamvaj ragini.* Its total number of lines is thirty-one.

Vehag-khamvaj-Ektala

Sakhi, bhabona kahare bole?
Sakhi, jatana kahare bole?
Tomra je bolo dibasa-rajani
bhalobasa bhalobasa—
Sakhi bhalobasa kare koy?
Seki kebali jatonamoy?
Tahe, kebali chokher jal?
Tahe kebali duker swas?
Tahe kebali dukher swas?
Loke tabe kare ki sukher tare
amon dukher aas?
Aamar chakhe ta sakali sobhan,
Sakali nabin, sakali vimal,
Sunil aakash, shyamal kanon,
Vishoda jochhana, kusum komal
sakali aamari mata
(Tara) kebali hashe kebali gaay
Hashia khelia marite chaay
Najane bedan, na jane rodan,
Na jane sadher jatana jata
Phool to hashite hashite jhare

Jochhana hashia milaye jaay,
Hashite hashite alok-sagare
Aakasher tara teyage kaay.
Aamar matan sukhi ke aachhe!
Aay sakhi aay aamar kachhe!
Sukhi hridayer sukher gaan
Shunia toder judave praan!
Pratidin jadi kandibi kebal
Ekdin nay hashibi tora,
Ekdin nay vishad bhulia
Sakale milia gahibo mora,

(Friend, what is thought?
Friend, what is suffering?
Day and night you tell about
love-love
Friend, what is love?
Is it suffering alone?
In those tears alone?
In those sighs of sorrow alone?
Why, for what happiness then, people hope for such sorrow?
Everything in my eyes is beautiful
Everything young, everything clear,
The blue sky, the green forest,
The vast moonlight, tender like the flowers,
Everything alike me.
(They) go on laughing and singing,
Want to die in laughing and singing,
Pain they know not, weeping they know not
Nor do they know the sufferings of desire.
Flowers wither in laughter,
Moonlight wanes in laughter, too,
Laughingly in the sea of heaven
Do stars of the sky their body leave,
Who is so happy as I am!
Come, dear, come to me!
The song of happiness of a heart happy
Would, on hearing, fill in your heart.
If everyday ye only weep,
Let one day laugh ye
Let one day we'll forget sorrow
And all sing together.)

These two songs are composed at a certain period in 1287 B.E. (1880). Formerly, this system of adding tunes in a poem of many lines was not seen in our country.

Towards the middle of the year 1289 B.E. (1882), Gurudev's second musical drama "*Kalmrigaya*" was composed and acted in the pattern of "*Valmiki-Pratibha*". From then onwards till the last day of his life, he turned a pretty few poems consisting of many lines into songs of indigenous tunes. For example—

1. Aamar praner pare chale gelo ke.
   (Who went away over my heart)
2. Tomra hashiya bahiya chalia jao.
   (Go ye laughing and flowing).
3. Eai to bhalo legechhilo.
   (This, indeed, appealed nice)
4. Esho Esho vasanta dharatale.
   (Come, spring, come to the earth)
5. E shudhu alasa maya.
   (It is only an illusion of idleness).
6. Ke aamare jena enechhe dakiya.
   (Some one, as if, has called on me).
7. Prangane more shirish shakhay
   (In the branches of *shirish* in my courtyard).

It is necessary to explain one or two points on the characteristics of adding tunes to these songs.

When the *raga* or *ragini* of the Hindi music of a high order, is spread in the pattern of *aalap,* then the orginal and permanent lyric emotion of the *ragini* attains a special motion. It does not stand in a fixed place; it goes ahead in many forms. The permanent emotion of the above-mentioned long poems of lyric emotion by Gurudev is mystified in that diversity of form; it did not want to be caged in a small area. When Gurudev added tunes according to the meanings and the idea of each line of these poems, it was naturally seen that the movements of these poems remained unchecked as a song also. These few songs are, therefore, to be finished by singing at a stretch from the beginning. The two songs "Aamar praner pare chale gelo ke ("Who went away over my heart") and "Esho esho vasanta dharatale" (come, spring, come to the earth) are of different types. The other songs are completed by singing at a stretch in the *tal* of stipulated rhymes. But the song 'Aamar praner pare chale gelo ke' should not be sung in that way. It will have to be sung in the pattern of speech in broken rhymes.

The total number of the lines of the song 'Esho esho vasanta dharatale' is twenty-three. It is composed in mixed tunes and in the beat of four accents, the *ragini* was not set in the usual pattern of division of lines; consequently, no opportunity is there in this song to come back to the tune of *aasthayee* again and again. Although the song is composed in the fixed beat, it will have to be sung at a stretch without stoppage by changing the *lay* of *tal* in accordance with the ideas of lines in slow, medium, or quick movements as occasion demands.

Madhya lay

Esho esho vasanta dharatale;
Aano muhu muhu navatan, ano nava pran, nava gan,
Aano gandhamadabhare alasa samiran.

Middle movement

Come, spring, come into the earth,
Bring new tunes again and again, bring new life, new songs/Bring indolent breeze burdened with fragrance of wine.

Drut lay

Aano viswer antare antare nivida chetana,
Aano nava ullas hillol,
Aano aano aananda chhander hindol dharatale,
Bhango bhango vandhana-srinkhal
Aano aano uddipta praner vedana dharatale.

Fast movement

Bring deep consciousness in every heart
Bring new waves of excitement
Bring, bring on earth the movement of rhyme joyous
Break, break the fetters of chains
Bring, bring the pains of boistrous heart on earth.

Madhya lay

Esho thara-thara-kampita : marmara mukharita, nava-pallava-pulakita
Phoola-aakula malati-valli-vitane, sukhachhaye, madhu-vaye,

Middle movement

Come, in the mildly trembled, enamoured with murmurs,
Joyous with new leaves,
Eager-for-flowers garden of *maalati* creepers,
in the shadow of happiness, in the air sweet.

Drut lay

Esho vikashita unmukh, esho chira utsuk, nandana-pathachirajatri,
Esho spandita nandita chitta-nilaye gaane gaane praane praane.

Fast movement

Come, the eager for blooming, come, the ever interested,
The eternal traveller of the garden of heaven.
Come in the abode of mind thrilling and dancing, in songs, in every heart.

Dhima lay

Esho aruna-charana kamala-varana taruna ooshaar kole
Esho jyotsna-vivasha-nishithe, kala kallola tatinitire,
Sukhasupta sarashinire.

Slow movement

Come in the lap of dawn—sunlike legged, lotus-coloured young.
Come at night mesmerized by moonlight, on the bank of the murmuring stream, in the water of the lake asleep in happiness.

Drut lay

Esho tarit sikha sama jhanjhavibhange sindhutarangadole.
Esho jagarmukhara prabhate, esho nagare prantare vane,
Esho karme vachane mane, esho esho.

Fast movement

Come like flashes of lightning in the dance of the hailstorm in the surging waves of the sea.
Come in the morn thrilled with awakening, come in cities, fields and forests,
Come in words in speech and the mind, come, come.

Madhya lay

Esho manjira-gunjara charane, esho gitamukhar kalakanthe,
Esho manjula mallika-malye, esho komala kiṣhalaya vasane.

Middle movement

Come with steps humming with the sound of *manjira,*
Come with the voice chirping with the sound of music,
Come with the sweet garland of *mallika,*
Come with the dress of tender new leaves.

Drut lay

Esho sundar jouvan-vege, esho driptavir, nave teje,
Ohe durmad, karo jayajatra, chala jara-parabhava samare,
Pavane keshar-renu chhadaye, chanchala kuntala udaye.

Fast movement

Come, Beautiful, in the speed of youth, come the emboldened hero, in new power,
O unvanquished, make the victorious journey, go in the War against disease and defeat
Spreading the pollens of *Nagkeshar,* waving the restless hair.

5 SONGS OF THE PATTERN OF SPEAKING

Gurudev said about "*Valimiki-Pratibha*" and "*Kalmrigaya*" as musical dramas :

> "Almost all its tunes are indigenous, but, in the musical drama, it has been drawn out of its prestige in conferences in a different sphere. All who have witnessed the acting of this musical drama would, I hope, admit that it has not become incorrect or fruitless to employ music in the work of acting in this way. This is the characteristic of "*Valmiki-Pratibha*",... that is a new experiment in music... Music itself has not dominated over it; its dramatic element is only acted in tunes.".

By conference-based songs, Gurudev wanted to indicate the various Hindi songs of the high order and Bengali songs, that were in vogue among the rich and educated societies of the then Bengal. Gurudev broke those Hindi and Bengali songs and turned them into one worthy of conversation of his musical drama. In the conversations of the different characters of the drama there are descriptions of anger, sorrow, laughter, tears, fear, fun, affection, empathy and such other emotions of the heart. But, at the time of acting, he sang in the pattern of words in many *raginis.* These did appear as current songs. In most of the songs there was no restraint of *tal* in accordance with musicology. For this reason, Gurudev wrote, "In '*Valmiki-Pratibha*', the restraint of songs was not totally averted, but in order to follow ideas, the *tal* has been dwarfed. As acting in fundamental, this exception to *tal* does not hurt the audience.".

Being encouraged by the success of the composition and acting of these musical dramas, Gurudev delivered a lecture, after a few months, at the Bethune Society in the evening of April 19, 1881 with illustrations through songs. With a view to explaining the ideas of his composing the songs of his two musical dramas and the reasons for singing these songs in the pattern of conversations, he published the essays "Sangit O Bhav", "Sangiter Utpatti O Upayogita" and "Sangit O Kavita" in the Journal *Bharati.* All the three essays were written at the time of the acting of the two musical dramas "*Valmiki-Pratibha*" and "*Kalmrigaya*". I would now try to show from the extracts of those essays how attempts were made to translate all those thoughts in the various emotional songs of "*Valmiki-Pratibha*".

1. "When we cry, the distance between the two tunes remaining side by side is very meagre. The voice of crying rolls over every soft tune; the tune becomes very much strained."

The two songs of "*Valmiki-Pratibha*"—'Ha kee dasa halo aamar' ('Ha, what a condition for me!') of the *ragini garabhairavi'* and "Valvo kee aar valvo, Khuro-ooh, ooh' ('Ooh, Ooh—What shall I say, uncle!') of *gouri ragini* are sung in the slow movement in the conversational rhyme by breaking the order. In expressing "Ooh, ooh" of the second song, it is the system to express the voice of crying realistically by maintaining *ragini.*

2. "When we laugh—ha, ha, ha, ha—there is not a single tender tune, nor even is there a single strained tune; there is a great distance between the two side by side tunes, and the tune appears at every stress of *tal.*"

Adjusting the *ragini* with the ha ha sounds of laughter, the two songs "Path bhulechhis satyi bate" ("Really you have forgotten the path") and 'Ha, ha bhaaya khappa" ("Ha ha, the brother is enraged") of *piloo ragini* and *Kanada raag* respectively are to be sung in comic acting exactly in stress. Moreover, the tunes of the whole two songs are composed by really maintaining a bit of distance between them.

3. "The *ragini* of happiness moves in very quick footsteps like happy days. It crosses two or three tunes. In our *raginis* there is the tune of excitement in joy. "The very mood of our music is gradual rise or gradual fall. There is no sudden rise or sudden fall. The tune of exaggerated hilarious excitement is very casual ..... There are tunes of terrible hilarious excitement in English *raginis.* In our *raginis* it may also be said that there is no such tune."

"Ekdore bandha aachii mora sakale" ("We are all bound in one string") in *Khambaz* and "Eai vela save mile chalo ho" ('O let's start together") in *Imankalyan ragini* are hilarious songs of the burglars. It is worth notice how the sudden rise and fall of tunes have occurred in these two songs.

4. "Many a time in case of composing a hilarious song, we set it in fast movement whatever type the *ragini* is"

"Eta ranga shikhechho kothay mundamalini" ("Where have you learnt such hilariousness, o one adorned with the garland of human heads") is a hilarious song sung by burglars in the fast movement.

5. With the change in ideas it is necessary to make *tal* fast and stretched. It is not proper that everywhere the *tal* will be the same or equal.

The above is clearly expressed in the song "Kali kali bal re aaz" ("Speak Kali Kali to-day") based on the English break-away songs. Besides this, I will , for instance, refer to a song to show how changes of *lay* have been made in accordance with ideas in it of the *Vehag raagini.* Valmiki has sung this song.

"Kothay judate aachhe thain
Kena pran kena kade re"
(Where shall I satiate my existence,
Why does the heart cry, O why?")

One will have to sing up-to this of the part of *aasthayee* in slow movement and in the rhyme of words.

"Jai dekhi shikarete
Rahiva aamode mete
Bhuli sav jwala vane vane chhutiye".
("Let me go ahunting
I will remain intoxicated in joy
By forgetting all burnings and making them afoot
From forest to forest")

One will have to sing these three lines of regulated rhyme in the fast movement of *antara* at a stretch and then will have to sing in the previous rule by returning to the lines "Kena pran kande re" (Why does the heart cry, O why ?") of the first part.

> "Apana bhulite chai, bhuliva kemane-
> Kemane jave vedana."
> ("I would like to forget myself, how would I,
> How would pain disappear?")

This *kali* (extract) of *Sanchaari* is sung in the middle movement in the pattern of words.

> "Dhari dhanu aani vaan
> Gahiva vyadher gaan,
> Dalval laye mativa".
> (Holding the bow and bringing the arrow
> The song of a fowler shall I sing,
> With groups shall I be drunk.").

After singing this part of *aabhog* in the fast movement and regulated rhyme, the song is to be completed by singing "Keno pran keno kande re" ("Why does the heart cry, O why") in accordance with the previous rules. The first line of this song is only sung in the beginning, it is not sung after every *kali* (part) in accordance with the system in vogue.

6. "Let the *tal* (beat) remain as it is, let the division of *matra,* remain the same. Only one will have to return to *sam* at a certain place. I do not see any disadvantage without having the advantage in such a regulation".

"It is better to do away with the rule that one must come back to *sam* by any means. It is enough if there is equal *matra* in *tal;* it does not seem to be good to be more rigid than that."

Most of the lines of "Chaarbo na bhai chhharbo na bhai" ("No, dear, I won't leave you") in *Misra Vageshri,* "Gahane gahane ja re tora" ("Go, ye, into the deep") in *vahar* and "Aar na, aar na ekhane aar na" ("No more, no more, no more here") in *Natanarayan* are sung in the rhythm of beats. In one or two places, that is divided. But as these are beats, there is no chance for repetition to specially show the stress of the regular *sam.* Every line will have to be finished by singing by maintaining rhythm. It does not stop in accordance with the rule of *sam* or gap even though the line ends.

7. "In a musical drama, what is to be acted from beginning to end necessitates absence of beats in accordance with places. Otherwise, it is impossible to accelerate enjoyment in acting."

Gurudev composed most of the songs of "*Valmiki-Pratibha*" and "*Kalmrigaya*" by breaking many Hindi songs current in that era and the Bengali ones known to him. For this reason, we call these songs translated songs; there is hardly any song of his own. There were some break-away songs of the European tune. The rest are all composed following indigenous songs. But when all the original songs were translated and sung in the drama, then those appeared in a new form. This is because they were sung in a tune in the pattern of speaking. To explain this speciality of songs of the musical drama, Gurudev said :

> "The subject-matter of the drama is only acted in tuning. It has very little beauty of music separately... In order to follow ideas, it has to shorten the *tal.* As acting is fundamental, this exception of the *tal* does not afford sorrow to the audience".

Thus, at the time of composing "*Valmiki-Pratibha*", the following fundamental principles on adding tunes came to Gurudev's mind permanently, and he knew it for certain :

1. The *ragini* of words with ideas of desolation, melancholy, separation or weeping will be rolling and very strained.
2. In lively, ennervating, humorous, happy and hilarious songs, the tune will march in quick footsteps, cross over two or three tunes or suddenly rise or fall.
3. The tune of words expressing reverence, submission, salutation and sombre emotion will not be a rolling one. The vowel sounds will be placed nearer and the movement will neither be very slow nor very fast.
4. In case of singing in the pattern of conversation of acting, differences in movements in the same song following ideas must be made.

Gurudev extensively utilized these few fundamental principles of adding tunes in accordance with ideas in his various types of songs composed in his later life. This continued till the end of his life. This is the remarkable aspect of his song that indicates the influence of musical thoughts of Herbert Spencer or European music.

The Indian music is a diverse and endless storehouse of *raga-raginis* and rhythm. So, Gurudev had not to beg for tune and rhythm to other countries. In our ancient music, too, there were some special strategies for applying tune and rhythm in accordance with the ideas of words. This attracted Gurudev's attention at the time of his composing musical dramas in foreign thoughts. Afterwards, it was for this reason that he had an advantage, in extensively applying the ancient musical treasures of India in the creation of music. A discussion, in brief, may be made on how songs were composed in ancient India in accordance with the ideas of words.

The movement of the Hindi classical songs composed in *choutal* is slow and its nature is sombre, the method of adding tunes being easy, simple and non-ornamental. There is no restlessness in this song. The songs are calm and favourable to widen meditation for religion. The untrembled tunes are greater in number in this song, but these are primarily *gamak* and *meed.* The singers pay strict attention to the purity of *raga-raginis* at the time of singing. They had no freedom to change the tunings of the *Vandesi* Hindi song. The current system of this song is to express every tune over words distinctly. In its early stage, *Kheyal* was a relative of *Dhrupad* (classical songs). This serenity of the ancient *Kheyal* and *Dhrupad* is expressed in all the serious songs of Gurudev.

Almost all the songs of calm and serene nature were composed by Gurudev in the rhythm of *Choutal, Dhamar, Dhima-tetala* and *Ektala* in the model of Hindi songs.

The tune of songs of excitement or hilariousness in the Hindi songs of ancient times having *Jhaaptal, Teora tal,* suddenly rises and falls by maintaining a pretty distance between the upward and the downward movements. Gurudev has used these *tals* in the songs of same ideas composed by him and his system of adding tunes is the same.

Kheyal is the song of restless joy. Specially, the stresses of rhythm of *Drut Kheyal* and *Top Kheyal* fill the mind of the audience restless in joy. In the Bengali songs composed in the rhythm of *Drut Tetala* by Gurudev, an emotion of restless joy is noticed.

Hindi or Bengali *Tappa* songs are not favourable to serene or exciting ideas. They are appropriate to express the ideas of the feelings of sadness arising out of detachment or separation. Whenever Gurudev has composed Bengali songs following the ancient *Tappa* songs, the emotions of the feelings of detachment or sorrow only have been expressed in these. There is no scope for restlessness in the system of application of notes and in the speed of rhythm.

Gurudev thus utilized the treasures of the Indian music at the time of composing his songs in diverse avenues. That was why, it did not take much time for him to eliminate the various shortcomings that he had felt about the Indian music in his early youth.

An evaluation of the storehouse of the songs composed by Gurudev will prove the point that at the time of composing songs of emotion like sombre, exciting, joyous, sorrowful and painful ones, he took the help of foreign thoughts but arranged them only with indigenous ingredients. In the few dance-dramas composed by him towards the last decade of his life, we get a successful stamp of the integration of thoughts of the two countries. In these, everything like the rhythm of *tal* in accordance with the ideas of words, break-away rhythm, rhythm of words and varieties of *lay* has been accommodated together. But their patterns of tunes and composition are completely Indian.

In Gurudev's songs of different categories, too, we get a very distinct evidence of this influence. As already mentioned, he introduced the new system of adding tunes in the long poems of the same nature. We have also come across examples of how the long poems, woven in the *ragini* or tune are to be sung by changing the movement of the same *tal* in accordance with ideas, in the song "Esho esho Vasanta dharatale" ("Come, Spring, come to the earth") already referred to. Besides these, towards the end of his life, he also composed songs of the pattern of speaking in the tune of the songs of *Valmiki-Pratibha.* The two songs "Krishna kali aami tarei boli" ("Krishnakali I call her alone") and "Tumi ki kebali chhabi" ("Are you merely a potrait") are examples of this type. I have heard so many songs in the voice of Gurudev as he had sung, completely in the pattern of conversation. A direct evidence to this is his songs composed in the middle period of his life and recorded in his old age "Tabu mane rekho" ("Remember me yet"), "Kangal aamare kangal karechho", ("Poor have you made me, poor") and "Esho he badhu, phire esho" ("Come, ye bride, return").

The avenue of emancipation for the Indian music that Gurudev showed in the above way through his own songs, is not born of imitation but of co-ordination as a consequence to the influence of the European thoughts on music.

6 A FEW CHARACTERISTICS OF DIVISION OF WORDS IN GURUDEV'S SONGS

A few statutory systems of adding tunes by arranging the words of the Indian Hindi and folk songs of high order from twofold to fourfold division of words have been going on for a long time. There are also songs of manifold division of words but tunes are added to these by turning tunes from two-fold to four-fold division. The normal system is to add tunes to the lines of Hindi classical songs by dividing them into fourfold parts. Classical songs of twofold division of words are also found but these are not songs of the existing system. The names of the four divisions of words of the *Dhrupad* are *Aasthayee, Antara, Sanchari* and *Aabhog.* In *Kheyal* songs, the number of division of words in vogue are two only—*Aasthayee* and *Antara;* sometimes songs of fourfold division of words are also found, but their last two divisions of words are sung in the tune of *Antara. Tappa* and *Thungri* are songs of twofold division of words. Many songs in the Bengali language were composed in this imitation. Bengal's own folksong and *Kirtan* are fundamentally songs of two-fold division of tuned words. As there are generally a great number of divisions of words in these songs, the rest divisions of words are sung in repetitions of the tune of *Antara.* Songs of fourfold division of words like the *Dhrupad* are not found in folk-songs or in *Kirtan* songs.

Just as Gurudev Rabindranath composed songs of fourfold and twofold divisions of words following the Hindi *Kheyal, Dhrupad* and *Tappa* songs, he also composed many songs following the current division of words of the folksong and the *Kirtan.* But we get the maximum number of songs of fourfold division of words like the *Dhrupad.* As he had a very great tendency towards a fourfold division of words, he arranged many songs composed by him in the models of *Kheyal, Tappa, Kirtan* and folksong into division of words and added tunes in the rule of the *Dhrupad.* But, besides these, we find a few songs in which he invented a few systems at the time of adding tunes to division of their words. For example, it is normally seen in Gurudev's songs of five-fold to ten-fold division of words that he has added tunes to the first four divisions of words in accordance with the rules of the Hindi *Dhrupad* and, in the succeeding divisions of words, he has used the tunes of *Sanchari* and *Aabhog* one after the other. Even in Gurudev's *Baul* songs or in those of the tunes of *Kirtan,* no exception to this was made. I shall now make an endeavour to elucidate the nature of these songs with some of his songs composed in four to ten divisions of words.

Let me begin with a song of five divisions of words. The first division of words of the song is *Aasthayee* and the second *kali* is *Antara.* The tune of the third *kali* is like that of *Antara.* For this, I shall call it the second *Antara.* In the succeeding fourth *kali* a separate tune like that of *Sanchari* is set. The tune of the fifth *kali* is the same as that of the second *kali* or *Antara.* It may be called *Aabhog* of the third *Antara.* The song of five *kalis* that I am referring to as a specimen is composed in the *Bhimpalasri raag* and in *Ektal.* It is Gurudev's "Aamay chhajanay mile path dekhay bale" ("As six persons show me the way"). The tunes as set forth in its five *kalis* are :

Aasthayee

Aamay chhajanay mile path dekhay bale
Pade pade path bhuli he!
Nana kathar chhale nanan muni bale,
Sangsaye tai duli he.

Ist. Antara

Toma kachhe jabo eichhilo saadh,
Tomar vani sune ghuchabo pramaad,
Kaner kachhe sabai karichhe vivaad—
Sata loker sata vuli he.

2nd. Antara

Katar prane aami tomay jakhan jachi
Aadal kare sabai draday kachhakachhi,
Dharanir dhulo tai niye aachhi—
Paaine charan dhuli he.

Sanchari

Sata bhaag mor sata dike dhay
Aapana –aapni vivad Vadhay
Kare samaliva, eki halo daay,
Eka je anekguli he.

3rd. Antara or Aabhog

Aamay ek karo tomar preme vendhe
Ek path aamay dekhao avichchhede,
Aandhar majhe pade kata mari kende,
Charanete laho tuli he.

Aasthayee

As six persons show me the way
O, at every step I forget it
Many experts deliver opinions diverse
O, in doubts do I retreat.

The First Antara

My intention was to go to you,
Hearing your words did confusions adieu
The quarrels of all are coming thro'
The ears, O, a hundred persons have a hundred sermons :

The Second Antara

When I make a piteous call
In shade do stand nearer all
The dust of the earth is what I recall
O, I've not yet been blessed with the dust
Of your feet sacred.

Sanchari

My hundred parts in a hundred directions rush
And quarrels in the self same style do crush

What an assignment, whom aside I brush,
O, one is indeed equal to legion.

The Third Antara or Aabhog

Stringing in your love, make me one,
Show me the way *sans* separation is gone,
Weep do I amid confusion,
O, let your feet be my holy bed.

The matter to be noticed in this song is that the tune of *Sanchari* has been set at the end of two *Antaras* of the same tune consecutively, which is normally not made. The current system is to set the tune of *Sanchari* after the first *Antara.*

"Gahana kusama kunja majhe", is a song of six *kalis*. Its first and second *kalis* are *Aasthayee* and *Antara* respectively and a separate tune like *Sanchari* has been set in the third *kali.* The tune of the fourth *kali* next is like that of *Antara.* We shall, therefore, call it *Aabhog.* Upto this, we are getting the song in four *kalis* like the *Dhrupad.* But instead of ending the song here, it has been completed by adding two *kalis* more with it. These two *kalis* are consecutively sung in the tunes of *Sanchari* and *Aabhog*.

Aasthayee

Gahana kusuma kunja majhe
Mridual madhura bangshi baje
Visari trasa lokalaaje
Sajani, aao aao lo.

Antara

Pinaha charu nila vasa
Hridaye pranayakusumaraasa
Harinanetre vimala haasa
Kunjavanme aao lo!

Sanchari

Dhaale kusuma surava-bhaar
Dhale vihaga surava-saar
Dhale indu amritadhaar
Vimala rajatabhaati re.

Aabhog

Manda manda bhringa gunje
Ajuta kusuma kunje kunje
Phutala sajani, punje punje
Vakula juthi jati re.

Dwitiya Sanchari

Dekha, lo Sakhi, shyaamaraay
Nayane prema uthale jaay
Madhura vadana amritasadana
Chandramaay nindichhe.

Tritiya Antara/Dwitiya Aabhog

Aao aao sajanivrinda
Heriva sakhi Srigovinda
Shyamko padaravinda
Bhanusingha vandichhe.

Aasthayee

Amid dense garden of flowers
On plays the soft and sweet flute
Forgetting fear and public shame
Come, ye come, O dear.

Antara

Dress thyself with the artistic new attire
Fill in thy heart with wedding flowers

Laugh with thy deerlike eyes
Come, ye in the garden of flowers
Fragrance do flowers shower
Essence of pleasant sound do birds shower
Streams of nectar does the man shower
O, the crescent silver lustre :

Aabhog

In the breeze do bees hum
In the garden of flowers unending
In clusters, O dear, bloom
Vakul, Juthi and others alike.

The Second Sanchari (Shyamaray)

O dear friend, Shyamaray, behold
Love in eyes does overflow,
A lovely countenance is a nectar bar
Is being despised by the moon.

The Third Antara or The Second Aabhog

Come, ye, come, dear all
Friends, we'll see *Srigovinda*
The feet of *Shyam* beautiful as the moon,
Bhanusingha is saluting.

Posterior to this *Kirtan* song of the *Jhinjhit raag,* I am quoting another song of six *kalis* of the tune of *Kirtan.* In the first four *kalis* of the song, the tune of *Kirtan* has been set in accordance with the rules of the *Dhrupad,* one by one, the tune of the fifth *kali* is that of *Sanchari Kali.* But they are not one and the same in toto. In the sixth *kali,* we get the tune of *Aabhog* in a slightly changed form. For example :

Aasthayee

Purana jaaniya cheyona aamare
Aadheka aankhira kone alasa anyamane

Antara

Aapanare aami dite aasi jei
Jeno jeno sei suva nimeshei
Jirna kichhui nei kichhu nei
Phele dei puratane.

Sanchari

Aapanare dey jharna aapan tyagarase uchhvali
Lahare lahare nutan nutan arghyer anjali

Aabhog

Madhavikunja vaar vaar kari
Vanalaksmir daala dey bhari
Vaar vaar taar daanmanjari
Nava nava kshane kshane.

Dwitiya Sanchari

Tomar preme je legechhe aamar
Chiranutaner sur
Sav kaje mor sav bhavanay
Jage chira sumadhur.

Dwitiya Aabhog

More daane nei dinatar lesh,
Jata neva tumi na pave sesh—
Aamar diner sakal nimesh
Bhara ashesher dhane.

Aasthayee

Look at me not, knowing me old
In the corners of your eyes half open, in an absent idle mind

Antara

When I come to submit myself
Know, know at that very moment auspicious
Nothing, nothing tattered is.
The old I leave off.

Sanchari

The fountain offers herself with the overflow of the stream of sacrifice,
In every wave is her new folded hands of offerings.

Aabhog

The garden of *Madhavi* again and again
Fills in the tray of the goddess of forest
Again and again her bowers of offering
At every moment turn newer and newer.

The Second Sanchari

In your love am I thrilled
With the tune of the ever new,
In all my acts and in all my thoughts
The over-pleasant peeps like the dew.

The Second Aabhog

No poverty does my offering kiss,
The more will you take the less you'll miss.
Every moment of my day is the bliss
Of the wealth of the endless.

We come across another type of song of six *kalis* in a different pattern in Rabindrasangeet. The first *kali* of this song is *Aasthayee* and the second *kali, Antara.* The tune of the third and the fifth *kalis* are exactly that of *Aasthayee.* The tune of *Antara* is set in its fourth and sixth *kalis.* In other words, every two *kalis* next to *Aasthayee* and

Antara is like the tunes of consecutive *Aasthayee* and *Antara,* composed in the *Misra Jogia Ragini;* this six *kali* song is "Nayana tomare pay na dekhite" ("Eyes cannot see you").

Aasthayee

Nayana tomare paay na dekhite
Rayechha nayane nayane.
Hridaya tomare paay na dekhite
Hridaye ryechha gopane.

Antara

Vaasanar veshe man avirata
Dhhaay dash dishe paagaler mata,
Sthir aankhi tumi marame satata
Jagiccha shayane swapane.

Dwitiya Aasthayee

Savaai chhedechhe nai jaar keha,
Tumi aacha taar aachhe tava sneha.
Niraasray jan, path jaar geha,
Seo aachee tava bhavane.

Dwitiya Antara

Tumi chhada keha saathi naai aar
Samukhe ananta jivanvistaar,
Kaalpaaravar karitechha paar,
Keha naahi jaane kemane.

Tritiya Aasthaye

Jaani shudhu tumi aachha, tai aachhi,
Tumi praanamay taai aami baanchhi,
Jata paai tomaay aaro tata jaachi,
Jata jani tata janine.

Tritiya Antara

Jaani aami tomaay paava nirantar
Lokalokaantare jugajugaantar,
Tumi aar aami maajhe keha naai,
Kono vadhaa naai bhuvane.

Aasthayee

Eyes cannot see you
In eyes you are,
The mind knows not you,
Secretly you remain there.

Antara

Ceaselessly does the mind in aspiration
Like a mad man run in every direction,
Always in the heart with eyes in fixed fashion
Remain, ye, awake in sleep or in dream.

The Second Aasthayee

All have left, none is there,
Remain you and your care
The homeless whose home the through fare
In your residence, he, too, remains.

The Second Antara

Sans you, no mate is there
In front is the expanse of life e'er
The sea of time you are crossing o'er
No one knows, O how.

The Third Aasthayee

Know I you remain alone, so am I,
I live because you are lively
The more I get you, the more to live I try,
The more I know, the more I know not.

The Third Antara

I know I will always have you in me
From the world beyond world from all eras free,
You and I alone, amid none we see,
No constraint is there on earth.

The song that I shall mention now is one of ten *kalis* but of a different quality. The song is "Aamar Sonar Bangla, Aami tomay bhalovasi". ("O my *Sonar Bangla,* I love thee") – an indigenous song of the old break-away *Baul* type. The first and the second *kalis* of the song are *Aasthayee* and *Antara* respectively. The third *kali* is *Sanchari.* In the fourth *kali,* the tune is set in the pattern of *Antara,* and so we may call it *Aabhog.* Upto this, the song is formed in the tune, *Baul,* of consecutive four *kalis* in the patterns of *Aasthayee, Antara, Sanchari* and *Aabhog* of the *Dhrupad.* By dividing the next six *kalis* into consecutive two *kalis,* the tune has been set in the pattern of *Sanchari* and *Aabhog.*

Aasthayee

Aamar sonar Bangla, aami tomay bhalovasi
Chiradin tomaar aakash, tomaar bataash,
Aamar praane vaajay vaashi.

Antara

O maa, phaalgoone tor aamer vane
Ghraane paagal kare (Mari haay, haay re)-
O maa, aghrane tor bharaa kshete
Aami ki dekhechhi madhur haashi

Sanchari

Kee shova ki chhaaya go,
Kee sneha ki maya go,
Kee aanchal vichhayechha vater mule,
Nadir kule kule.

Aabhog

Maa, tor mukher vani aamar kaane
Laage sudhaar mata, (Mari haay, haay re)-
Maa, tor vadankhaani malin hale,
Aami nayanjale bhaasi.

The Second Sanchari

Tomaar oi khelaghare
Shishukaal katilo re
Tomaari dhulamaati ange maakhi
Dhanya jivan maani.

The Second Aabhog

Tui din phoorale sandhyakaale
Kee dwip jwaalis ghare (Mari haay, haay re)-
Takhan kheladhula sakal phele,
Tomar kole chhute aasi.

The Third Sanchari

Dhenu-charaa tomar maathe,
Paare jaabar kheyaghaate,
Saradin paakhidaka chhayay-dhaka
Tomar pallivate.

The Third Aabhog

Tomaar dhaane-bhara aanginate
Jivaner din kate, (mari haay, haay re)-
Omaa, aamar je bhai tara savai
Tomaar rakhaal tomar chaashi.

The Fourth Sanchari

Omaa, tor charanete
Dilem ei maatha pete-
De go tor paayer dhulaa, se je aamar
Maathar manik have.

The Fourth Aabhog

Omaa, gariver dhan ja aachhe taai
Diva charantale, (Mari haay, haay re)-
Aami parer ghare kinvo naa aar
Bhusan vale galar phaansi.

Aasthayee

O my sonar Bangla, I love thee.
Thy firmament and thy air
Play on the flute eternally.

Antara

Mother dear, in thy mango-groves in *Phalgoon*
With perfumes make me swoon (Ah ha, ha, ha)
Mother dear in thy paddy fields in *Aghraan*
What a lovely smile in thee do I see.

Sanchari

Ah, what a scene and the shade
Ah, what a care and an enchantment parade!
What a covering have ye spread beneath the banyan tree
On the banks of rivers gay and free.

Aabhog

Mother, the words of thy mouth reach my ears
Like drops of juice (Ah ha, ha, ha)
Mother, thy countenance wry and ematiated
Speed forth floods of tears within me.

The Second Sanchari

In the house of play
I did pass my childhood away
I adorn the dust and soil of thee alone
And blessed I think of me.

The Second Aabhog

At the close of the day at even-time
What light do ye trim on in the room :(Ah ha, ha, ha)
Leaving, then, all my games and sports
I return to thy lap hurriedly.

The Third Sanchari

In thy fields where cows graze
In thy *kheyaghaat* to cross over the river-phase
In thy daylong bird-screamed shade-kissed rural place.

The Third Aabhog

In thy paddy-field courtyard
Do pass my life's days, (Ah ha, ha, ha)
O Mother, brothers of mine are they all-
The cowboy and the ploughman of thee.

The Fourth Sanchari

O Mother, on feet thine
I place this head of mine,
Offer me, please, the dust of thy feet, that would be
The jewel of my head.

The Fourth Aabhog

O Mother, whatever treasure do I have, the poor one,
At thy feet, I'll offer (Ah ha, ha, ha)
No more shall I buy from the one unknown
The hanging rope to adorn me.

In spite of the fact that this song was composed in imitation of the tune of the old Baul song of Shelaidah, it slightly differs from the original song in adding tunes with division of words at the beginning.

7 THE INFLUENCE OF BENGALI SONGS ON RABINDRA-SANGEET

From the second half of the eighteenth century to the end of the whole nineteenth century, the history of the extensive culture anew of the Hindi songs of the high order in Bengal that we come across, signifies that many great *Ostads* (Masters) of the Western India came at that time to Bengal on invitations from rich *Zamindars* (Landlords). The Bengalees learnt singing from them with great sincerity and eagerness. Again, for the same purpose, many also went out of Bengal. The original centres for cultivation of the Hindi music were set up in some famous towns of Bengal. One of them was set up at Bishnupur, the capital of the *Malla* kings of the district of Bankura. The second was at Krishnanagar, the district of Nadia; Burdwan, the third, and the fourth was established in Calcutta. In the learning of songs of the high order, this endeavour became most fruitful with the efforts of Sourindramohan Tagore, the rich *Zamindar* of Calcutta and his band of musicians and with the inspiration of the famous musical assembly of Wazed Ali Shah of Metiaburuz, the captive Nawab of Ayodhya. In the *Durbar* of the captive Nawab, many eminent singers and percussionists of the erstwhile Western India were employed. With the help of these centres of music, many well-known Bengalee singers ushered in the middle part of the nineteenth century. The city of Calcutta was the principal centre for this movement for music. We would like to mention the names of a few famous singers of the above-mentioned four localities about whom we hear even now. They are Ramsankar Bhattacharya, Kshetramohan Goswami, Anantalal Bandyopadhyay, Jadubhatta, or Radhikaprasad Goswami of Bishnupur, and Bishnu Chakrabarti of Krishnanagar. He was the singer of the *Adi Brahmo Samaj* and music-teacher of the house of Gurudev. In Calcutta, there were Sourindramohan Tagore, Kaliprasanna Bandyopadhyay, Krishnadhan Bandyopadhyay and other eminent musicians.

Along with the above, we should mention two names more, which are not often heard to-day. But they were very known to the world of music in Calcutta towards the beginning of the nineteenth century. One of them was Kaliprasad Mukhopadhyay. He was called as Kali Mirza. The Second person was Radhamohan Sen. He was a singer and composer of songs and he has made his position permanently secured in the history of the music of Bengal by first publishing books on Hindi music of the high order in the Bengali language. The name of his book is *Sangeet-taranga* (The Waves of Music). It is written not in prose but in poetry.

Towards the middle of this period, a strong aspiration was seen anew among the educated Bengalees towards the history and scientific discussion on the Indian music for the endeavour of Sourindramohan and his group. New books of notations including collections of Hindi songs of *Dhrupad*, *Dhamar*, *Kheyal*, *Tappa* etc., were published. Musical institutions were set up. Discussions and meetings were held. Attempts were made to invite and to unite the *Ostads* by arranging musical assemblies. Books containing analytical discussions on music, whose values have not yet been lessened, were brought out. In this way, an extensive movement was launched in Bengal to re-introduce Hindi songs of the high order.

But the Bengalee singers did not remain satisfied with learning *Ostadi* songs or by fully controlling their rules and regulations. They were strongly inspired within themselves to arrange those songs in the language of their own and to make the same their very own. A new image of music came out with the very launching of this activity. The first man who introduced this new era of music was Ramnidhi Gupta whom Bengal knew as Nidhubabu. When, towards the earlier part of the nineteenth century, he began to compose songs anew in the Bengali language with the help of the Hindi Tappa songs, the appreciators of the Bengalee society were charmed at hearing those songs. From that time onwards till the whole nineteenth century, whoever composed music were all followers of Nidhubabu. Even *Jatra* and *Panchali* songs also changed their patterns with that encouragement. The new pattern of *Dhap Kirtan* that Madhusudan Kinnar or Mudhukhan, the famous *Kirtaniya* (the specialist in *Kirtan)* introduced after learning songs in Hindi from the Muslim *Ostad* was also influenced by the Bengali *Tappa* songs. Nidhubabu extensively used Hindi *raga-raginis* in Bengali *Tappa* songs. He did not at all utilise the indigenous tunes in vogue in Bengal. Besides pure *raginis* in his songs, then were sufficient *Misra raginis* (Mixed tunes). He imitated not only the *Misra raginis* current in Hindi at the time of composing songs but, with the emotion of composing songs, himself created many *Misra raginis* also. Being inspired by his songs of *Misra raginis,* the later composers extensively used *Misra raginis* in their songs.

The rich and the educated communities of those days had a great attraction for the *Tappa* songs of Nidhubabu. One of the major reasons for this was the subject-matter of the songs. Nidhubabu composed songs of love but we get ideas of the lives of love of the men and women of those days from the picture of love that he portrayed in his songs. He did not draw the picture of love through Radha and Krishna like the poets of the previous era. Nidhubabu very boldly brought about a change in that existing system. He was a pioneer in this respect. The later composers of songs have easily composed many songs after the avenues shown by Nidhubabu.

Analysing the trend of the unison of words and *raginis* in Bengali songs, Gurudev said that in our country there are expressions of two ideas in our music, one is in the form of pure music and the other in the form of a mixture of poetry. There are differences of nature in man. In accordance with these differences, these two kinds of expressions take place. The evidence of this is seen in and outside Bengal. No doubt, music in Bengal is a follower of poetry, if not a companion. In Bengal, music has no separate place, it has its seat beside words. For these reasons, the words of the song are to compromise in the interest of tunes and to be appropriate with the latter.

Where music prevails with its own uniqueness, its purity of rules and restraints is expressed there. However, its purity cannot be maintained lackadaisically as a song in association with words but if one masters over the system of music out of continuity, one is appropriately empowered within oneself to bring about changes of rules.

Gurudev has expressed, within these few words, the nature of everyone associated with Bengali songs and their composers in the nineteenth century. It is true that those who achieved fame as composers of songs in the Bengali language in the nineteenth century practised Hindi songs of the high order under any *Ustad* (Master) of those days. As they achieved complete mastery over the *raga-raginis* and *Tal,* they were able to mix words with *raginis* easily and beautifully and this unison of *raginis* was easy to them for the same reasons.

The language of the *Tappas* of Nidhubabu was Bengali. So the rules of the *raga-raginigs* of Hindi songs and their strategies for singing were not given importance in these songs. As he was able to mix words and *raginis* in the same proportion, he omitted much of the strategies of singing the *Tappas* in original. As a result, the Bengali *Tappa* was comparatively easy to a certain extent. Considering the aspect of union between the words and the *raginis,* he easily broke the rules of the *raga-raginis* of Hindi songs. In spite of that, it was not very easy to sing Nidhubabu's Bengali *Tappa.* It was necessary to undergo practice for many days and to have a good knowledge of *raga-raginis* and *Tal* for singing those songs. But gradually that pattern of singing was made easier in need of the public. This very easy pattern extensively made room in the *Jatra,* the *Panchali* and in the theatre. Even now, easy songs of this type are heard to be sung by the rural singers of Bengal. The Bengali songs of this easy method composed with the help of the *raga-raginis* of the *Uchchanga Sangeet* has been greatly given prominence in the compositions of Gurudev. The songs of *Misra raginis* that we get in Gurudev's compositions are not a casual outcome as I think. I would like to say that the songs of Gurudev were impressed by the model of the Bengali songs of the nineteenth century. He was born in the era when the songs like the Bengali *Tappa,* the *Jatra* songs of Gopal Ure and the *Panchali* song of Dashuray were on the lips of every Bengalee. His infancy and childhood were spent in the midst of the songs of these types. It will be highly erroneous to say that he was brought up amidst the Hindi/*Ostadi* songs alone. Gurudev has himself said that he could himself sing *panchali* songs he had heard from the servants in his infancy. The tunes of those songs were strung in the *raga-raginis* of the Hindi songs of the high order. He also noticed the same thing in *Jatra* and in *Kathakata* as well. The influence of Gopal Ure's *Jatra* songs was there in the songs of the dramas and others composed by the elder brother (Jyotirindranath) and the aged relatives. Jyotirindranath played *raga-raginis* on the piano, and the songs in which he told Gurudev to set words in accordance with ideas, appeared to hear like the erstwhile Bengali songs of pure and mixed *raginis* simple and easy *tal.* Vishnu Chakrabarti, the first master of music in the life of Gurudev, imparted the first lesson on music to the latter at the age of six and that song was a nursery rhyme of easy rhythm in the Bengali language. Its tune was strung in *raga-ragini.* Such an atmosphere of music encompassed the early life of Gurudev. This is why it was possible for him in his later life to compose songs easily by making a balanced fusion of words and *raginis* and by the manifold mixtures of *raga-raginis*. From a good assessment of the Bengali songs of the nineteenth century, it can easily be said that in composing songs, Gurudev was the most successful and best personality of that era that introduced the trend through Nidhubabu.

8 RABINDRANATH AND PANDIT BHATKHANDE IN THE THOUGHT OF SANDHIPRAKASH RAGINI

It does not necessitate to tell musicians anew that Sri Vishnunarayan Bhatkhande is the best of the experts on *Uchchanga* Hindustani music. His book entitled "*Hindusthani Sangit Paddhati*" ("Methods of Hindustani Music"), "*Laksha Sangit*", "*Abhinav Ragmanjari*" and "*Kramik Pustak Malika*" are epoch-making in the North Indian Music. It can be said without hesitation that he made his permanent position along with the ancient musicians like Srangadev and others for these few books.

Bhatkhande was educated in the university of the British era. So we encounter with his argumentative attitude like the European scholars, in his thoughts and discussions. Perhaps, for this reason, it was particularly seen that he wanted to assess the North Indian music through arguments. That he did not stick to the principles of six *ragas* and thirty-six *raginis* of the musicians of the past era without assessment, gives an important evidence to this very attitude. He, therefore, ventured to divide into the original ten parts by evaluating Indian Hindustani Music of the high order and its *raga-raginis* anew, and arranged for mass campaign of the music named "Lakshan Geet" which is especially helpful to the beginners. Besides these, he drew the attention of the experts in the North Indian music to some *raginis* and said that those were "Sandhiprakash" *raginis*. We think that by expressing this word he has unfolded the doors of the innermost mystery of the origin of the *raga-raginis* of the Indian Music. With the analysis of the *raga-raginis* of "Sandhiprakash", he expressed the idea and clearly elucidated how the *raga-raginis* of India are closely associated with the expression of the nature of every day, month or season. It would be helpful for the readers if a brief discussion is made on what a "Sandhiprakash" *ragini* is.

The meaning of the word "Sandhi" is union. Day and night comprise 24 hours,. In these, day and night unite twice : once at dawn and then, in the evening. This time of union may be called "Union-period". Just as it takes time to begin and to end solar or lunar eclipse, the time of union of the day and the night is of the same type. It seems that they slowly come closer to each other towards union. After union, they slowly recede to be separated from each other. It takes nearly three hours to be united and to be separated in this way : from 4 a.m. to 7a.m. and from 4 p.m. to 7 p.m. In three hours each in the morning and in the evening, the *raga* or *raginis* of the Hindi music of the high order scheduled to be sung are called 'Sandhiprakash" *ragini*. These fall under the *raginis* of the first class category. The *raginis* to be sung in the juncture of the morning are all of the category of *Bhairav* that is *Bhairav, Kalengda, Ramkeli, Jogia* and *Vibhas*. Again, the *raginis* of the categories of *Marva* and *Puravi* are to be sung in the evening. For example, *Sri, Purevi, Puria, Dhanesri, Vasanta, Paraj, Sohini, Lalit* and *Marva* are to be sung in the evening. In the fourteen *raga-raginis* of the categories of *Bharavi, Puravi* and *Marva,* the notes like the tender *ri,* pure *ga* and *na* remain the same. No change takes place.

We do not know exactly how this thought of the "Sandhiprakash" ragini first came in the mind of Pandit Bhatkhande. But a question similar to this arose in the mind of Gurudev in his early youth. His "Sangit O Bhav" ("Music and Ideas"), an old essay on music, was published in the "Bharati" in Jaistha, 1288 B.E. (June, 1881). Gurudev in his memoirs, wrote on the subject-matter of the essay that on Baisakh 8, 1288 B.E. (April 19, 1881), he first read out this essay in a meeting of the Medical College held under the auspices of the Bethune College. As a token of examples, he himself sang songs by applying different kinds of tunes. The meeting was presided over by Rev. Krishnamohan Bandyopadhyay.

The main subject of Gurudev's lecture was "Geya Sangeet" ("Music to be sung"). In this lecture, he said—

> "The purpose of (the Indian) *raga-raginis* is to express ideas only. But what is the present condition now? Now *raga-raginis* have become the purpose. The *raga-ragini* on whom the idea was placed has now become the supreme by treacherously killing it. Today, whenever anyone hears a song, one wants to see whether *Jayjayanti, Vehag* or *Kanada* is maintained..."
>
> "Now, if the music-experts begin to discover with special attention the identification of expressions in different *raginis,*

there will be the real benefit of music. Where will the idea inherent in our *raga-raginis* go?... Let our experts in music draw the attention of everyone towards that idea. Let them find out why a particular idea arises with a particular *ragini*. Take, for example, why one remembers evening through *puravi* or recalls morning through *Bhairon*. In both *Purvai* and *Bhairon*, there is affluence of the tender tune. Why, then, both bring forth different results? Is that an outcome of ancient rules? That is not true. There are deeper reasons. First, in both the *raginis* of the morning and evening, a tender tune is necessary. Just as morning slowly and gradually opens its eyes, so the evening slowly and gradually closes its eyes. Therefore, the tender tunes, that is, the tunes that have little distance among themselves, the tunes that slowly marge with one another unnoticed, predominate in the *raginis* of the morning and that of the evening. Then, in what respect should there be a difference between the morning and the evening? In one, there should be a gradual manifestation of the tune, and, in the other, a gradual waning of the tune. This difference is maintained in the *Bhairon* and *Puravi* and hence the presence of the morning and the evening in these *raginis*."

After a persual of the above extract of the lecture, it seems that the thoughts of the Sandhiprakashi *ragini* of Pandit Bhatkhande are the reply to the above-mentioned question of Gurudev. Many years after Gurudev's call to the experts on music to discover the appropriate marks of identification of the ideas contained in *raginis*, in between 1909-1914, Bhatkhande, as if admitted that call, as if he directly posed before everyone the same string of thought with his critical analysis that had been hinted at by Gurudev. Now my question is : How did the unity between one's thought and the other's action take place ? Is it the outcome of the same result through following different avenues or is the origin of the same thought elsewhere? We are yet to know.

9 THE REMINISCENCE OF GURUDEV

In the few years of the beginning of the Santiniketan Vidyalaya, Gurudev himself taught students how to sing. Dinendranath was with him, and a few years afterwards, Ajit Chakrabarti joined.

When the number of students increased after 1912, Gurudev had very little time to teach singing. But often he himself taught the songs of functions and festivals. He taught students and teachers together.

When I was a boy of five or six years, I began to learn singing Gurudev's songs at that very period from Dinendranath along with the seniors and the juniors together. I learnt the songs of *Gitanjali* (Song Offerings) in that evening class. Very often Gurudev came, sat and taught all together in ease there was a new song. Afterwards Dinendranath taught us that song and succeeded in making us how to sing that well in our voice. We have all thus learnt from the guidance of Gurudev and Dinendranath together how to sing many new songs of various functions, festivals and dramas. When we were pretty grown up and when Gurudev called on Dinendranath at the time of teaching new songs, Dinendranath often called us together to learn those songs. I have got the first opportunity to learn singing new songs alone from Gurudev off and on a few years before 1930. Afterwards, from 1935 till two months before his death I have learnt singing alone from him at a stretch. In this period, during my tour abroad, there was a discontinuity in my learning singing for about a month only, but on my return, he himself taught me singing those few new songs. From 1935 ordinary songs, songs of dance-dramas, and those of musical dramas—everything I learnt from him. Afterwards I taught others those songs, made Gurudev hear those songs with them and also myself sang. Sometimes Gurudev also taught new songs by taking all together in this period like the days of yore.

Whenever I learnt singing from Gurudev alone especially the new songs, I received from him a copy of his songs written in his own hand-writing. He wrote those on papers of superior or inferior types and kept them for me in advance. He also signed his own name in many songs. I precisely put different marks of tunes and beats on the very paper that contains the song so that I might learn the song and remember its tune. Afterwards, on returning home, I made fair-work in the exercise book from that manuscript.

I had to face inconveniences in making Gurudev hear my songs as I did not arrange beforehand the papers, after learning the songs of the new dance-drama "Chandalika" completely. Seeing this, Gurudev wrote the dance-drama in a good exercise book in his own hands, and handing it over to me on the next day said :

> "As the songs are not systematically arranged in one place, I understood your difficulties, and so I wrote all these in exact order last night in this exercise book. Now you will feel no inconvenience in singing one after the other."

That exercise book is still with me. In this way, in learning new songs from him, I had the good fortune to receive more than a hundred songs in his own hand-writing. I have kept that exercise book with care. Often I browse over it and think of those good old days.

I had no fixed time to learn singing from Gurudev alone. Whenever he composed songs either by day or at night, he called on me to learn those songs. I had to go early at dawn and again, I received his call many times after 10 P.M. He had a fear, lest he forgot the tunes of the songs.

I recall a day's incident related to the composition of 'Tasher Desh" ("The Kingdon of Cards"). On that day he gave tunings to five songs simultaneously throughout the whole noon. At about 3 p.m., one of his servants informed me to immediately go to Gurudev to learn new songs. Then I was teaching the singers the new songs I had learnt from him the previous day because it was already decided to make Gurudev hear those songs in the rehearsal of the evening. I told the servant that I was going a bit afterwards. At that time Gurudev lived in the house named "Konark"; I was late by nearly half an hour to go there. Reaching there, I saw that he had remained silently seated alone in his chair by opening the exercise book of songs, in his writing room. His face was sombre, I assumed that something had happened. But I could not understand what had actually happened. I stood silently. He neither spoke nore did he look at me. Nearly eight to ten minutes spent in that way. Then handing his few hand-written songs over to me he told me to sit beside him on a "Mora" (Palm-stickleaf chair). I understood that he had been irritated, but I had no courage to ask him of reasons. Sitting beside him, I was silently reading the words of the songs one after the other. Then, what he said in his poignant voice was that by composing the tune of the five songs throughout mid-day, he was tired of singing those songs continually to remember tunings. It was impossible for him to exert labour in that way and to remember tunes. I was informed but I came late. Why I did not come by discontinuing the work, if any, and such other matters pained him. Then I understood the reasons for his anger. But my mind was totally relieved, hearing those words, I said, "Truly, I beg to be execused for my delay in arrival, but I will pick up those songs as early as possible. I won't give troubles at the time of learning." Within half an hour, I learnt all the songs, gave tunings and marks on his hand-written papers of songs and sang those songs before him more than once, and then I found him greatly pleased. In a pleasing mind, he called Vanamali and told him that I had laboured very hard and I would be fed well. Immediately arrived my food. Conversations on many topics went on between us at the time of taking food beside him. In course of these, I began to sing this or that division of songs. Gurudev heard attentively. At the end of taking food, I said to him, "Perhaps I shall be able to present before you the songs today in the evening by singing them well." I was also able to please him by singing those songs in the evening.

10 RABINDRANATH AND RURAL CULTURE

Villages were the centres for Indian civilization. The very heart is in them. Every arrangement for culture of humanity was preserved everywhere in every village. There was not a single village *sans* any institution for universal primary education. Within four or five villages, there was at least one scholar adept in scriptures, whose askesis was to impart education to the learners. In this way, the all-embracing vitality of life has spread from village to village. The mind of man had to remain starved. The-then society knew every item of social science to be worth learning and preserving. The special culture of education was in *Toles* and *Chatuspathis* but the role of learning was spread all over the country. There was constant give and take between special and general knowledge. There was not a single neglected part in the country where the *Ramayana,* the *Mahabharata,* the stories of the *Puranas,* the religious discourses did not continually spread through different channels. Even those theoretical knowledge and philosophy which are discussed under strict perseverance, were continually irrigated in the mind of the public. Theories on the physique, creation and emancipation were heard in the song of *Baul-Vairagis* (homeless wanderers and singing renunciators) and in discourses. The swift, enamoured symphony of dance, music and fun accompanied these. The audience heard with diverse sense of appreciation the episodes of Dhruba and Prahlad, the banishment of Sita, the offerings of the armlet by Karna, the sacrifice of everything own by Harishchandra etc. Moreover, different artistry and dance, music and percussions were spontaneous in every village through manifold *vratas* (askesis), *Parvanas* (Periodical Divine service), *Pujas* (Prayers) and in occasions on birth, death, marriage and so on. Temples were built in every village and although they are almost broken, their architecture and the artistic excellence in burnt soil even now create wonder in our mind. The artists of all these lived in villages. We see an expression of a very refined artistic taste of those days in the day-to-day used clothes and in various articles of the village community.

Much sorrow was also there in those days associated with injustice and uncertainties of livelihood at every step, but at the same time there was a flow of education that had showed unbarred avenues of the inner treasures of mankind amidst unfavourable atmosphere of fortune and has enlightened the fact that man's uniqueness cannot be dwarfed by untoward circumstances.

The arrangement for all-embracing education of the village community was voluntary. It has neither any law nor any demand from outside. Its spontaneous flow was there from house to house like circulation of blood throughout the body. In this way, the villagers were able to create a completely lively atmosphere of culture in the villages by making a union of knowledge and joy with activities and cultivation.

Some are of opinion that the picture that we draw today of the ancient village community was not really true. The village society somehow survived by sticking to the undesirable attitude towards caste-system and narrowness in every aspect. In other words, that society was polluted like the flowless, closed reservoirs of water, We may perhaps admit the truth of the statement by looking at the conditions of the villages in the British era. But we cannot accept it to be true for the village societies of the era prior to that. I would like to say a few words in support of the fact that villages were the embodiments of the Indian civilization upto to the end of the Muslim era.

Originally, Indian civilization is always religio-centric. In the very ancient period, the Saints and the Rishis of *Varnashram* led the Indian society. In the Buddhist era, the big and the small educational centres—the *Bouddhavihar* led by the Buddhist monks directed the Indian society, while, in the middle era, the Hindu and the Muslim Saints and *Sufi* mediators and the Gurus of big pilgrim centres led the Indian society. All those who led the society in the British era were the Gurus of any particular community or real followers of any religious opinion; the last examples of these in the modern era are Gurudev Rabindranath and Mahatma Gandhi. It is seen that the religious-minded great men have led the society, keeping pace with the era, and have tried to solve various problems of the society. Till the era prior to the British one, almost all religious preachers were creations of rural culture. Their birth and education took place in the rural atmosphere. Only Buddhadev was born in the city and was brought up in that atmosphere. But he had to flee away from that urban atmosphere to the village locality. He himself preached his meditation in villages and in pilgrimages which were centres for higher stratas of meditations. In ancient times, studies on numerous art and artistry, music, dance, histrionics were made from village to village. That is why, in order to adorn their own *Durvars* (Courts), the kings of those days had to bring the wise, the learned and the artistes from the villages. Krittivas was the poet of the village, Fulia. When he went to the court of the king of Gour, his name as a poet was then well established in the village society. If villages were centres of narrowness, Chandidas, the rural poet, could not write; "Sunaha Maanush Bhai, Sabaar Upare Maanush Satya Tahar Upare Nai" ("Listen, O men, the highest truth of all is man, beyond him there is nothing"). The birth, education and the centres for dissemination of religion of Chaitanyadev are in the village, in pilgrim centres and in holy places and villages respectively. The birth and the education of Sankaracharya, the religious preacher of monism are in the village; his preachings were made not in the capital but in holy places and in villages. The Guru of *Bhaktimarga* (The path of devotion), Madhavacharya's life and activities are in the village. Sankardev, the Vaishnavacharya of Assam was born in the village. The *Mutts* (Centres of religous teachings), his places of preachings, were also far away from the capitals of kings. He preached dance and music, histrionics and visual art with the help of those Mutts in association with rural artistes. The Sants like Kabir, Nanak etc. were born in villages and villages alone were their centres of activities. The religious leaders came to fulfil the need of the age. Their activities accelerated through the help of the rural societies only.

Through assessment as made above, it will be seen that the picture Gurudev has drawn of the ancient village societies was neither an outcome of mere sentimentalism nor fascination for the old. As that society was lively, changes were made unhesitatingly as and when occasions arose. This was the real picture of rural life till the end of the Muslim era. The first jolt came when the British imposed the civilization centering the cities, upon India. Being deprived of the opportunity to make contact with the neo-civilization, the villages remained stagnant. The villages had nothing to do besides sticking to what these had so long received in living on them.

During the era of the British rule, it was seen from the condition arising out of the limitation of the European civilization, that although villages encircled towns, these were poles apart. Whatever we orally say, what we, the residents of towns, mean by the country is one of gentlemen. We call the public as mean people and to them every standard is mean. The mean are followers of the shadows of the gentleman. Their exposure is ematiated, but they are the majority of the country, and so at least seventy-five per cent people of the country are devoid of light. The society of gentlemen does not clearly see them.

To sum up, the people having intelligence, learning, and respect in the small part of the country maintain more than a gulf of distance from those seventy-five per cent people. We are in the same country but our country is not one. We have not even the appropriate curiosity to have an exact idea of villages. They are mean people. Whatever empathy we have for man fails to make them visualized before us. Many movements are going on among our public but these are behind the sight of our educated people. There is no curiosity for knowing these, because it would not bring forth marks for passing the examination. For this very reason, beauty is banished from the country, nor is there health nor even learning. The flow of joy is at a low ebb, very little of life has remained. The reservoirs of water of the village are dried up, her air polluted, paths impassable, store empty, social ties loose. Envy, altercations, ill-behaviour are making the pollutions of the locality more polluted.

It was Gurudev who said the above words. The reasons for his saying these words are his living in the rural locality in the then East Bengal for more than twelve years at a stretch and having a closer account with love of the social system, health, economy, education of the village and her joyful life. With that idea, he could easily understand how the English civilization had affected the Indian urban and the rural societies. He began to think over the means of arresting this and understood that however bright and lively for their own country, the imitation of foreign civilization was a failure. We have put on their dress, learnt their language but it was not possible for us to become pure Englishmen. We could accept nothing of the qualities in the British character. He thought that we would have to look back to the social system with whose influence our ancient civilization or culture achieved excellence. Thinking over building up the civilization of the new era, he called the gentlemen living in towns and told them through lectures on 'Swadeshi Samaj" [1311 B.E./ "The Indigenous Society" (1904)] and "Chhatrader Prati Sambhasan" (1312 B.E.) ["Address to the Students" (1905)] to look back to the village and to feel her heart with sympathy. However little the rural people might be in education, health, wealth and honour, the true identity of India is still surviving amongst them. There lies the real India. He said that a few societies of gentlemen of cities were not the only India. If the country's independence is to be achieved, the inherent power of the rural society is to be awakened not by neglecting the village but by unison in love with her. Let the people living in the town and the village say together : 'We do not want to live depending on the foreigners. Whatever need we have will be met by our own strength.' Perhaps the leaders of the country did not accept his advice. But when Gurudev said anything whatsoever addressing, he never waited for hearing whether the country accepted that or not. He always tried to give shape to his thoughts by working in his own hands. He started his own work in seclusion in the villages of East Bengal (now Bangladesh) with a few devoted followers. He decided that he would set up an ideal centre anywhere in India in the method in which the extensive effectiveness of efflorescence of Indian culture occurred, which would be the centre of manifestation of Indian culture and not a blind imitation of the old. In fact, from such a thought, Santiniketan and Sriniketan came out, and with the combination of these two is the Visva-Bharati University; the method of education is run here with the help of routine and the syllabus introduced in the British era. It could not be discarded in need of the towns. But the human society that was seen at Visva-Bharati with the assembly of students and members of the staff can be calmly seen by any one to visualize the trend of life. The conjoint atmosphere created here through various knowledge, activities, service to mankind and cultivation of joy is closely associated with this society. This society treasures up strength from within. There is a constant endeavour going on to meet everything one needs by one's own effort, and this may be voluntary. Gurudev wanted that the cultivation of knowledge might flourish in different branches through manifold conferences and symposia, functions and festivals besides studies in schools and colleges in this society. Let the daily necessities of the society be met by devotion to duties in diverse ways. Let arrangements be channelized through diverse avenues and let this society be set as an example to India. This thought on his part was not derived from the civilization introduced in India during the British era. It has no similarity with that society from any aspect. It is only a transformation of the picture that he had portrayed in his mind, of the ancient rural society, whose short description is the beginning of this discussion. Visva-Bharati has developed on the basis of genuine indigenous ideals.

By this, Gurudev has sincerely proved that he was not merely a sentimental poet but a truly patriotic worker.

There was a longtime belief in our gentlemen's society that rural life was about to die; its former dynamic current of life had stopped. It was neither possible for it to help the new era nor was it possible in its end to go ahead in keeping with the latter any more. But it was Gurudev who first made effective protest against this thought and showed by proving the fact that if the strength latent is rural culture in awakened, the India of today *in toto* will be benefitted. To justify the truth of these words, I am presenting only a few examples.

The main part of the annual festivals of Santiniketan and Sriniketan is the fair. I have not heard of any university in India where the fair is given such a position in her main functions. In this aspect, Visva-Bharati is singular. Gurudev got this idea of introducing fairs by witnessing the fairs in the rural localities of our country and hearing about these. Understanding that fairs have enriched the Indian rural societies from manifold ends from time to time, he told the leaders desirous of the country's independence towards the beginning of the twentieth century in his written speech entitled "Swadeshi Samaj" (The Indigenous society). It was in accordance with his desire that the fair has been accepted as the main part of Visva-Bharati's two principal festival items. By making a sphere of unison between the 'Bhadralog' (gentlemen) and the 'Chhotolog' ('Uneducated') this fair is going on exchanging knowledge, activities and joy. The proposal that Gurudev made to arrange the fairs as a major means for all-round rural development in his lecture "Swadeshi Samaj" is directly visualized by us in practice at present through these two *melas* (fairs) framed on that ideal and effectively introduced at every time.

Everyone knows about Gurudev's songs. From this point, he has offered much to the country. The two ancient Indian trends of music that helped him especially in course of this massive creation are first, the Hindi music of the high order and secondly, the numerous easy and simple songs that are in vogue in the rural society of Bengal. Of these—the latter—the songs of the Baul communities are especially remarkable. The influence of Baul songs in ideas, languages, tunes and rhythm are spread in Gurudev's songs in various ways. Besides this, his songs have also gone ahead with the help of the songs of this community. He gave prominence to the lives in these *Bauls* in his dramas as model characters. We are also not ignorant of their spiritual thoughts that deeply moved Gurudev's spiritual life.

There is a special trend of decoration in all the functions and festivals, meetings and assemblies of Visva-Bharati. The main part of that decoration is *alpana* (drawing). The study of this art is going on from time immemorial among the women of the village. It was Gurudev who first felt its life-force in this era and encouraged to decorate all festivals, meetings and conferences of Visva-Bharati with this *alpana.* Today, almost everywhere in the country, this unknown and inglorious rural art is presented by the leadership of Nandalal, the artist-principal.

Gurudev himself is the master of the dance-movement of the educated society of this era. At the backdrop of this movement, there is the influence of easy, simple dance of the rural societies of different countries. As he was also inspired by the ideals of the *Baul* dance of Bengal, he composed the character of the blind *Baul* in "Falguni" (1916) and himself acted on the role. Gurudev pleased the audience with his dance, songs and acting.

When 'Raybeshe' dance was known anew to the educated society, Gurudev brought the 'Raybeshe' dancers to teach us. As a dance, this is a very ordinary male group dance. But its value did not avert his attention.

He (Gurudev) said that he liked the *yatras* of rural Bengal. One of its main reasons is the stage without having any background. The thought that there is no need of decorated background for the acting of a drama, arose in the mind of Gurudev after attending this *yatra.* He, therefore, abolished the use of decorated background in the acting of his dramas at Visva-Bharati.

In his dramas, he accepted the system of introducing songs to a great extent to words for the *Yatras.* In this way, with the inspiration of Gurudev, rural culture achieved the opportunity to strongly flourish in different dimensions and proved that she was not conservative and she also knew how to keep pace with the time.

If we do not tread on this avenue and appear before the rural people as gentlemen of the town to give advice to them only, then they will not know us as alien people as they did in the past. They will think that they are inferior people, and everything of them is mean. Being affected by this attitude, they will try, at every moment of opportunity, to eliminate their littleness and to be '*bhadralog*' (gentlemen), and to forget and neglect their own society.

I know about many rural people whose forefathers have been cultivating the practice of different arts like dance and music, histrionics etc. in need of their own society from one generation to the other; but it was their own descendents of this era who have become *bhadralogs* by undergoing school and collegeate education and have felt ashamed to participate in dancing, singing and percussions together. Even after independence, no change of this situation took place. We are always encountering the fact that the son of a farmer feels ashamed at ploughing after being educated. A boy of the Santhal society has refused to return to his own parents on holidays of the school after learning the three R's. Such type of incidents has also occurred. It is, therefore, seen that the method we have now adopted for the service of the rural poor smacks of shortcomings somewhere. If we would advance step by step and keep pace with the all-round development of the rural society in our assignment, the results would have been different. No work will succeed unless we eliminate the superstition within themselves to think themselves inferior to others for the last two centuries.

It is often seen that, to bring back joy of the village, the educated societies themselves arrange for soirees of dance drama and music from village to village. There is need for such activities to broaden knowledge but the union of hearts does not take place with these because the rural people by being inferior, are witnessing all these arranged by the *bhadralogs*.

It has been thought to instil Gurudev's songs among these rural people. But if these songs appear before them with the pride of aristocracy, it would be disastrous. The song of Gurudev is of a high strata but she also wants to sit on the same platform along with the song of the village. Let her be allowed to enjoy mass feast. Let no separate arrangements be made for her dinner by bringing tables and chairs.

Attempts are going on to introduce some newly launched festivals of the towns in the village-areas. But those who are engaged in that work do not give honour to the festivals that are in vogue in the villages. They want to remain a bit aloof from the latter. This is why one cannot admit that the rural people are being able to accept the newly introduced festivals as their very own. Till now, I have understood from whatever I have seen, that they are yet to accept. They have congratulated and thanked the *bhadralogs* in order to please them and show them courtesy. But they have not accepted these festivals as their very own.

11 RABINDRANATH AND THE BAULS OF BENGAL

Once Gurudev Rabindranath had to live for nearly ten to twelve years in the rural area of his *Zemindari* on the bank of the river Padma in East Bengal (now Bangladesh). He had his first genuine relationship there with the rural society, culture and Nature of Bengal. Gradually, that relationship turned into intense love. How true that love was can be known from the confessions made in the form of innumerable letters written by him from there, and from many stories, poetry and through development of his spiritual life. At the outset, I am stating an excerpt from his own confession. Then I shall discuss other matters.

Thinking over a special day during his stay at Shelaidah in Bangladesh, Gurudev writes :

> "During rains, the canal remained full of water. During dry days people walked on it. On this bank was a market with diverse crowd. I greatly enjoyed the mystery of human habitations from the room of the first floor. My way of living on the Padma was aloof from the crowd. The sand-banks of the river, the unending stretch of sand, at places water-bourne birds encircling water-springs. There is beckoning of the banks of the Padma in the short stories I have written there. When I would come to Sahjadpur, I could visualize the picture of rural life, the diverse endeavour of rural activities. These find expression in stories like "Postmaster", "*Samapti*" ("The end"), "*Chhuti*" ("The Holiday"), etc. In these, the scattered moving scenes of human habitations have been filled in with imagination."

"I remember a day of that period. The little, dry and old canal is filled in with water. The *dingis* (Rural boats) were half-sunk in mud. With the approach of water, these were made afloating. The boys are thrilled with the sound of the new flow of water. They are plunging on water ten times in a day.

"Standing beside the window of the first floor on that day, I saw clouds burdened with the water of the new rainy season in the sky ahead, and below is the wavy screams of life among boys. All on a sudden, my mind slipped out of its own open doors towards the vast distance outside. A feeling came within my heart very intensely. In front of me, I saw, an incessant flow of all-embracing feelings from time immemorial, an undivided mystery synchronizing diverse mysteries of different lives. Whatever I am feeling and enjoying in my own life, whatever understanding between man and man in every house going on at every moment has become one in a great experience.

"In this way, the burden of my own existence had been decreased by being separated from myself and placing the part upon the whole. The mystery of life had, then, been seen in the form of appreciation by being one with an appreciater. This feeling of mine on that day intensely appeared to me as a miracle."

"I found a joy of emancipation. Once I stood beside the window for a little period on my way to the bath-room out of fun to spend leisure. That little period appeared great in front of me. Drops of tears were then rolling down. I wished I would submit myself before anyone and salute him by bowing down on the ground. Who is that most intimate companion of mind who is accepting all my transitory moments into his eternity? Immediately I felt I had come out of one aspect and had been introduced with the other. *Eshohasya param ananda*—This and he stand within me : When that 'this' stands towards that 'he', he gets pleasure."

When Gurudev was in Calcutta, once he first felt this everlasting companion in prime of his youth at dawn. He named him "Jeevan-Devata" ('The God of life'). It was this God of life through whose support the existence of his own self bloomed on that day within everything. All differences were wiped out of the mind.

To Gurudev, nobody or nothing was then unendearing. To him, the style of movement on the road by labourers, their physical structures, facial beauty appeared very surprisingly beautiful. He also considered the passing of youths placing hands on the shoulders of one another and laughing to be a remarkable incident. In front of his residence, he saw that a kine was licking the shoulder of a donkey's offspring. Seeing the silent affectionate welcome of that little animal, the message of mystery encompassing the whole universe rang within the reeds of his breast. In this way, Gurudev was pleased at the music of movement of everything at every moment. He appeared to have visualised the festival of unquenchable cadence that falls in the form of a fountain all around in the unfathomable depth of the universe.

Gurudev found a group of lover-devotees of this type as his companions in the rural areas of Shelaidah. They are today famous in the name of *Bauls* in Bengal. They are a special community. Very few in number of this community existed till then. Both the Hindus and the Muslims are in that community. But in religion, they were neither the Hindus nor the Muslims. Their spiritual life was built on the harmony of these two religions. They are mediators of love. They receive enjoyment by loving a special object of love unknown, strange and bereft of physique. They name "Maner Manus" ("The man of the mind"). Unlike other gods and goddesses, that man of the mind is not a symbol of any spirit. He does nothing good or bad to man of the real life. He is existent. In secret he is existent in every man. They receive the message of that inherent man of the mind through meditation of love. But they cannot catch hold of Him. So, in the language of their songs, the unending pain of not knowing that known man of the mind is always expressed. The more are they advancing towards the avenue of knowing him, the more they feel that the distance of not knowing is as if going on increasing. They do not find the signal to its end. The *Bauls* think that through the pains of non-receiving and unknowing, one finds out that avenue. The mind is filled with the feelings of knowing the unknown through depth of pains. So they do not aspire after alleviating the sorrows of not knowing the unknown. The meditation of the *Bauls* of the locality of Shelaidah is one of such a mixture of sorrow and joy closely related to love that does not necessitate any extrinsic support. When this pain of love becomes intense to the *Bauls* for the man of the mind, they go beyond any sense of distinction of caste. Perhaps this is why they are called *Sahajiya* ('The simple followers'). They easily unite with everyone in the society irrespective of caste and creed. They crate an intense bond of unity with the universe.

Gurudev felt this similarity with the *Bauls* from this point of view and while introducing his *Jeevan-Devata* (The God of life), he writes in one place :

> "The God of the universe is existent. His seat is from man to man, in planets, stars and in the moon. The God of the universe is specially existent in the seat of every life, His holy seat is on every heart and He is at the centre of all feelings and all

> experiences. He is what the *Bauls* have called the man of the mind. I have tried to tell about this man of the mind, the *Jeevan-Devata* of every man in the lectures titled : 'Religion of man'."

Finding out the unison between the God of life and the man of the mind, Gurudev deeply attracted was towards the *Bauls* and their meditations. How true that attraction was and how he accepted that trend of ideas in his own life are proved in his letters. He writes :

> "Those who have read my writings, know that I have expressed my devotion to *Baul Padavalis* in many of my writings. When I was at Shelaidah, I always met and talked with the group of *Bauls.* In many of my songs, I have accepted the tunes of the *Bauls,* and in many songs the unison of the *Baul* tunes with other tune-patterns with or without my knowledge. From this, it may be understood that the tunes and words of the *Bauls* have, at a certain period, easily mingled within me. I remember, in the very Shelaidah area, a *Baul* sang with an *Ektara* (a single string instrument of the *Bauls*) :
>
> Kothay pavo taare
> Amar maner manush je re.
> [Where shall I get him,
> The Man of my mind.]

The words are very simple but their meanings brightened with a unique lustre in association with tuning. I heard from the non-scholar in his rustic tune and in simple language the pain of not knowing Him least whom one should know most has been tuned in his voice. "*Antaratar Yadayamatma*" ('That this soul is more endearing') When I heard this message of the Upanishad from their voice as "Maner Manush" ('Man of the mind'), I was greatly astonished. I have heard such a *Baul's* song as is incomparable in respect of simplicity of language, intensity of ideas and in empathy of tune. Just as it is in unison with the theories of knowledge, so is the composition of poetry coupled with the poignancy of *Bhakti* (Devotion). I do not believe that there is any such brilliance as available in folk literature".

In his lecture on *Brahmotsav* ('The Brahma festival') delivered on 1317 B.E. (1910), Gurudev says in connection with the *Bauls :*

> "A few days ago, I met two *Bauls* of a special community in the village. 'Would you tell me on the speciality of your religion?' said I to them. One said, 'Difficult to say, can't be said aright'. The other said, 'Of course, it can be said. It's easy. We say this : you will have to know yourself at the very outset in accordance with the advice of the *Guru* ('Master'). When I know myself, I find Him within that myself'. I said, 'Why don't you make all people of the world hear the words of your religion?' 'One who will be thirsty', he said, 'would himself come to *Ganga'*. 'Are you seeing that?' said I. 'Is anyone coming?' With a very peaceful smile, the man said, 'Everyone will come. Everyone will have to come'."

Prior to the beginning of the activities of the Rural Reconstruction Department of Sriniketan, Gurudev, while making a discussion in detail with my father on the ideals to be followed in connection with rural service, said something about his intimacy with the *Bauls.* I quote that extract from the dictation of my father. Gurudev said :

> "You have seen how I was deeply engaged in conversation for hours with the disciples of Lalan Shah Fakir of Shelaidah. They are poor. They have no dress. There is no scope to understand how great they are by looking at them. But how simply they could say about so many intense subjects! I have not seen any degree holder like an M.A. or a B.A. of any university discussing in that manner. The same is true in case of that *Vaishnavi* of my story. Looking at them it appears how deprived they are. But at the back of their apparent poverty, a trend of ancient culture has flowed like a stream within them. That is to be understood. They will have to be drawn nearer with love and then you will see that they will unbar their doors of the heart. I want that family relationship."

We have so long heard about the influence of the *Bauls* in Gurudev's personal life. Now let us hear from him an account of how the life and meditation of the *Bauls* were useful in building a better society in Bengal. He has written :

> "The history of our country is not related to our needs till today. Instead, it has been going on disseminating the

> meditation for unity through the innermost intense truth of mankind. In Baul literature we see that meditation of the Baul community. This is both for the Hindus and the Muslims. They are in unison but they never hurt each other. With this union, no assembly or samity has been established. With this union, songs have ushered forth. With the language and tunings of those songs, the voice of the Hindu and that of the Muslims are united. There was no feud between the *Koran* and the *Puran*. In this very union, the true identity of India is existent; in altercations lie barbarities. These *Baul* songs give us an account of how the inspiration of superior civilization is working on by itself behind the notice of the schools and the colleges in the intense mind of rural Bengal, and how it has endeavoured to create the same platform for the Hindus and the Muslims."

Let us come back to the point of Gurudev and the *Bauls.* He has said in one place that his songs are, to be more specific, composed by Rabindranath, the *Baul*. They are not imitative. Let me clarify the point.

It is seen that Gurudev has repeatedly expressed the intense pain of the absence of an intimate person like the *Bauls* in many songs of the categories of love and nature. This is why we can say so easily in the language of a song :

> "Amar kee vedana se ki jano, ogo mita sudurer mita."
> ["Do you know what pain do I have, O friend/friend abroad?"]

Many songs of this type so overflowed from the intense corner of his mind out of one emotion of pain that these have expressed anew the inherent words of the *Bauls*. Hearing these, it will be easily understood how the songs of Rabindra-Baul are written out of sincere emotional sensibilities. These are not amateurish imitative type of songs. For instance.

1. 'Ami tarei khoonje vedai'
   ('I tread on finding him out',)
2. 'Ami kaan pete rai',
   ('I am eager to listen,)
3. 'Se je maner manush, keno tare vasiye rakhis'
   (He is the man of the mind, why do you keep him seated,)

4. 'Amar hiar majhe lukie chhile"
   ('Hidden art thou in my heart')

In spite of having Gurudev's originality of thought and composition in these songs, there is a clear evidence of the influence of the Bauls in ideas, tunes and method of composition.

Leaving aside the influence of songs, let us discuss on dramas. The main characters of Gurudev's dramas like *Prayaschitta (Penance). Falgooni,* and "*Dakghar*" ("The Post Office") are created on the model of the Bauls. Through these characters of the dramas and through successful action by himself in these characters, he wanted to make us understand that it is very necessary to have ideal personalities like Dhananjay Vairagi, the blind Baul and the *Fakir* for the well-being of the twentieth century human society, for they alone are able to show the avenue of emancipation from every type of impediments of the petty human mind.

Perhaps those magnanimous Baul community of Shelaidah will not be found out any more. But their great message has still remained immortal. In this era, a new life has been instilled in that message by Gurudev Rabindranath. In Murshida and Marafti songs of the Muslim meditators of East Bengal (now Bangladesh), the same flow still continues. Otherwise, would it be possible for them to say in the medium of the language of Murshida songs :

> "Manushe manush biraje khoonje neoya vara daay
> Manik chine duek jane se mahajaner kripaay
> Manush aachhe prati ghate, dure nay ati nikate,
> Phooler kali aapni phoote bhramar chhoote kaachhe jaay.
>
> [Man heralds man, difficult it is to find out or trace,
> The jewel is identified by one or two, even that, too, by the Great Man's grace,
> Man is existent, be it far or very hear, at every place,
> The flower-bud blooms by itself, the bee runs forward and embraces."]

A group of *vairagis* of West Bengal, who are devoted to the Vaishnava religion, delivers that trend of idea to the rural people through singing songs. One of their songs is :

"Jar tare pran kendechhe se to tomar hride aachhe.
Vaaire theke daakchho kaake, pavena taare khoonjchho michhe
Naam dhaam naa jaanle pare keman kare dharve taare
Dekhte saadh hay antare, thikana taar sadhur kaachhe".
[He for whom your heart aches, in your heart he does remain.
Whom do you call from outside? You won't have him,
Seek ye in vain,
You know not his whereabout. How, then, would you find him out?
If the desire to see does sprout, his address from the saint you'll gain."]

Today, Bengal is divided and besmeared in the conflicts of caste and religion. This is the main problem of the Bengalees of this era. If they could feel the existence of a special Man in every animal from a generous and bold outlook like the Bauls, they could have achieved freedom from this curse.

Today, I would like to sum up by saying that it is high time to have joint meditation of the Bauls of the Shelaidaha locality and Rabindra-Baul of the previous era to the Bengalees of this era. Let the divided, detached Bengalees be united through this meditation alone and let them heighten the glory of the country by setting a glorious instance in front of the whole country.

12 RABINDRASANGEET : A STUDY

My father came to Santiniketan in 1907 as a teacher of the school.

Six months after my birth, in 1910, we came to Santiniketan. Since then, I have been living in Santiniketan at a stretch. When I was five or six years old, I got the opportunity to grow up amidst the atmosphere of music and histrionics in Santiniketan. I still remember those days. Then Dinendranath resided at the ground floor of the residence, named "Dehali" on the upstrairs, Gurudev himself lived, and we were also among a few teachers who lived with their families in "Natun Badi" ("The New House") that was well-known in those days and was adjacent to "Dehali". At that time I saw that Gurudev was teaching new songs to Dinendranath after composing them. Dinendranath taught the aged and even the children as well of Santiniketan, those songs at hours of recreation. I, too, was in that group of children. Very often Gurudev himself was present there, heard songs and taught all new songs together. Different types of learners were there in that group. Most of them had no education in music. That everyone is gifted with a tuneful voice is also not correct. Learners from other provinces were also in that class. Some of them had learnt the Bengali language, while some of them had started learning the same and nobody was perfect in pronunciation and in the styles of music. But as they were enthusiastic in learning Rabindra-Sangeet, Gurudev and Dinendranath did not debar any one of them from participating in that class.

I remember Bhimarao Shastri. He was a Maharastrian Sanskrit scholar, He was equally expert in Hindi songs like Dhrupad, Dhamar, Kheyal, Tappa etc. and in playing on percussion instruments like Tabla and Pakhoaz. In 1914, he came to Santiniketan as a teacher of Music in Hindi for the students of the Santiniketan Vidyalaya. He served as a teacher for fourteen to fifteen years as a teacher. Immediately after arriving at Santiniketan, he began to learn the Bengali language and Gurudev's songs with ardent sincerity. He learnt many songs and could sing those, too. Gurudev made him sing songs in solo in many functions and festivals. He also made notations of Gurudev's songs. As he was a singer of Hindi *Uchchanga Sangit* (classical music) and Maharastrian, his Bengali pronunciation was not always appropriate. If anyone would hear him singing Gurudev's songs, he would understand a non-Bengali singer was singing. In spite of that, Gurudev himself told him to sing Rabindra-sangeet and teach his students those songs.

From 1898 onwards, Mr. Shyam Bhattacharya was appointed on monthly payment to sing everyday in the morning and in the evening religious songs composed by Gurudev and other members of his family at the Santiniketan Upasana Mandir (Prayer Hall). The patterns and the tunes in which he sang Gurudev's religious songs had a great deal of difference from usual notations. But Gurudev neither told Mr. Bhattacharya to sing those songs in accordance with notations nor did he terminate the latter's service in singing. Mr. Bhattacharya continued singing in his own pattern till his death at an old age in 1940.

Towards the beginning of the First World War in the twentieth century, professional songsters and songstresses of those days started singing Gurudev's songs in the records. In those days, any endeavour to sing in accordance with the tune as set forth in the notation was rarely seen. Almost all the artistes of the records sang Rabindra-Sangeet in the patterns and the tunes as they desired. In that era, Gurudev had heard the recorded song of most of these artistes. He said nothing to the authorities of these record companies for many years. In 1926, after the inception of Visva-Bharati, Gurudev first gave attention to this aspect. He ordered to stop selling the old records containing songs sung in tunes and patterns as desired. It was decided with the companies that whenever one would sing, one would have to properly learn the tune of the song and then one would sing. From that time onwards, the record-artistes of other songs have tried to sing Gurudev's songs after learning in appropriats tunes. Gurudev had also generously permitted for circulation of their records in the market. In support of this generosity of Gurudev, I would like to mention the names of a few famous artistes of different nature who sang Rabindra-Sangeet in records and received Gurudev's recommendation afterwards; e.g., Kundan Saigal, Kanan Devi, Pankaj Mallik, K.C. De, Niharbala, Santa Apte, Renuka Das Gupta etc. We never saw Gurudev thinking over the appropriateness and inappropriateness of Rabindra-Sangeet in their voice.

Even now I remember Gurudev's 70th birth anniversary celebration in 1931. The festival was held in Calcutta. On that occasion a function for a few days was also held. Singers of different patterns of Calcutta participated in this function. Dinendranath and Indira Devi were in charge of teaching the songs of this musical function and directing the same. They prepared singers for individual and choric songs. Gurudev and Dinendranath did not hear the songs of most of the singers of this group. Prior to the function, they did not learn singing from Dinendranath or Indira Devi, to Gurudev notwithstanding. In spite of that, they were all included in the group of music. Nobody was left out. I hope my point will be clear if I mention the following names of songsters and songsteresses who sang in the 70th birth anniversary festival :

Songsters

1. Sri Gopeswar Bandyopadhyay
2. Sri Satyakinkar Bandyopadhyay
3. Sri Rameshchandra Bandyopadhyay
4. Sri Umapada Bhattacharya
5. Sri Gopalchandra Sen Gupta
6. Sri Anadikumar Dastidar
7. Sri Haripada Chattopadhyay
8. Sri Pashupati Bhattacharya
9. Sri Sushilkumar Basu
10. Sri Pankajkumar Mallik
11. Sri Anil Kumar Bagchi
12. Sri Santosh Kumar Ghosh
13. Sri Kanan Kumar Mukhopadhyay
14. Sri Haripada Roy
15. Sri Rabi Basu
16. Sri Sashi Kumar Chattopadhyay
17. Sri Prabhat Dev Mukhopadhyay
18. Sri Sagar Lahiri
19. Sri Sachindranath Bhattacharya
20. Sri Benoy Krishna Ghosh
21. Sri Nirmal Chandra Baral
22. Sri Dipak Choudhury
23. Sri Ajit Kumar Mallick
24. Sri Asoke Mitra

25. Sri Sudhir Kar
26. Sri Pinakin Trivedi
27. Sri Sailen Hom

Songstresses

1. Srimati Arundhati Chattopadhyay
2. Srimati Malati Basu
3. Srimati Kanak Das
4. Srimati Rama Kar
5. Srimati Savitri Govind
6. Srimati J. Begam
7. Srimati Latika Roy
8. Srimati Sujata Mukhopadhyay
9. Srimati Manjushri Chattopadhyay
10. Srimati Bani Chattopadhyay
11. Srimati Sumita Chakraborty
12. Srimati Amiya Tagore
13. Srimati Amita Sen (Khuku)
14. Srimati Purnima Choudhury
15. Srimati Dipti Chattopadhyay
16. Srimati Saraswati Dutta
17. Srimati Arundhati Ghosh
18. Srimati Uma Chattopadhyay
19. Srimati Rama Chattopadhyay
20. Srimati Sefalika Palit
21. Srimati Sulekha Ghosh
22. Srimati Anjali Das
23. Srimati Gita Das
24. Srimati Amiyomukul Choudhury
25. Srimati Ilarani Ghosh
26. Srimati Lila Mitra
27. Srimati Karuna Choudhury
28. Srimati Amala Dutta
29. Srimati Manika Dhar
30. Srimati Gita Roy
31. Srimati Lalita Sen
32. Srimati Kalyani Sarkar
33. Srimati Mandira Gupta
34. Srimati Sudha Das

35. Srimati Anubha Tagore
36. Srimati Aruna Sen
37. Srimati Rama Chattopadhyay
38. Srimati Ishita Chattopadhyay
39. Srimati Mala Das
40. Srimati Sangjukta Sen
41. Srimati Gayatri Bagchi
42. Srimati Rubi Chattopadhyay
43. Srimati Sibani Sarkar
44. Srimati Monju Bosu
45. Srimati Hasi Basu
46. Srmiati Usha Majumdar
47. Srimati Abha Chandra.

Of the above group of male and female singers, nearly twenty went from Santiniketan, and the rest were all of Calcutta.

Dr. Arnold Bucke, the scholar of foreign music, spent many years (1925-1934) at a stretch at Santiniketan, learnt many songs from Dinendranath and made notations of many songs. Like the European singers' voice, he always sang Gurudev's songs with the help of the piano. He had a piano at Santiniketan. The pronunciation of Bengali song was also Europeanized. Seeing encouraged by Gurudev and Dinendranath, he sang Gurudev's songs at Santiniketan, in Calcutta and in many towns of India. In spite of variations in pronunciation and voice, I never heard either from Gurudev or from Dinendranath any derogatory remark about his songs.

Let me now refer to another incident related to the era at the acting of dance-dramas of Gurudev. There was a South Indian student at Siksha-Bhavana, Visva-Bharati. His name was Kondamuni Reddy. His voice was very sombre and tuneful. But he could not ever eliminate defects of pronunciation. Gurudev placed him in the group of singers for the dance-drama "Chitrangada" due to his tuneful sombre voice and he had sung along with the group of singers for the dance-drama in Calcutta, Delhi, Patna and Lahore. Gurudev himself was the president of this group.

I have seen and known the last twenty-five years of Gurudev's life of music and histrionics at Santiniketan. As I was able to make a little bit of room in this aspect of his life to the best of my abilities, I have got this opportunity to unfold this picture of his musical life. Nobody has yet paid attention to this part of his life. But, today, it has become highly necessary to do so because many types of alterations have started on the issue of the right to sing Gurudev's songs. The unnecessary debate that has been allowed to spring up on the right to sing Rabindrasangeet today badly necessitates termination, and this could have been easily done if this picture of the generous mind of Gurudev was clearly revealed to one and all.

It is now often heard about the special trend of songs in the name of "pure Rabindrasangeet". It means that whatever we mean by "Rabindrasangeet" is, as if, not the "pure Rabindrasangeet". The preachers of "pure Rabindrasangeet" think of the necessity of a special type of the mode of singing in the songs of Gurudev. They think that, not to speak of Hindi songs, this mode of singing has no similarity with any other Bengali songs. It is completely of a different type. It cannot, therefore, be considered to be at par with other songs. If Rabindrasangeet is sung by alien singers, it will lose its identity. As there was no right for the non-Brahmins to read the Vedas, it has also become identical with the same condition. I never think that there is really any reason for thinking over such differences of this type with regard to Rabindrasangeet because if there was any difference in the mode of singing in Gurudev's songs and if Gurudev would think of its importance, then he would certainly have written something about it. But we do not come across any such discussion in his written form. Nor did he give any direction or order about the right to sing his songs. In fact, the very opposite is seen from a study of his activities. He encouraged all to sing, without making any assessment. He wanted that those who earn bread by working hard, who attend offices, who have no opportunity to sing like an *Ostad* by meditating on voice, who want to derive enjoyment in mind out of singing in a simple and matter-of-fact manner, all of them will sing his songs. He said :

> "I do not hesitate to say that my songs have found their place in the heart of my land, along with her flowers that are never exhausted, and that the folk of the future, in days of joy or sorrow or festival will have to sing them".

Elsewhere, he said :

> "The Bengalees will have to accept my song. My song shall have to be sung by all, at every house in Bengal, in the meadows and on the banks of rivers."

Did Gurudev not know that, with this extensive circulation, mediocre or low type of artistes are seen more than the good ones in number? He knew very well but he also knew that the good singers would come up by their own merit and would survive, while the bad ones would by themselves be extinct.

It is also true that he earnestly wanted every good or bad singer to notice how he composed the songs out of his deep appreciation and emotional inspiration. They might make an endeavour to enter into the world of ideas of the songs. So he had to say :

> "Teach music with a bit of empathy and appreciation. This is the speciality of my song. If you drive steam rollers on them (empathy and appreciation), my song will become flat."

In other words, whatever I have understood from a direct experience of the activities of Gurudev and from his written statements is that everyone has the right to sing Rabindrasangeet. Everyone will try to sing out of the need of his own joy and sorrow, but it would not be an endeavour to memorize like a tame bird and sing accordingly. The purpose will be to sing oneself and to enchant the mind with the cadence of music. From such an ability to enchant with the essence of music, the interested audience will be contented. This is the last word of all songs. Failure to pay heed to this purpose welcomes various complicated arguments. Of late, this has appeared in Rabindrasangeet.

13 RABINDRASANGEET FROM THE PERSPECTIVE OF THE AUDIENCE

To answer the question : In which meaning should one use "Rabindrasangeet", I shall say in accordance with the opinion in vogue that every song composed by Gurudev Rabindranath is "Rabindrsangeet". It is used in the same way in which we use expressions like Baulsangeet, Ramprasadi, Nidhu Babu's Tappa, Dashu Roy's Panchali, Songs of D.L. Ray, Atulprasadi, and Nazrul Geeti.

The litterateurs did not differentiate Gurudev's poerty and literature of early, middle and last periods by different names. To them, everything is known as the poetry of Rabindranath or the composition of Rabindranath. When have they admitted this in case of poetry and literature, why should there be an exception in case of music? The compositions of Gurudev's early life are not of an expert's creation in comparison to those written in mature years. Even, then, nobody says that they are not the poetry of Rabindranath or the literature of Rabindranath or again, they should be given separate names.

The little stream of the water of a river that comes out of the cave of the mountain in a little size, expands itself more and more until it unites with the sea. Can any one deny its first stream of water? If one can do so, then the "Gangotri" could not be turned into a place of pilgrimage. Gurudev's poetry and songs will have to be seen and known by us from that very perspective. Although it appears like a little stream of water at the outset, it has also a value as a part of the whole. The early era to the last one of Gurudev's songs is a part of that same trend of ideas.

The grandeur of the note of simple, easy emotions of the heart that we encounter in the songs of Gurudev's early life, is not a matter to be neglected. Like easy, simple folk-songs, these songs instill appreciation in the minds of persons who are really appreciators to music. The songs of musical dramas like "*Valmiki Pratibha*" etc.

cannot be sung like other songs of lyrical emotion by dissociating them from the dramas. But in case of songs in ordinary dramas, this rule does not hold good. There are many songs that he composed out of his own emotion before these are associated with the dramas. He attached these songs to the dramas later on. First, at the time of composition, the songs were expressions of Gurudev's own emotions of the heart, and these later appeared as songs of the dramatis personae consequential to the needs of the dramas. These songs cannot be called musical dramas.

Gurudev has composed many songs that indicate through their meanings the words of a certain woman's mind. Those songs are also sung in male voice. Gurudev and Dinendranath sang these, too. But if there is any objection to this, we will face a few difficult questions out of these. For example : Is it possible to say anything about any woman's mind in case of a male person? Do males possess the power of appropriate expression of the joys and sorrows of a woman's mind? It might appear that it is impossible from the standpoint of physical and mental differences between them. But, even then, the male persons have expressed the words of a woman's heart from time to time in songs and poems. Has any woman been able to express her own words so poignantly as men? There are many such poems and songs by Gurudev. If these songs are sung by men by exposing their inner themes, why will that be unnatural? In case of the Hindi Kheyal, Tappa and Thungri songs, we encounter the various points of separation of a woman's heart. The best songsters and the best composers of these songs are all male persons. When Bade Golam Ali Khan sang the song "Bajubandh khul khul jaay" ("The armlets gradually open") in 'thungri' of the Bhairavi Ragini, then, by feeling the emotional pangs of the adolescent Radha's heart in his songs, everyone of the audience had been in tears. They never complained of betrayal of appreciation or objected to listen because that was sung by a man having a pair of moustache and a big physique like Mr. Khan. From this, it is understood that when we hear songs, our minds do not give so much importance as to who is singing or whether the words of the song are meant for the male or the female persons. Our ears and minds are eager for appropriate expression of the original emotion of the songs.

"Mari lo mari amay banshite dekechhe ke" ("Ah, who has called me in the flute!") is one of the most favourite songs of Gurudev. In his youth, he very often sang this song; I have also heard him singing this song with emotion. Nobody ever thought it unnatural after hearing the song composed and sung by him on the pang of Radha's separation. The male *Kirtaniyas* (Singing Appreciators) sing many couplets on the adolescent Radha's union and separation for hours together and charm the devout audience. If these are not natural to the audience, how have they been singing these songs in the assembly of Kirtan from time to time? The female audience also did not raise any objection to this.

The argument in connection with making the song "Megher kole rod hesechhe" ("The sunlight has laughed behind the veil of the cloud") sung by the seniors instead of doing so by the juniors as it is meant for them, is the same. Formerly, Dinendranath Tagore sang the song in a chorus by taking a group of boys like us at the time of the acting of a drama. If we do not accept this argument, what would happen to the poetic creation of Gurudev entitled "Sishu" ("The child")? It is true that he has composed many songs and poems keeping in mind the children's world. Even then, it is not possible for children to make a total appreciation to these poems. Gurudev has said about this type of his songs, poetry and drama that, though he composed these with a view to providing the children with enjoyments, he has primarily endeavoured to expose his own emotions of the heart through these compositions.

I agree with the revered Parimal Babu that in order to sing Gurudev's songs, it is necessary to have an intimate acquaintance with the sentiments of these songs. The more the artistes can advance towards this avenue, the more will it be possible for them to discover avenues for appreciation to music. But are vocal meditation and pronunciational accuracies only necessary for marching ahead in this avenue? That is not correct. For this, another aspect that is much beyond these two, is needed. That is the appreciation to and empathy for music. An artiste necessitates ability, like Gurudev, to enjoy worldwide love and joy to reach there. He had endless love for everything of Nature and the material world. So he has heard the tune of joy as well as pain in everything. That tune has struok the heart of Gurudev again and again and has been expressed in his songs and poems. It has spread in his hundreds of songs and poems. We have not yet encountered that extent of meditation for music and poetic pursuit necessary for singing by understanding these numerous little lyrical emotions. We are only dependent on the structure of his songs. We have our own joy and boistrousness only on that. How many artistes of empathy in this era who know how to instill life in these songs have we come across?

One cannot be a true evaluator to appreciate this by learning and reading from a teacher. None can create an appreciator. An appreciator is self-created.

Deformation of words in Rabindrasangeet or singing in erroneous words or unrefined pronunciation necessitate caution. This is applicable in case of every song. When the Bengalee artistes cultivate Hindi classical songs, then, naturally, they are to pay attention to faultless pronunciation of Hindi or Urdu words. Inspite of that, it is not correct that defective pronunciation never takes place. As these are unwillingly committed, the audience forgive these little bits of errors.

Gurudev has composed songs in the Bengali language. These are composed in very simple and easy words. Every educated Bengalee of this era uses this language in his/her studies, speech, hearing and in conversation with one another. I cannot even think that they will sing Gurudev's songs in deformed and erroneous words or in unrefined pronunciation willingly or knowingly. I have not yet heard any specimen of complaint of this type in the radio or in recorded songs. But even if that occurs, the artistes concerned will definitely correct that error. Nobody is adamant.

A few districts of Bengal have their own typical pattern of pronunciation. Sometimes that impression unknowingly persists among the singers of that district. The artistes cannot but correct that due to the pressure of cautious attention of today's audience. If anyone wants to sing according to his own will, the audience of Bengal will never admit him as a singer.

14 THE GRADUAL DEVELOPMENT OF RABINDRA DANCE–DRAMAS

One of the remarkable aspects in Rabindranath's life was that he placed in his own hands as an example through activities before everyone and the country on whatever he thought. He did not discharge his duties by merely preaching the massage of big ideals like intellectual scholars. He put these in black and white and proved that whatever he thought or said was not unrealistic. There is truth in it. That fine arts, music and dance should have special places along with general education is not only preached by him as a big ideal but their importance in the human society was also proved by him by making an honourable room for them along with the general education of Santinikatan. He laboured enough to actualize this thought at the very outset. He danced with the students, encouraged them in dancing, and patiently directed rehearsals day after day by composing dramas suitable for dance. He had neither a bit of boredom nor neglect in this work. He loved dancing much. As he looked upon it as a great means for enjoying pure pleasure, he had special endeavour towards enjoyment of the same by others as well. In this respect, he remarks :

> "I am the messenger of diversities. I dance and make others dance, laugh and make others laugh, sing and paint pictures. We are the messengers of the expression that is restless in the unreasonable exposure of the universe........ I have accepted the duty of a messenger of the diverse cadence of the manifold that goes on playing, by becoming numerous, towards every direction, in tunes, songs, dances, pictures, colours, appearance, in turmoils and triflings of happiness and sorrow, in the conflicts between the good and the evil. I wanted to become a companion of the mysteries of these tender boys and girls in the blue sky and in the ground of sunrise and sunset of the *Ashrama*. The very endeavour to awaken the

minds of these children in joy by harmonizing with the mysterious rhythm of the ever mysterious through dance and music signifies my pleasure and success."

I am quoting an extract to show how Gurudev specially considered the art of dancing. He remarks :

> "The first role of the art of dancing lies in meaningless cohesion of physical movements. There is only pleasure of rhythm in it.
>
> "Our physique carries the burden of limbs and other parts and it is guided by the velocity of the latter. When these two opposite elements are turned into mystery through fusion, dancing dawns. The speed of the body makes the burden of the body diverse in different postures. It gives the body a moving, artistic form not out of the needs for livelihood but out of the desire for creation. We call it dance.
>
> "Not a single style of dancing remains static; it is continually becoming diverse and different. And yet, one who is seeing is saying joyfully : I am seeing dancing. Every transitory style of dancing is expressing a continual truth restrained in beats and a standard. We are not seeing the style of dancing as the fundamental one, we are seeing its truth and, therefore, we are becoming pleased.
>
> Girls begin to sketch on the tune of the song through zigzag lines of the movements of limbs. I think within myself : what does it mean? Every day of ours in stained, torn and tattered full of innumerable errors. Where is harmony within these?..... If the poverty of everyday is the only truth, this dance would not at all be liked by us. We would call it an eccentricity. But when I visualize this complete mystery of form of the rhythm, the mind begins to say that it is very true—more intensely and intimately truthfully than what the eyes arrest what are scattered in a haphazard manner all around."

To Gurudav, the art of dancing received honour as a moving art of the body. The joy of this rhythm has enamoured his mind. For this very reason, he unhesitatingly steered a living movement of dance. Gurudev noticed how it took shape keeping a synchronized relationship with the ideal of education for fullness of life and said :

> "During my tour in many places of the eastern countries, I have got the opportunity to see the art of dancing in Java, Bali, Shyam, China and Japan, and in Cochin, Malabar and Manipur in our country. I am familiar with the folk dance of Europe and other dances. I have experience in this regard and I have the authority to say about this. I won't hesitate to tell you this : in our Ashrama, all these trends have instilled in our art of dancing. The meditation, sense of artistry and manifestation of the beauty of the revealed in it are rare anywhere."

From the above statements of Gurudev, it is fairly clearly revealed that he felt the art of dancing as an honourable educative discipline. In Bengal, its absence was profusely seen in the urban educated society from the nineteenth century. The art of dancing was then a matter of luxury only. So its pursuit was limited to professional *vaijees, khemtawalis* and dancers and danseuses of the *Yatras* and the theatres. The urban educated society totally lost the sense that, apart from luxury of a low standard, dancing has a special role in the human mind. This is why, we do not know if there was any pursuit of dancing among the men and women of the urban society in those days, But, in the rural society, the prestige of the art of dancing remained untarnished, and it has still remained so. We encounter its evidence through extensive introduction of the Indian folk dance. Owing to the neglect of the urban educated society, many social dances of the village were gradually undergoing extinction. In spite of this, whatever is still existent is a matter of pride from the point of diversities. Gurudev considered this neglect by the educated society towards this art of dancing that caters to enjoyment of pure pleasure to be a serious limitation from the standpoint of total development of the society. And he also understood that whatever he spoke, he would not be supported by the urban educated society. So he gave attention to the spread of the pursuit of dancing among the students and teachers of Santiniketan.

Nobody is aware of the exact history of Gurudev's sincere endeavour and labour behind the new dance-movement that he introduced through the Santiniketan Vidyalaya and which culminated in the full-length dance-dramas composed by him towards the end of his life. When it will be published we will see that whatever he said orally or in writing on dance was not only an overflow of temporary emotion of his poetic mind, but also a necessary truth of his own development of life.

15 THE DRAMA " TAPATI"

Rabindranath's drama "Tapati" was first staged in 1929, in *Aswin* 1336 Bengali era, by erecting a stage in the southern corner of the old building for worship of the residence at Jorasanko. There is a history behind the composition and the acting of the drama.

In February 1929, Gurudev had to spend nearly four months abroad touring Canada of the North America. He returned to his country on the 3rd July. The route for Canada was through Japan. He could not forget on his way abroad that the *Vasantotsav* (The Spring Festival) would take place in Santiniketan in March next. It was also not possible for him to forget because he introduced the different festivals of Santiniketan throughout the year as a compulsory part of the educational life here. For this reason, he always tried to make these festivals beautiful in all respects. He could not at all tolerate any slackness or inattention to these. He had to remain all the time at the centre of these festivals. He would himself actively participate in these festivals with great enthusiasm and eagerness. This is why he could not forget about the ensuing spring festivals on his tour aboard. Recalling the spring festival before the ship reached Sanghai, he wrote a letter on *Chaitra* 3, 1336 Bengali era to Pratima Devi :

> "I came across in the almanac that the full moon of the Spring Festival would be on *Chaitra* 11. It is not at all far. This time I will be deprived of attending your festival. Are you trying anything for acting? It is better if you stage "Natir Puja" with new girls. Have you seen the acting of "Raja O Rani"? I regret, we could not stage that."

Though Gurudev's desire is expressed in this letter, Pratima Devi could not arrange any of these in the Spring Festival due to shortage of time. A totally different programme of activities has already been fixed for the night of the Spring Festival.

Towards the end of the month of *Asad* (July), just after his return from abroad, Gurudev was reminded of the acting of "Raja O Rani." In the evening of *Sravan* 7 (July 23) he read out the old drama composed in blank verse before a few teachers and senior students. On that day he read out the drama in the very name "Raja O Rani".

At that time, preparations for the festivals of *Varsamangal* (Rains), *Vriksharopan* (Tree Planting) and *Halakarsan* (Ploughing) were going on under the direction of Dinendranath. Mrs. Pratima Devi was getting ready for the acting of the drama "Natir Puja", taking new girls. On *Sravan* 25 (August 10) it was acted in the evening at Singhasadana in an abridged manner. The *Halakarsan Utsav* at Sriniketan was held on that day. The next day the functions of *Vriksharopan* and *Varsamangal* were performed at Santiniketan. Meanwhile, Gurudev was going on with the work of turning into prose and enlarging "Raja O Rani." On 22 *Sravan* (August 7), in the evening, he read out the drama "Raja O Rani" in its changed form.

Discussions were also held with the old teachers on the change of the old name of the drama. It was decided that instead of the name "Raja O Rani", he would select one out of the names "Sumitra." "Savitri", "Tapati" and "Kalbhairav". In a letter of *Sravan* 23 (August 8), Gurudev writes on the drama :

> "My pen gave birth to an all perfect drama yesterday... I think that it did not take more than ten days.... I would emphatically say that the drama has become all perfect..... It is my new composition, a changed version of "Raja O Rani." That name and that glamour still persist..... "Sumitra" is the name that I have decided."

At the end of the *Varsamangal* and *Vriksharopan Utsav*, Gurudev very enthusiastically paid attention to the rehearsal of the new drama. The work for selections of persons for the acting of the drama in its different characters started. In another letter of *Bhadra* 3 (August 28), he states with a bit of hint :

> "I corrected and revised "*Sumitra*" and yesterday read, but needless to say, everyone is in praise of it. But I can't hope that it can, all on a sudden, be acted. Ajin will not be able to play the role of Vikram. Who will be able? Where shall I find out the appropriate person? Arguments are going on in this regard."

On *Bhadra* 7 (August 24), handing the first act of the manuscript of the drama over to me, Gurudev instructed to copy the whole of it. He would immediately start rehearsals after selecting persons for acting. In the manuscript, the name of the drama for the time being was "Sumitra". Regular rehearsals started from *Bhadra* 8 (August 25). But Gurudev had to ponder over much as to whom he would select for the role of Sumitra. He tested a few among the female teachers and students for the character of Sumitra. Many failed. Meanwhile, he changed the name "Sumitra" into "Tapati". It was more or less decided before *Bhadra* 21 (September) who would play their parts in the main characters. Srimati Amita Tagore, Shri Ajin Tagore and Srimati Sumita Chakraborty became Sumitra, Naresh and Vipasha respectively. Some selections for the mob and the female characters still remained due.

When the hand-written manuscript of the first act of Gurudev's drama "Sumitra" came to us on *Bhadra* 7 (August 24), then its beginning runs as follows :

Sumitra

Act I

Devadutta and Vikram

Devadutta

Your Majesty, the worship of Anangadev! In this garden of worship of Rudrabhairavdev!

Vikram

Yes, the altar is ready under the Nagkeshar tree.

Devadutta

How daring! In his very forest of worship, by dint of whose meditation panchasar has been burnt!

Vikram

Last time Kandarpa came hidden like an accused. Now I'm openly calling him. He would come unhesitatingly befitting to gods, with the head raised and flags flying.

Devadutta

Your Majesty, from the very early times, there is a conflict between those two gods.

Vikram

It's man who suffers from that. One god deprives him from the gift of the other.

Devadutta

Anangadev never allows any other god to enter the room blessed by his own footprints. And for that, envy creeps in the mind of the revered.

Vikram

It seems that the words are directed towards me, courage is aggravating.

Devadutta

Friendship with the king is the climax of adventure. As ill luck would have it, the king's friend is outspoken.

Vikram

Open your mouth, then. Speak out clearly what the subjects are speaking about me!

Devadutta

They are speaking that under the coverings of the harem, there's darkness in the morning today throughout the stage. The affluence of the kingdom is ematiated in the shadow of the queen.

Vikram

O outspoken, is there the necessity of the banishment of Sita once more for the contentment of the subject!

Devadutta

It's you who alone want her banishment in the harem. The subjects want her in the royal throne. The whole of her heart does not belong to you; a part of it is for the subject. Is she merely a royal bride? The people's mother is she, too.

Vikram

Devadutta, it's division alone that spurts all conflicts. There she comes. In the part of a royal bride, or a people's mother?

Devadutta

Please allow me to depart then, your Majesty. (Exit).

Gurudev made many changes of the dialogues of the characters of this drama at the time of taking rehearsals. Most of the time he had to make so, thinking over the mode of speaking of the actors or their abilities to act. He ordered to print the revised drama quickly in the book form for the necessity of rehearsals. The work of printing also began at the Santiniketan Press. Towards the end of the month of *Bhadra* (September), he arranged to bring a few copies of the final proof and distributed those among the main actors. He gave a copy of the same to me, too. My assignment was to prompt and sing in the music group. Besides this, Gurudev also entrusted me with another serious assignment. This is to attend him now and then, and help him to memorize the part of Vikram. He went on saying the part of Vikram and I read out the words of the other characters.

What stood as a part of the beginning of the final proof copy "Tapati" by being changed from the manuscript was the following :

Tapati

Vikram, the head of Jullandhar, and friend Devadutta.

Devadutta

Your Majesty, the worship of Anangadev? In this garden of worship of Rudrabhairavdev?

Vikaram

Yes, the altar is ready under the *Nagkeshar* tree.

Devadutta

How daring! In his very forest of worship, by dint of whose meditation panchashar has been burnt?

Vikram

Last time Kandarpa came hidden like an accused. Now I'd openly call him. He would come unhesitatingly befitting to gods, with the head raised and flags flying.

Devadutta

Your Majesty, from the very early times, there is a conflict between those two gods.

Vikram

It's man who suffers from that. One god deprives him from the gift of the other. You have eternally made business with the worship of gods by combining the Brahmins and the scriptures, and so you know nothing about God.

Devadutta

That's right. My acquaintance with God is through scriptures. I am fed up with the meleé of *slokas,* I receive *dakshina* (honorarium), but I don't get time to come nearer to them.

Vikram

My 'Minaketu' is unscriptural. It does not obey the barriers of 'anustubh' or 'tristubh'. The Lord Siva has been in disguise with his bow of flowers.

Devadutta

I fear hearing this. But the reason for that which invites

incidents is the room which Anangadev marks by spraying the dust of his feet is banned for the gods to enter. And, for that, envy breeds in the minds of the revered.

Vikram

It seems that the words are directed towards me only. Courage is aggravating.

Devadutta

Friendship with the king is the climax of adventure. As ill luck would have it, the king's friend is outspoken.

Vikram

Open your mouth, then. Speak out clearly what the subjects are speaking about me.

Devadutta

They are speaking that under the coverings of the harem, there's darkness in the morning today throughout the state. The affluence of the kingdom is ematiated in the shadow of the empress.

Vikram

O Outspoken, is there the necessity of the banishment of Sita once again for the contentment of the subjects :

Devadutta

It's you who alone want here banishment in the harem. The subjects want her in the royal throne of everyone. The whole of her heart does not belong to you; a part of it is for the subjects. Is she merely a royal bride? The people's mother is she, too.

Vikram

Devadutta, it's division alone that spurts all conflicts that alone bring forth *Kurukshetra* (feud). There she comes. In the part of a royal bride or a people's mother?

Devadutta

Your Majesty, please allow me, then, to depart. (Exit).

Just a few days before the acting of the drama in Calcutta, Gurudev made a major change of the drama at the very beginning in the second page. From pages 51-55 of the first impression of "Tapati", where there is a fair extent of conversation between Kalindi and Maharaj Vikram; it had been fixed that Kalindi would recite the Bengali sloka 'O Puspadhanu, leave off the bed of the ashes of humiliation" ("Bhasma apaman shajya chhado puspadhanu)". As Kalindi could not manage to recite, Gurudev omitted the whole of the three-page conversation. But he retained the sloka 'Bhasma apaman shajya' in the beginning of the drama, on the second page, with reference to the dialogue between Vikram and Devadutta. In the first impression of "Tapati" on page two, we find the following statement of Maharaj Vikram :

> "My 'Minaketu' is unscriptural; it does not obey the barriers of 'anustubh' or 'tristubh'. It has its affinity of heart with the Rudrabhairav. The Lord Siva has taken disguise in his bow of flowers."

A new part has been added to the above :

Devadutta

Your Majesty, I don't understand this god well, but I don't find any sufficient resemblance of dress between him and Bhairav.

Vikram

That's because, Rati one day dressed him. He is brought up by women, enamoured and encircled by women, and so, he is ashamed in the assembly of tunings. That's why the fire of the manliness of Rudra burnt him.
That episode is over. Why this symptom again with that burnt god? Will he be burnt again?

Vikram

No. he will have to live in a new life through death. Today the festival of mine indicates that only. The power of the hero is required to make him alive. Unless I add chanting of my 'Minaketu', your chanting of Bhairav would not be complete.

Bhasma apaman shajya chhado, Puspadhanu,
Rudra agni hate laho jaladarchi tanu!
Jaha maraniya jak mare,
Jago chira-smaraniya dhyanmurti dhare.
Jaha sthul, jaha klanta tava,

Anga sathe dagdha hok, hao nitya-nava :

Mrityu hate jago, Puspadhanu
He atanu, virer tanute laho tanu.
Vandhu tava daityajayee dev vajrapani,
Puspachchhale tari agni dao tumi aani,
Sei divya dipyaman daha
Antare karuk kshuvdha duhkher pravaha.
Milanere karuk prakhar,
Vichchhedere kare dik duhsaha sundar.
Mrityu hate otho Puspadhanu,
He atanu, virer tanute laho tanu.
Timir toran rajanir
Spandive ahavane mor nirghos-gambhir.
Jak dure dvidha lajja traas—
Aay vakshe sarvanasha prachanda ullash.
Mrityu hate otho, Puspadhanu,
He atanu, virer tanute laho tanu

Leave off the bed of the ashes of humiliation,
Puspadhanu
From the fury of fire, accept thy arm that
is worshipped by the cloud,
Let it die that is worth death.
Awake, the one Ever-remembered with thy
meditative image.
What is crude and tired within you

Let it be burnt with limbs, be ever new,
Awake from death, Puspadhanu
O the armless one, accept thy arm in the arm of the hero.
The winner of demons is thy friend, Vajrapani,
Bring his fire in the show of flowers
That hevenly lustrous blaze—
Furious let it make the flow of sorrow in the heart
Let it make union ablaze
Detachment unbearably beautiful.
Arise from death, Puspadhanu,
O the armless, accept thy arm in the arm of the hero.

At the time of reharsal, the above few stanzas stand as follows after minor modifications :

Bhasma apaman shajya chhado, Paspadhanu
Rudra vihni hate laho jaladarchi tanu;
Jaha maraniya jaak mare
Jago abismaraniya dhayanmurti dhare.
Jaha rudha, jaha mudha tava,
Jaha sthul dagdha hok, hou nitya-nava.
Mrityu hate jago, Puspadhanu,
He atanu, virer tanute laho tanu,
Mrityunjay je mrityure diyechhen hani
Amrita se patra hate dao tumi ani.
Sei divya dipyaman daha
Unmukta karuk agniutser pravaha,
Milanere kurak prakhar,
Vichchhedere kare dik duhsaha sundar,
Mrityu hate otho, Puspadhanu,
He atanu, virer tanute laho tanu.
Duhkha sukhe vedanay vandhur je path—
Se-durgame chaluk premer jayrath!
Timir prangane, he ratrir
Jatri: ano arghyadip naisha aratir.
Ullanghiya tuchchha lajja trash—
Ano vanya atmahara udvel ullash.
Mrityu hate otho, Puspadhanu,
He atanu, virer tanute laho tanu.

[Leave off the bed of the ashes of humiliation, Puspa-
dhanu],
From the fury of fire, accept thy arm
that is worshipped by the cloud.
Let it die that is worth death
Awake in the unforgettable image of meditation
Whatever is rude and stupid in you
Whatever is blunt, let burnt be it, be eternal and new
Arise from death, Puspadhanu,
O, the armless, accept the arm in the arm of the armless.
The Winner of death who has killed death
Give from that deathless bowl
That heavenly blaze enkindling
Let that flow of the source of fire make open,
Let that make union ablaze.
Detachment unbearbly beautiful
Arise from death, Puspadhanu,
O the armless, accept thy arm in the arm of the hero.
The path pitched with sorrow and joy and pain.
Let the chariot of the victory of love in that path advance.
O the traveller of darkness,
Bring in the dark courtyard the lamp of the worship for
the night.
Crossing over futile shame and fear,
Come, O Flood, being beside yourself with over-flowing
joy.
Arise from death, Puspandhanu,
O, the armless, accept thy arm in the arm of the hero.]

Before acting in Calcutta, Gurudev totally omitted many dramatic statements of the first impression, and added some new ones. I am separately stating a list of these changes :

Act I

Page	1	—	Set new dialogues for Sankar and Vikram.
Page	7	—	Made minor omissions of the dialogues of Vikram and Sumitra.
Pages	32-34	—	Omitted the dialogues of Ratneswar and Devadutta.

Pages	36	—	Made minor omissions of the dialogues of Devadutta and Sumitra.
Page	46	—	Omitted the dialogues of Vipasha and Naresh.
Pages	50-51	—	Omitted the dialogues of Vipasha and Naresh.
Pages	52-55	—	Omitted the dialogues of Vikram and Kalindi.

Act II

Page	63	—	Omitted the dialogues of Sumitra and Pratihari.
Pages	66-73	—	Omitted many statements of Narayani, and Devadutta, Vipasha and Sumitra.
Pages	113-117	—	Omitted many statements of Narayani and Devadutta.

Act III

Pages	120-128	—	Omitted many statements of the crowd and admitted minor new statements in the beginning.
Pages	136-137	—	Omitted a few portions of the statements of the crowd and Naresh.
Pages	150-154	—	Ommissions made in case of the statements of the crowd, Naresh and Vipasha along with the song 'Jamer duar khola peye' ('Finding the doors of the King of Death open').
Pages	156-160	—	Omitted the statements of the crowd and Devadutta.
Pages	163	—	To the end of Act III — The statements of Vikram, the messenger and Chandrasen were added anew.

Act IV

Pages	164-165	—	Omitted the statements of the pilgrims and Bhargav.
Pages	172-173	—	Omitted the statements of Naresh and Vipasha.
Pages	182	—	Introduced the new statements of Devadutta, Sankar and Sumitra.

Nearly a week before the beginning of acting in Calcutta, that is on *Aswin* 2 (September 18) the song 'Sarva kharva tare dahe tava krodhadaha' (Thy fire of anger burns all dwarfness) was composed. The incident as the backdrop of the composition was the following :

> At the time of the composition of the drama "Tapati" anew, Jatin Das, the revolutionary, had been observing fast for about two months in his resolution to embrace death as a mark of protest against the ill behaviour of the authorities of the Lahore jail. At the news of his fast unto death, the minds of the country men were very restless. Everyone was impatient to save Jatin Das. But the British Government stuck to their adamant attitude. Jatin Das kept to his promise and sacrificed his life. This news reached Santiniketan on *Aswin* 2 (September 18). Everyone right from Gurudev was grieved at this news. Being pained at this sacrifice of Jatin Das, Gurudev composed the song 'Sarva kharvatare dahe tava krodhadaha' ('Thy fire of angar burns all dwarfness') and decided to retain it as an inaugural song. As the incident occurred after the publication of the drama "Tapati" in book form, the song was not included in the first impression. But it was placed first as a song of the worshippers of Bhairav of the temple of Bhairav in the supplement published at the time of acting.

On the second night of acting the song of Vipasha of the drama "Tapati", Act II, 'Diner pare din je gelo' ('Day after day passed') was omitted. Instead, he made her sing his new song 'Amar andha pradip' ('My blind lamp'). Although the song 'Jamer duar khola peye' ('Finding the doors of the King of Death open') was in the supplement, it was not sung at the time of acting. No other song was also retained as an alternative to it. The following ten songs were there in the first impression of "Tapati" :

1. 'Man je vale chini chini'
   (Know I, I know, says my mind')
2. 'Aalok-chora lukie elo'
   ('The thief of light came in disguise')
3. 'Jago he rudra, jago'
   ('Awake, O Fury, awake')
4. 'Vakul gandhe vanya elo'
   ('The fragrance of *Vakul* surged flood')
5. 'Pralay nachan nachle jakhan'
   ('When you started the dance of devastation')
6. 'Diner pare din je gelo'
   ('Day after day passed')

7. 'Tomar asan sunya aaji'
   ('Vacant is thy seat today')
8. 'Jamer duar khola peye'
   ('Finding the doors of the King of Death open')
9. 'Jago aalasasayan'
   ('Awake the moments of the idle slumber')
10. 'Subhra nava sankha tava'
    ('White and new is thy conchshell')

All the songs of Vipasha were acted in the pattern of dancing. The girls sang those songs from the background.

"Tapati" was acted on *Aswin* 11, 12, 13 and 15 (September 27, 28, 29 and 30) consecutively and the *dramatis persona* are :

Vikram	—	The king of Jullundhar : Gurudev.
Sumitra	—	The Queen of Jullundhar : Srimati Amita Tagore.
Naresh	—	Vikram's step brother : Sri Ajindranath Tagore.
Vipasha	—	Sumitra's fried : Srimati Sumita Chakrabarti. (Sumita Bahadur Singh).
Devadutta	—	The king's friend : Dinendranath Tagore.
Gouri	—	Srimati Rama Majumdar (Kar).
Kalindi	—	Srimati Nirupama Devi.
Manjari	—	Srimati Chitra Tagore (Buzu).
Kumar Sen	—	The Prince of Kashmir : Sri Kalimohan Ghosh.
Chandra Sen	—	Kumar's Uncle : Sri Nalin Mitra.
Trivedi	—	The Royal priest of Jullendhar; Sri Nitai Vinod Goswami.
Maidens	—	Srimati Rama Majumder, Srimati Chitra Tagore, Srimati Nirupama Devi, Srimati Amita Sen (Khukoo) and Srimati Niharkana.
Bhargav	—	The priest of the Martanda Temple, Kashmir : Sri Kalimohan Ghosh.
Minister	—	Sri Satyen Bishi.
Sankar	—	Sri Kanak Tagore.
The Commander in Chief	—	Sri Nitendranath Ganguly (Nitu).
Shikharini	—	Shrimati Nirupama Devi.
Kunjalal and Ratneswar	—	Sri Anathnath Basu.
The door-keepers	—	Sri Aryanayakam, Sri Vinayak Masoji.
The Brahmin Pilgrim	—	Sri Satyen Bishi.
Messengers	—	Sri Vinayak Masoji, Sri Sagarmay Ghosh.

The Crowd	—	Sri Sagarmay Ghosh, Sri Anathnath Basu, Sri Santosh Mitra, Sri Sachchidananda Roy (Aaloo), Sri Nishikanta Roy Chowdhury (Pondicherry), Sri Deben Ghosal, Sri Banabihari Ghosh, Sri Koko Tagore, Sri Nitaivinod Goswami.
Music Group	—	Sri Dinendranath Tagore, Sri Santidev Ghosh, Sri Sudhir Chandra Kar, Sri Sagarmoy Ghosh, Sri Banabihari Ghosh, Sri Moni Roy Chowdhury, Sri Deben Ghosal, Srimati Rama Majumdar (Kar), Srimati Amita Sen (Khukoo), Srimati Nirupama Devi, Srimati Chitra Tagore (Buzu), Srimati Niharkana, Srimati Savitri Krishnan.

I would like to recall one or two special incidents related to the acting of the drama "Tapati" :

> A big group of students and teachers from Santiniketan reached Calcutta a few days before acting. Regular rehearsals were going on at Jorasanko. A special request was made to Gurudev one or two days before acting to allow Silpacharya Abanindranath Tagore to play the role of 'Trivedi' of the drama. For this role, Nitaivinod Goswami, a teacher of Santiniketan came prepared. Gurudev had no intention at all to make this type of change two days before the beginning of acting, but in the earnest interest of the proposers, he called on Abanindranath and requested him to participate in the drama. Although time was short, Abanindranath could not neglect Gurudev's intention. He took the stage copy from me and wrote the statements of Trivedi on the paper in his own hand in order to memorize, but as he could not memorize well, he could not act easily and boldly at the time of rehearsal and so it was Sri Nitaivinod Goswami who remained as "Trivedi".

My assignment was mainly to prompt at the time of Gurudev's acting and, at the time of songs, I had to sing along with the music group. When Gurudev would play his role during acting by moving right or left on the stage, I went on prompting by standing very near him behind the wings. For this reason, I had to run often from this side of the stage to the other. During acting on the first night, Gurudev delivered fairly well his statements for a long time in the beginning but, in the first scene, after the entrance of Naresh and Vipasha on the stage for the first time, Gurudev skipped his statements covering nearly a page and a half, to be made after seeing them. He could not understand what Naresh would say in response to that, but as soon as prompting from behind reached his ears the matter of the error made Gurudev aware. He immediately composed new statements orally, returned to the beginning of the left out portion and went on speaking the whole of that correctly. Afterwards, conversations consecutively went on without any interruption. No disturbance occurred till the end.

The total responsibility in regard to the constumes and decorations of the drama "Tapati" was entrusted with Sri Nandalal Bose, Srimati Pratima Devi and Sri Surendranath Kar. Sri Abanindranath also assisted them in this matter. I quote here the description of Abanindranath in his memoirs on the decoration of Gurudev, He writes :

> "*Tapati*" will be acted : Rabikaka has dressed himself as a king. He dressed as much as he could.

The dress rehearsal of *Tapati* will commence; Suren, Rathi and others have brought boxfuls of colour. Rabikaka picked up a few black colours from these and entered the dressing room. He would himself blacken the beard.

What Rabikaka has done! He has profusely rubbed black colour on the cheek. As a result, his beard turned black and looked very ugly.

However, the dress rehearsal ended. Lying on bed, I was thinking what could be done, Rising in the morning, I said to Pratima : Bring a yard or two of the cloth of black colour that you, girls, often put on the head. Those, the *memsahibs* wear to stick on hair. Light, appears very much the same as hair from a distance. That cloth, however, came. Before acting I said to Rabikaka : Don't apply colour on the beard today. I shall blacken your beard. Saying this, I put that cloth fairly well, stuck on the beard like gallup and tied on two sides of the ears. I stuck some portions of cloth in the same way on the moustache also and cut off near the mouth. Everyone was surprised at its show from the stage, and appreciated the beard as marvellous, Rabikaka had to face no trouble also; it was over, if the gallup and the cloth were put off after acting.

Just before acting, the first impression of the drama *Tapati* was published twice in two forms within a span of a few days with changes of covers and inclusion of notations. Gurudev's own drawing in sketches of black ink of the title *Tapati* was on the cover of the first that was printed. The names of the publishers, the printer and the press were on the third cover inside including the date of the month of *Bhadra*, 1336 (September 1929). The price was rupee one and a half. The list of the characters of the drama were stated on the fourth cover followed by an introduction. At the end of the introduction the date 19 *Bhadra*, 1336 (September 5, 1929) was there inserted.

It was a four-act drama

Act I	:	Pages 1-62,
Act II	:	Pages 63-117
Act III	:	Pages 118-163 and
Act IV	:	Pages 164-185
Appendix	:	Translation of the *Mantra* (Chanting), p.1-3.

The two names 'Tapati' and 'Sri Rabindranath Tagore' on the cover of the second book of the first edition of *Tapati* were painted by Gurudev and published in a coloured picture. From the next page, everything including name, date, characters of the drama, introduction, pages of the four acts and the *mantra* at the appendix with its translation is the same as that of the first book. The notations of the songs of *Tapati* were first given towards the end in this book separately from pages 7-42. But the name of notation-composer was not mentioned. The songs with notations are :

1. 'Man je vale chini chini'
   (Know I, I know, says my mind)
2. 'Aalok-chora lukie elo'
   ('The thief of light came in disguise')
3. 'Vakul gandhe vanya elo'
   ('The fragrance of *Vakul* surged flood')
4. 'Pralay nachan nachle jakhan'
   ('When you started the dance of devastation')
5. 'Jago he rudro jago'
   ('Awake, O Fury, awake')
6. 'Diner pare din je gelo'
   ('Day after day passed')
7. 'Tomar asan sunya aazi'
   ('Vacant is thy seat today')
8. 'Jamer duar khola peye'
   ('Finding the doors of the King of Death open')

9. 'Jaga aalasasayan'
   ('Awake, the moments of the idle slumber')
10. 'Subhra nava sankha tava'
   ('White and new is thy conchshell').

At the time of acting in Calcutta, a souvenir was published for the convenience of the audience. It was as follows :

Tapati

Sri Rabindranath Tagore—Price : Four annas.
First show : 10 *Aswin*, 1336
Jorasanko, Calcutta.

Act I

The song of the worshippers of Bhairav in the courtyard of the temple of Bhairav :
'Sarva, kharvatare dahe tava krodhadaha'
(The fire of anger burns all dwarfness)
Vikram, the king of Jullundhar. His Brahmin friend, Devadutta. The Queen, Sumitra. The king's step brother, Naresh, and the Queen's companion, Vipasha. The Minister, guards, complainants, subjects, and Ratneswar. The ladies of the harem, Kalindi, Gouri, Manjari, Trivedi, the Royal priest.

Song

'Man vale je chini chini'
('Know I, I know, says my mind')

Song

'Aalok chora lukie elo oi'
('There came the thief of light in disguise')

Song

'Jago he rudra Jago'
('Awake, O Fury, awake)

Song

'Vakul gandhe vanya elo'
('The fragrance of *Vakul* surged flood')

Song

'Pralay nachan nachle jakhan'
('When you started the dance of devastation)

Act II

The crowd, Kumarsen, Naresh and Vipasha, Chandrasen, Devadutta.

Song

'Diner par din je gelo'
('Day after day passed')

Song

'Tomar asan sunya aazi'
('Vacant is thy seat today')

Song

'Jamer duar khola peye'
('Finding the door of the King of Death open')

Act III

Kasmir-The temple of Martanda
Bhargav, the priest, the pilgrims, Vipasha, Sumitra, Sikharini, Kunjalal, Naresh, Kumar, Devadutta, Sankar, Vikram.

Song

'Jago aalasa sayan-vilagna
('Awake, the moments of the idle slumber')

Song

'Subhra nava sankha tava gagan bhari'
('White and new is the couchshell throughout the sky').

The slokas and the Vedic hyms used in the drama were included. The total number of pages of the souvenir was eight. On the cover was a sketch by Silpacharya Nandalal Basu of a woman encircled with fire in linocut, and printed in red colour.

That the Indian political movement of those days specially influenced the mind of Gurudev at the time of writing the drama *Tapati* by changing *Raja O Rani* in 1929, is clearly revealed from a few portions of the drama. I have already referred to this fact related to the history of the composition of the song 'Sarva kharvatare dahe'. Besides this, the coversations among Ratneswar, Devadutta and Sumitra at pages 30-45 of the first edition also clearly reveal this fact.

In the drama *Raja O Rani,* the character of Ratneswar was not at all there. It is not difficult to understand that the picture of oppression by Siladitya, the foreigner, on the subjects that he has drawn in the drama *Tapati,* centering this character, was actually that of the British rulers in those days. Whatever Gurudev has made the Queen Sumitra speak on the role of the public to negotiate this oppression is the very echo of his political opinion. About this foreign oppression, Sumitra says to Devadatta :

> "O the revered one, confrontations certainly are there, but why is the timid mind screaming, standing in front of him? Do they not know that those whom God ignores are not fovoured by Him? Let the doors be broken by them. As they pray for judgment in fear, they are deprived of the same. The more forcibly the king demands taxes from them, the more forcibly is their right to demand judgment. The prescription of religion is not the gift of human favour."

16 THE INFLUENCE OF THUMRI ON THE SONGS OF RABINDRANATH

More than a hundred years ago, books on classical Hindi songs and discussion on their *raga-raginis* in detail in Bengali language were composed for the first time. From that period till now, many books have been published. From a thorough study of these books, it will not be difficult to know the principles, in vogue, of beats and *raga-raginis* of the classical Hindi songs towards the end of the nineteenth century. It is fairly undestood that a great deal of change has taken place in the music of this era from that of the previous one. Before making any discussion on the influence of Thumri on the songs of Rabindranath, it will not be easy, without taking help of these books, to properly assess what the Thumri song of the nineteenth century in Bengal actually meant and what changes have at present taken place in it.

It is known about the Thumri songs of yore that a beat named Thumri was greatly in vogue at that time, and as it was well-known to the persons who were appreciators to music in those days, the discussion on the beats of Thumri have been made in all books. First, I place a few specimens of the Thumris of those days as referred to in the authentic books on rural music the nineteenth and the twentieth centuries of Bengal.

Radhamohan, Sen, referring to Thumri as a *ragini* in his book "*Sangit Taranga*" printed in 1225 B.E. (1818) writes :

> "Thumri Raginir Dhara.
> Thumri name Shyam-Kalyaner promodini
> Jati-lakshanete sampuran vidhayini
> Ruper adhar dui-varoa vehag.
> Gaaner samay nishi kimva diva-bhaag."
>
> Thumri by name amuses with *Shyam-kalyan*
> By species and symptoms does make completion

A two-fold cascade of *varoa* and *Vehag*
To be sung at night or by day as you hug.

In this book, the author published two songs of Thumri ragini and *Aada-Tetala* composed by himself.

In the book *Gitaratna* (1244 B.E./1837) by Ramnidhi Gupta (Nidhubabu) songs of Thumri *tal* are found, but there is no song of Thumri *ragini*. Dasarathi Roy has also used Thumri as a *tal* only in his *Panchali* songs.

In the book *Ragakalpadrum,* a collection of Hindi and other songs, published in 1843, many songs of Thumri *tal* with *raga-ragini* are available, but in this book there is no source-analysis of Thumri songs of Thumri *tal.*

In 1869, Kshetramohan Goswami first published the identity of Thumri in his book and said :

> "Thumri is composed of very little *raga* and *tal.* Its precision is so pleasing that it soon captures the mind of people."

In course of discussion of the Thumri *tal,* he said :

> "Thumri is a tetra-accented *tal.* In it, a *tal* and a blob are there. The *theka* (gap) for example, is the following :

I+	I		I		I	
"Dhadha	ge	dhin	ta	ddha	ge	dhin"

In the division of two accents, it is shown as a *tal* of four accents. In the first accent there is *sam* and in the third *matra* (accent) there is *phank".*

Kshetramohan Babu also said :

> "There are various types of *Tappa;* of them, Thumri, Gazal, Vekta, Rubai, Sahela, Hori, Zigar, etc. are more famous."

From this statement, it is known that in those days, Thumri was considered to be a branch of *Tappa.* Krishnadhan Bandhyopadhyay, the eminent theoretician on music in Bengal, writes about Thumri in his book "*Gitisutrasaar*" .

"The songs that are sung in the ragini of *Tappa* and in *Aaddha Kaoali* and *Thumri tal* are called *Thumri* songs. Captain Williard has referred to the fact that there is a separate *raga* named *Thumri.*

> "A type of song named *Thumri* is in vogue in Hindusthan. That is sung in different *ragas*. In Lucknow, Thumri songs are greatly favoured...... Many people believe that *Shori* might not be the inventor of *Thumri* raga but it is the inventor of *Thumri* songs as a method..... It is so believed that as the *Tappas* of Shori are shortened, *Thumri* songs have come out of these. The songstresses of *Tarfakaoali* of Hindusthan always sing Thumri songs...... From a study of the tunings of *Thumri* songs, two aspects of beauty are observed : One is the style of singing and the other, diversity. The significance of diversity in the tuning of *Thumri* is that, it has more diversity than its appearance. In colloquial language, this diversity is called 'Jangla'. It means that there is a combination of two or three *ragas* in the same *Kali* of the same song. That combination is performed in such a surprising strategy that, for this, it does not seem incoherent when heard.... A person inexperienced in music can never understand the appropriate use of the *ragas.....*"
>
> "There are some differences in *Thumri* songs, e.g. *Khemta, Kaharba, Dadra* etc. As these songs are sung in the *tals* like *Khemta, Kaharba, Bharanga* etc., they are thus named."

Although we do not hear any such *raga* or *ragini* as *Thumri* in this era, in the beginning of the nineteenth century, Captain Williard referred to such a *raga* of that name and, towards the second half of that era, Dakshinaranjan Sen, a genius in music, published a Bengali song of *Thumri raga* along with its tuning in one of his books. Explaining this *raga*, he says :

> "*Thumri* is a kind of song. In it, there is an assembly of two or more *ragas*. This type of *ragini* of the song is called the *Thumri ragini.*"

The song published by Dakshina Babu is :

Thumri Aaddha

3 0 1 +
Sa pa ! ma pa aa aa ! pa sa aa ndha ! pa aa aa ma !
ga aa aa aa !
Sa dher pre me o o o na o pu ri o o la
sa o o o

3 0 1 +
! Sa ga ma pa ! ma aa jna jna ! sa aa ra na ! sa aa aa aa !
o o o o dh o e ki re o o bi sa o o o

3 0 1 +
! Sa aa ma pa ! na aa aa na ! sa sa aa aa ! na aa sa aa
d o a pa ra o o dhi ni ra o o ba o dhi o

On *Thumri tal* Krishnadhan Babu has written in a separate discussion :

> "This *tal* is only a different type of *Kaoali,* that is *prasvan* and beats fall at an interval of four short accents in it also...... The letters of the song of the tetra-accented beats that become light and prominent again and again in which there is a natural tendency to impose *prasvan* strongly at an interval of every fourth accent, ... the Bol of a more *prasvan* (force) applied in that *Theka* is called *Thumri.* If the movement of the song becomes any one of the rhythms as referred to above, it will be included under the *Thumri tal*........ As every *Prasvan* is forceful in *Thumri*, *Sam* takes place just after one beat, that is at the second beat. The rhythm of its *Theka* is, therefore, completed within two beats and so the half of *Kaoali* has become....... *Theka,* e.g.

+ 2
dha dha kete tak ! ne dha kete tak

"*Sam* is on the very first 'dha'. The song is seen to begin from every place of this *tal.* The following is the rhythm of the Urdu song of Lucknow *Thumri* :

+ 2 + 2
Dil ! Khu o shu da ! lag o jo g ! Ja o hai me ! ra o

"If the number of *Prasvan* of each *Kali* of the Thumri song is a division of four, then in accordance with three beats and one gap, the *theka* of *Kaoali* is given to it. It is also seen in the *Asthayee* of many songs of the beats of *Thumri* that in order to make the *Prasvan* strong, no letter remains upon the *Prasvan* that preceeds. For example—

2 + 2 +

! o gha o re ! rai o te o ! o na o di ! le o o o

2 + 2 +

Hindi ! o ko o hi ! na o hi o ! o aa o p ! na o o o"

I am quoting from old books two specimens of Urdu songs of the beats of *Thumri* that was introduced in Bengal towards the end of the nineteenth century, with notations. It is said that Nawab Wazed Ali Shah himself composed the first one while he was imprisoned in Calcutta. The second one was composed by a famous *Tappa* singer of Lucknow named 'Sarasar'. It is heard that he achieved fame like 'Shori' and 'Hamdam' in composing songs.

(1) Khambaz-Thumari

Jab chhor chale Lakhnou nagri
Kahun hal adan par kya guzri
Adam guzri sadma guzri
Jab ham guzre, dunia guzri.

\+ 2 + 2

ra ga ! sa ra sa na ! ga aa ga ga ! ma aa ma dha ! pa aa ma ga !

Ja b chho o d cha le o la kh nou o na g ri o ka han

\+ 2 + 2

ma aa pa pa ! pa dha sa na ! dha aa pa ma ! ga aa ra ga !

ga o ga da m pa r kya o gu z ri o ja v

\+ 2 + 2

ma ga ! ma aa dha dha ! dha aa dha dha ! na na ra sa na dha !

pa na ma ga !

aa da m o gu z ri o sad ma o o gu z

ri o ja v

\+ 2 2

ma aa pa pa ! pa dha sa na ! dha aa pa ma ! ga aa ra ra !

ha m gu z re o du ni aa o gu z vi o ja v

(2) Khambaz-Thumri

Bhala nimak haramme muluk dubaya
Hazrat jate hain London ko
Mahal mahal me begam royan
Gali gali royen paturia.

+ 0 + 0
ma ga ! ma dha dha dha ! dha na sa aa ! dha sa aa na ! dha aa pa aa !
bha la ni ma k ha ra m ne o mu lu k du ba o ya o
+ 0 + 0 1
! pa dha ma pa ! ma ga ra ga ! ma aa na aa ! dha aa ma ga !
ha z ra t ja o te hen la n do n ko o bha la
+ 0 + 0
aa aa ! ma ma dha dha ! dha dha na aa ! sa aa ka aa ! sa aa sa aa !
o o ma ha ma ma ha l me o be o ga m ro a yen o
+ 0 + 0
! dha dhna sa na ! dha pa ma ga ! ma aa dha pa ! dha aa ma ga !
ga li o ga li ro o yen o pa o tu ri ya o bha la

In the first song, *Thumri* is a *tal* of eight accents in toto. The notation-composer of this song has shown beats without giving *phank* and *sam* in the fifth and the first accents respectively. The notation-composer of the second song has, of course, said that the *Thumri tal* is a combination of eight accents, but he has marked *sam* and *phank* in the first and fifth accents, respectively.

The writer of "Sachitra Visva-sangit" says :

> "*Thumri* is the name of a kind of *Tal.* The *Tappas* sung in the *Thumri tal,* are normally called *Thumri.* Besides this, *Thumris* are also sung in *Aaddha-kaoali.* The *Taraf-kaoalis* of Hindusthan sing this song. For this, the artistic *Ostads* do not like it. A typical quality of *Thumri* is that, in its one *Kali* association of two or three *raginis* is observed. This union is called 'Jangla'."

"*Thumri* is a beat of four accents. In it, there are a beat and a blank, *Theka*, for example, is :

1+		1		1		1⁰	
dha	d'dha	ge	din	ta	ddha	ge	din."

It seems that discussions in this book are made in accordance with the opinion of Kshetramohan Goswami.

Dakshinacharan Sen, an author of numerous books on music and eminent exponent of the Indian choric songs, has discussed on the songs and beats of the *Thumri raga* in the following way :

> "It is a beat of eight accents and is divided into two parts of four accents each. In most cases, it has a long letter at the beginning of the part and the short ones at the end. The rhythm of *Thumri* is mostly that of *Karpa,* but the special point of difference is that in many places of *Karpa*, there is a di-accented or tri-accented letter from the word of a certain *Sam* to the end of every fourth word, but in *Thumri,* there is almost no such analysis. The *theka* of *sangat* for this is as follows :

+	1	1	1	1	1	1	1	1	1
I	dha	dha	kete	tak	I	ne	dha	kete	tag."

The *theka* is exactly like "Gitasutrasar".

Now let me quote a few examples of the songs that were composed in those days in imitation of the Lucknow *Thumri.*

Govinda Chandra Roy, a resident of Agra, composed his famous national song "Kata kala pare bala Bharata re' in Laucknow *Thumri Tal* in imitation of Wazed Ali Shah's 'Jav chhor chali Lucknow nagari' in the *Khambaj ragini* in need of the Hindu Mela in the seventh decade of the nineteenth century. I quote a notation of this song composed in the *Thumri Tal,* from the book "*Sangit Sutra*."

Jhijhit-khambaz (complete, ni) - *Thumri*
Composed by Shri Gobinda Chandra Roy.

ra ga II sa ra ga ma I ea maga ra ga I ma aa ma dha I pa dha pa ma ga I
ka ta ka o la pa re o o ba la bha o ra ta re o o du kha
I ma aa pa pa II pa dha sa na I dha ma dha pa ma I ga ma ga ma ga I
sa o ga ra sa o ta ri pa o o ra ha be o o a ba
I ma pa ma na I dha na dhapa dha I sa aa na dha I pa dha pa ma ga I
sa o da hi me o o du bi ye o du bl ye o o o ki
I ma aa pa pa I pa dha sa na I dha na dha pa ma I ga ma ga ra ga II
se o sa ni be o sa ra ba o o ba la re o o "Kata"

The notation of the song made by Dakshinacharan Sen is as follows :

Kahambaz-Thumri

```
sa sa   I ra ga ma pa ma pa ma ma I  ga aa  ga ga  I  ma  aa pa  ma  I pa ma
ka ta     ka o o    o     la pa     re o   ba la     bha  o ra   ta     re
garga  ga ga I ma aa pa pa  I padha padha   sa sa   nadha I pa dhap  amapa
o oo  duk kha sa o ga ra     sa    o o               ri     pa  o     o o
ma ma I ga aa sa sa I
ra ha   be o 'ka ba'
```

In connexion with the discussion on the rhythm of songs as above, I would like to refer to the fact related to the *Thumri tal.*

In Sanskrit scriptures on rhythm, there is a rhyme called "Totak". In Bengali poetry, most of the poets of the nineteenth century have used this rhyme. From an analysis of the 'Totak' rhyme used in Bengali poetry, it will be found that the total number of accents of its every line is 16. Altogether twenty-four words in equal pattern are there in its two lines, and every word beginning with every 3rd, 6th, 9th, 12th, 15th, 18th, 21st and 24th letter is grave and the rest are light,. This means that of the 12 letters of the first line, the poems are to be recited by giving a special stress on 3rd, 6th, 9th and 12 letters. Let me clarify this point by taking the lines of a poem, in Bengali, of the nineteenth century.

```
'Tuni   panka  jini   muhi   bhaskar 10
Bhay    na     karo   na     karo    10.
```

If these two lines of the poem are analysed in the principles of the 'Totak' rhyme, its division of accents will be the following :

```
11      11 1   1 11   11     1ì 1 1          11
tuhi    panka  jini   muhi   bhaskar na karo 10.
```

This means that at the time of reciting this poem the stresses of rhyme fall on the letters 'pa', 'ni', 'bha' and 'lo' of 3rd, 6th, 9th and 12th letters. The following are other examples of old Bengali poems composed on the rhyme 'Totak' :

```
          1             1          1         1
(1)   Ramanimani      nagar       raj       kavi
          1             1          1         1
       Ratinath     Vinindita   Charuch     habi
```

(2)		1	1	1	1	
	Sara	nirnaya	duskara	karya	hate	
		1	1	1	1	
	Ati	asruta	martya	amartya	sabe	
		1	1	1	1	
	Jadi	rakshaha	anguri	atma	sane	
	1		1	1	1	
	Labhibe	sthira	kumbhaka	santa	mane	
(3)	1	1	1	1		
	Atirosa	mane	rajputa	sabe		
	1	1		1	1	
	jabanere	hare	bal	ghora	rabe	
		1	1	1	1	
	Nara	rakta	chhata	tarabara	pare	
		1	1		1	1
	Rabi	rasmi	bhara	kata	raga	kare

Let us compare with the above, the following famous lines of the poet Govinda Chandra Roy :

	1	1		1	1
Kata	kala	pare	bala	bharata	re
	1	1	1	1	
Dudha	sagar	santari	para	habe	

If we recite the above two lines of the song of *Khambaj ragini* and *Thumri tal,* we will see that it is a Bengali poem of the rhyme "Totak". Its every line is complete in twelve letters and is divided into sixteen accents. For example :

1	1	11	1	1	11	1	1	11	1	1	11
Ka	ta	ka	la	pa	re	ba	la	Bha	ra	ta	re
1	1	11	1	1	11	1	1	11	1	1	11
Du	dha	sa	ga	ra	sa	ta	ri	pa	ra	ha	be

In this connection, I am trying to express the identity of the rhyme of the song "Jab chhod chale Lucknow nagari" composed by the Nawab Wazed Ali Shah, by putting the sign of accents on the top of the letters :

1	1	11	1	1	11	11	11	1	1	11		
Ja	ba	chho	ra	cha	le	Lack	now	na	ga	ri		
1	1	11	1	1	1	11	1	1	11	1	1	11
Ka	hu	ha	la	aa	da	m	pa	ra	kya	gu	ja	ri

Every line of this song composed in the Urdu language is complete in 16 accents. At the time of recitation, the stress of rhyme in it comes automatically like the Bengali poem. A remarkable special feature of the two songs 'Kata kala pare bala Bharata re' and 'Jab chhod chale Lucknow nagari' is that the words of these to be sung in the stress of rhythm are exactly the same as that of poetry. For this it seems that, for this very rhyme, the *Thumri Tal* in Northern Indian music was originated. Perhaps the Sanskrit rhyme "Totak" has been turned into *Thumri Tal* in Hindi songs. It also seems that in the song of the rhyme "Totak" the use of *Thumri Tal* has been going on in Northern India from a long time ago.

In a book entitled "*Tabla Siksha*" ("Learning Tabla"), there is a reference to four *bols* of *Theka* along with a short description of *Thumri Tal.* The author collected those four *Thekas* from four eminent Tabla-players of those days : In introducing *Tal,* the author writes :

Thumri is a tal of four accents. Of these three are *tals* and one is blank. The *thekas* are the following :

	1^+		$1'$	1^0	$1'$		
1.	Dha	dha	gedhen	tadha	gedhen.		- *Theka* - Hossain Box.

	1^+		$1'$	1^0		$1'$	
2.	Dhet	dhage	trekut	ta	dha	gedhen	- *Theka* -Ata Hossain

	1^+	$1'$		1^0	$1'$		
3.	Kat	dhage	den	dha	dhage	dhen	- *Theka* - Salari Khan

	1^+		$1'$	1^0	$1'$		
4.	Dha	dhen	dha trekut	ta	dhen dha	trekut	- *Theka* -Ahmani Khan

In the book " *Sangit-Sutra*", the reference made to another *Theka* of the *Thumri Tal* of the previous era is the following :

"Thumri is a *Tal* of two accents. It was made into four accents by doubling it. Between two divisions there are a stroke and a blank in the first and the second respectively. The *bol* of *Theka* is as follows :

1^+		1	1^0		1
Dhak	thena	kete,	Nak	ghena	kete"

On *Thumri,* we come across the very same opinion of the previous era in the Bengali books on music at the beginning of the twentieth century.

Ramprasanna Bandyopadhyay, the master of music- *Sangitguru-* of Visnupur, has said on *Thumri Tal :*

"*Thumri* is a *tal* of eight accents. In it, there are one stroke and one blank. The *Theka* is as as follows :

1^+	1	1	1	1^0	1	1	1	
Dha	dha	kete	tag,	Na	dhi	dha	tere	kete."

The notation of a Bengali song of *Thumri Tal* in medium movement that he has given in his book is :

+ 0 + 0
"ra ga I sa ra sa ma I ga aa ga ga I ma aa ma dha I pa aa ma ga I
sa ma re aa na che ra o kar e o ra ma ni o na shi
+ 0 + 0
I ma aa pa pa I pa dha sa na I dha mapadha pa ma I ga aa
chhe o ti mi re o ti mi ra o o o ba ra ni o"

The song is composed in accordance with the 'Totak' rhyme of Bengali poetry. Besides this, the song reminds one of the *Thumri* song of Wazed Ali Shah in the formations of tuning, rhyme and *tal.*

Ramprasanna Babu also made the notation of a separate Hindi song of *Thumri tal.* For example :

Khambaz - Thumri

+ 0 + 0
I aa sa ga ga I ma ma pa aa I ga ma pa pa I mapa dhadha pama gaga I
o bu nda na ba ra khe o o aa ju gh na o oo oo oo
I aa mapama dhaI dha dha dha dha I na dha na sa I dhasa madha pama gaga I
o chala tu pa ba n ba n sa n sa n bo o oo lio o

Ramprasanna Babu has a separate book on *Tals* of *Mridanga* and *Tabla.* In it, he has referred to altogether five kinds of *Thumri Tals.*

It is a *tal* having eight short accents. There are a beat and a blank in it. The *Theka* is as follows :

		1^+	1	1	1		1^0		1	1
1.	I	dha	dha	kete	tag	I	na	dhi	dha	terekiti
		1^+	1	1	1		1^0	1	1	1
2.	I	dhi	dha	gi	ta	I	na	dhi	kiti	tak
		1^+	1	1	1		1^0	1	1	1
3.	I	dha	dha	dha	tin	I	na	dhi	dha	tin
		1^+	1	1	1		1^0	1	1	1
4.	I	dhah	dwa	gi	ta	I	na	dhi	dha	treke
		1^+	1	1	1		1^0	1	1	1
5.	I	dha	ti	dhag	di	I	na	dhi	dhadha	ti"

Thumri songs as Ramprasanna thinks are :

> *Chhepka, Kaharba, Thumri, Kabali* etc., are the halves of *Tetala* (Tri-beats), ...*Kabali* and *Thumri*- these two rhymes are the same. It is seen in the book on music entitled *Hindusthani Talpaddhati* that, as the Kabals use this *Kabali Tal* it is called so. Again, that very *Tal* is known as *Thumri* in Lucknow. So the same *Tal* has changed its name in the changes of places. Some persons in these places have divided *Thumri* into four parts like *Tetala*. But that has not become appropriate."

Gopeswar Bandyopadhyay has said in his book "*Sangit Chandrika*" :

> "The song that is sung in the *ragini* of *Tappa* and in the *tals* like *Kabali, Andha, Thumri, Khemta, Kaharba* etc., is called *Thumri.*"

Referring to the *Theka* of *Thumri Tal,* Nabinkrishna Haldar, in his book "*Behala Darpan*" remarks : "*Thumri* is of four accents."

1+	1⁰	1'	1⁰
Dheddha	kiti	neddha	kiti."

Manilal Sen, in "*Git Upakramanika*", says : "*Thumri* is created in the city of Lucknow. Nawab Wazed Ali Shah of Lucknow first created the *Thumri* song and Sanad and Kadar, the two eminent musicians, disseminated it in different ways. These three were singers and composers of *Thumri*...... A few musicians like Dayasakhi, Kripasakhi etc. composed excellent *Thumri* songs and became famous.

"Thumri is a *tal* of eight short accents. The rhymes in which there is a natural stress after every fourth accent is included in *Thumri.* There are four accents in every *pad* of *Thumri*. There is no gap in it. The very first is *Sam.* The *Theka* :

	+					2			
I	da	dhin	dha	dhin	I	ta	dhin	ta	dhin

The book, "*Sangit Parikrama*", is not old. What is written about the *Thumris* of the old and the of present eras in this book is as follows :

> "Some persons have indicated the meaning of the word 'Thumri' as a song delineating with light emotions. There is

> also a *tal* of this name and, probably, the song at first sung in the *Thumri tal* was called *Thumri*. For instance, the song belonging to the *Thumri* group and sung in the *Dadra tal* are now called 'Dadra'.

"The *Thumri* song is also enriched mainly in the beat of *Tappa,* and in the joint embellishments of *Kheyal* and *Tappa.* Although the emballishments like *Meed, Murchhana* and *Tal* etc. are widely used in it, the use of *Gamak* is rarely found. *Krintan* and an association of little notes make it specially audible. In this song, there is a special expression of the dancing (*Lasya)* style of the tune. *Tals* like *Trital, Yat, Addhakaoali, Dadra, Thumri, Kaharba* etc. are used in *Thumri.*

"In *Thumri,* the grammar of *raga-s* is not properly carried out....... The singers of *Thumri* use many tunes beyond the domain of *ragas. Raga-s* like *Bhairavi, Piloo, Manda, Jhinjhit, Khambaz, Desh, Vehag, Kafi, Bihari, Tilak-Kamod, Gara* etc. are particularly appropriate for *Thumri* songs.

"*Thumri* is mainly of two types—*Ostadi* or Classical, and *Baiji Thumri.* In *Ostadi Thumri, Vilamvit Tal* and embellishments of *Kheyal-Tappa* are used more. In other words, in *Ostadi Thumri,* the influence of *Margasangeet (*Classical music*)* is great. In *Baiji Thumri*, the use of *Drut-tal* and little *Kartav-s* are legion, the *Baiji-s* express the ideas (*Bhano*) of songs through physical movements.

"The *Thumri* songs have thrived by encompassing Nawab Wazed Ali Shah and Lucknow Kadarpiya, Sanad, Kripasakhi and other distinguished personalities were the great exponents of *Thumri* of the old era. In the later era learned personalities like Maijuddin, Bhaia Saheb etc. have introduced many *Thumri* songs."

In his book "*Sangeet-Jnan-Pravesh*", Satyakinkar Bandyopadhyay writes :

> "*Thumri* songs were in vogue in dance only. Realising specially the luxuries of Wazed Ali Shah Bahadur, the Nawab of Lucknow, towards music, the type of songs that the two eminent singers of his court (*Durbar)* composed songs in the tune of *Tappa* songs through analysis of light fine artistry of tunes, and by means of simple words on love and in easy *tal-s* in the style of dancing, is disseminated as '*Thumri'*.
> That there is a *tal* named *Thumri* is not admitted by many musicians today...... In our country .... in the midst of beats also, a beat named '*Thumri'* has been going on for a long time."

"At the first stage of the creation of (*Thumri*) songs, once the *theka* of *tabla* arose in such a beautiful emotion of ideas with dance in a new type of rhythmic song as, from that day onwards, that beautiful *theka* became a separately characteristic *tal* of the *Thumri* song, and was introduced as a 'Thumri-tal' by being synonymously named for that type of song. The songs framed in its rhyme have no resemblance with its tetra-accented *tal.*

"The application of *Thumri tal* is seen in the songs of the tune of *Thumri* alone. This *tal* consists of eight accents. It has only two *tal-s :* one is the *tal* of *Sam,* and the other, *Phank tal.* There are four divisions of accents in *tal.* Its rhyme is a bit tightened. The *theka* to play on is as follows :

+	1	1	1	1	0	1	1	1	1
I	dhan	dhi(n)	gi	ta	I	na	dhi	dha	terekete

Variation

	1^{+}	1	1	0	1	1	1	1
I	dhi	gi	ta	I	na(n)	ti(n)	na	ta.

In "Sangite Abidhan", Apurbakumar Choudhury, the author, has informed us of a separate type of *theka* of the *Thumri tal.* He has written - 8 accents, 3 strokes, 1 gap, *Sam* in the second *tal.*

Theka

1	1^{2}	1^{3}	1	1		1^{0}	1	1^{1}	1
I	dha	dhi	dhadha	dhin	I	ta	dhin	dhatak	dhin

In the eighth edition of the year 1340 B.E. (1933) of the book "Nava Sangeet Kalpataru", Krishnadhan Vidyapati has referred to more than one *theka* of *Thumri Tal* and has divided them into two groups. In the first group, the *bol* of *theka* consists of three beats and one gap.

	1^{+}		1^{3}	1^{0}	1^{1}
(1)	dhe	dha	kiti	nedha	kiti
	1^{+}		1^{3}	1^{0}	1^{1}
(2)	dhad	dha	dhaten	taddha	dadhen

The *Thumri* of the second group is a beat of four accents- two beats and two blanks. For example :

	1^+	1^0	1^+	1^0
(1)	dhedha	kiti	nedha	kiti
	1^+	1^0	1^+	1^0
(2)	tatraki	jun,	na	junna
	1^+	1^0	1^+	1^0
(3)	dhak	dhin,	dhedha	gedin
	1^+	1^0	1^+	1^0
(4)	dhage	dhindhin	dhage	dhindhin

In the book "Bharatiya Sangite Tal O Chhanda" by Sri Subodh Nandy, *Thumri* is called a *Tal* of eight accents. 1 beat and 1 gap. The rhyme is tetra-accented. The *theka :*

	+					0			
I	dha	dhin	nege	tete	I	dha	jun	nana	tete

Whatever is known about *Thumri* from a study of the books published in the Bengali language during the period from the middle of the nineteenth century to that of the twentieth one may be summed up as follows :

1. *Thumri* is a song of little *raga* and *tal.* This song easily charms the listeners. It was known as an easy branch of *Tappa* songs. A separate *ragini* is also available in this name. The *Tappas* that are sung in *Thumri-tal* were called *Thumri* songs. As these are songs of *Tarfawalis,* the *Ostads,* at one time, did neither sing nor like these. In these songs, an assembly or mixture of more than one *raga* is seen.
2. *Thumri* was once a *tal* that was very much in vogue. It is a *tal* of eight accents in all, and is divided into two or four parts. One opinion is that *Sam* falls on the first accent and *Phank* is on the fifth accent. In the second opinion, there is no *Phank* in this *tal.* The beat falls on the fifth accent. In the third opinion, this *tal* is divided into four parts in two accents. There are three beats and one gap including *Sam.* The fourth opinion is that it is a tetra-accented *tal.* There is *Sam* in the first accent, and the gap lies in the third accent. One of the fundamental characteristics of this *tal* is the stress of rapid rhythm of *Sam-matra.*

The family of Gurudev Rabindranath was not aloof from the influence of *Thumri.* The words of the *Thumri* songs composed by them were arranged keeping an eye to the *Thumri-tal* and its rhyme of yore. The seniors of Gurudev liked the *Thumri-tal* of eight accents in divisions of twos. In this rhythm, there are three beats including the *Sam* and one gap.

Dwijendranath Tagore, Gurudev's elder brother, composed the song 'Kara tara nama gaan' almost at the time of Gurudev's birth in *Jhinjhit ragini* and in *Thumri tal.* By dividing the *tal* of eight accents into four parts of two accents each, its notation was made in the following way :

	1	2	0	3	1	2	0	3
ra ra II	ga ga I	aa pa I	pa dha I	pa dha I	ma aa I	aa aa I	aaaa I	sa sa I
ka ra	ta o	o ra	na o	o ma	ga o	o o	o n	ka ra

At a certain time closely related to this period, Satyendranath Tagore, Gurudev's 'Mejodada' composed a few Brahmasangeet in *Thumri tal.* One of these songs has divisions of *tal* and accent similar to the previous one e.g.

	1	2	0	3	1	2
sa II	ri pa I	ma ma I	ma ma I	ma pa ma I	Jnah rah I	Jha ma I
da	ya o	gha na	to ma	he o na	ke o	hi ba

0	3
Jnama Jnari I	sa sa I
Ka o o o	ri 'da'

Jyotirindranatha Tagore, Gurudev's another elder brother was an expert in classical music. In one of his writings in 1298 B.E. (1891), he says "As grave accents—*gurumatra*-appear at regular intervals at every foot of *Thumri*, more sound than that of *Kaoali* takes place."

In "Svaralipi Gitimala", a book written by Jyotirindranath Tagore, it is stated : "The *tal* varies in accordance with the varience of light and grave words of the song or with the varience of its stress. Some of these *tal-s* are tetra-accented e.g. *Kaoali, Thumri, Adatheka* etc."

"*Thumri, Adatheka* etc. are produced with the differences of the rhyme and the pause of *Kaoali.* The difference between *Thumri* and *Kaoali* is that, as grave accents appear with every division of beats of *Thumri* at regular intervals there is greater stress in *Thumri* than *Kaoali.*"

He has also informed us that *Thumri* is a *Tal* of *Drut-Lay.*

The *Theka* of the *Thumri Tal* as given in the "Svaralipi Gitimala" is as follows :

	1					2			
I	dha	dha	kete	tak	I	ne	dha	kete	tak

It seems that he has accepted this *Theka* from the book written by Krishnadhan Bandyopadhyay. But the notation for the song composed by himself of *Thumri Tal* as given in "Svaralipi Gitimala" by Jyotirindranath has no similarity with the given *Theka* so far as the division of accents of its *Tal* is concerned. He has followed his elders in the notation of this song. The song is :

Lum-Jhinjhit-Thumri

II	nadha	dha	I	sara	sara	I	gaga	rasa	I	saga	rasa	I
	ki o	ka		ri o	swa o		jani	o o		se o	bine	

Gurudev's song 'e ki akulata bhubane' is in "Svaralipi Gitimala." Jyotirindranath has earmarked this song as one of *Thumri Tal.* But in spite of being a *tal* of four accents, the words have been arranged like *Trital* of 16 accents. There are altogether three beats and one gap. We do not know why he has called it a song of *Thumri Tal.* In the notation, the song is as follows :

						2					3					0				
I	aa	aa	dha	dha	I	dha	nadha	pa	ma	I	mapa	aa	jna	aa	I	ma	jna	ma	jna	I
			e	ki		aa	co	ku	la		ta	o	o	o		o	o	o	o	
	1					2					3					0				
I	jnana	aa	dha	aa	I	aa	aa	na	na	I	nasa	aa	aa	aa	I	aa	aa	sa	sa	I
	o	o	o	o		o	o	bhu	ba		ne	o	o	o		o	o	e	ki	

At the age of 22, the total number of songs composed by Gurudev stood nearly two hundred. Of these, there was not a single song of *Thumri ragini,* but there are a few songs of *Thumri Tal.* A specimen of the same is quoted below. The song is 'Varisha dhara majhe santira bari' included in the religious songs. This song is composed in imitation of the tune and beats of the song 'Dayaghana toma hena ke hitakari' composed by his 'mejodada', Satyendranath Tagore. For example :

Sa	II	re	pa	I	ma	ma	I	ma	ma	I	mapa	ma	I	jna	ra	I	jna	ma	I
ba		ri	o		sa	dha		ra	o		ma	jhe		sa	n		ti	ra	
jnadha		jnari		I	(sa	sa)	I												
ba		o		o	ri,	'ba'													

In Kangalicharan Sen's " Brahmasangit Swaralipi" in six volumes (1311-1318 B.E./1904-1911) under the supervision of Jyotirindranath, we are acquainted with a few more notations of *Thumri Tal* composed by Gurudev. They are similar to the song 'Varisha dhara majhe'. The following notations are given from that book :

Bhairabi Thumri

1 2 0 3 1 2 0 3
I To ma I ra pa I ta o I ka o I ja re I da o I ta o I re o I

Jhinjhit Thumri

1 2 0 3 1 2 0 3
I sa n I ta ha I ye o I ma ma I chi o I tta oni I ra o I ku l I

Lum-khambaz-Thumri

1 2 0 3 1 2 0 3
Aa zi I ja ta o I ra o I ta ba I aa o I ka o I she o I sha be I

Kalangda-Thumri

1 2 0 3 1 2 0 3
I I o I chha o I be o I ja be I la ai I yo o I pa o I re o I

Sri Surendranath Bandhyopadhyay, one of the singers of the *Adi Brahma Samaj,* published from 1910-1918 a book of notations in six volumes of the religious songs composed by Gurudev and titled as "Gitalipi". We get altogether eight songs there composed in *Thumri Tal.* Of course, Surendrababu has showed division of accents of *Tal* in these songs in accordance with the opinions in vogue in his family, which refer to *Sam* and gap in the first and the fifth accents respectively. He did not make notations in divisions of two accents like Kangalicharan Sen. A specimen of the notation of Surendrababu is as follows :

Khambaz - Thumri

1 0 1
II gama padha nahsa na I dha aa dha ma I ma dha padhana na I
ru o o o op sa ga o re du o o o b di
o
nanaa dhadhaa paga I
ye o o o chhi o

Pandit Bhimrao Shastri, a Maharastrian, former professor of music at Visva-Bharati, singer of classical Hindi music published in 1920 a book of notations named "*Sangit Gitanjali*" written in Devnagri scripts and in notations introduced by Bhatkhande of Gurudev's "*Gitanjali*" and a few other songs. There are five songs of *Thumri Tal* of "Gitalipi" in this book. But Bhimrao Shastri did not mention the songs as ones of *Thumri Tal.* Instead, he called them "Dhumali" *Tal.* He has introduced it in the following way :

"Dhumali matra 8 I Bhag 2 matra men"
(*Dhumali :* No. of accents : 8, in divisions of two)

1	2	–	3	4		5	6		7	8
dhi	dhi	I	na	dhi(n)	I	nak	dhi (n)	I	nagi	trik

Dhumali is a *tal* used in the theatres, light dramas and in the Marathi *Kirtan* songs of Maharastra. But Bhimrao Shastri did not accept this *theka* at the time of making notations of Gurudev's songs. He showed *Sam* and *Phank* (Gap) in the first and the fifth accents respectively by dividing eight accents into two equal parts. For example :

***Raga :* Khambaz II *Tal :Dhamali* II *Madhyalay* II B Accents**

1					0					1				
II Gama	padha	nasa	naa	I	dha	aa	dha	ma	I	ma	dha	padhma	naa	I
ruo	o	o o	p	·	sa	ga	du	o		o	o	b	di	
nanak	dhadhaa	pa	ga	I										
ye o	o o o	chi	o											

Although Bhimrao Shastri has shown the division of accents and *Theka* of *Dhumali Tal* separately, in spite of the fact that there is a reference to the *Dhumali Tal* on the song, it is clearly understood that, in case of notation, he has totally initated Surendranath. From this it appears that in those days the followers of Bhatkhande were not perhaps desirous of admitting *Thumri* as a *Tal.*

From a discussion on the *Thumri Tal* as above, the specimen of division of the accents of *Tal* may be arranged as follows :

		+		0							
1.	I	1	2	3	4	I	=	*Tal* of 8 accents in total			
		+				"					
2.	I	1	2	3	4	I	5	6	7	8	*Tal* of 8 accents in total

		+					0						
3.	I	1	2	3	4	I	5	6	7	8	*Tal* of 8 accents in total		
		+		2			0			3			
4.	I	1	2	3	4	I	5	6	I	7	8	I	*Tal* of 8 accents in total

That Gurudev himself knew *Thumri* as a *Tal* is categorically known from one of his letters. In his old age, he wrote this letter to Indira Devi on May, 9, 1931.

> "You have written on my songs. What is there to say about this on my part? A little remark may be made. The list of *Tal-s* with which I am composing my songs is as follows. You may try :
>
> > *Rupak, Rupkada, Jhaptal, Jhampak, Ektala, Kaoali, Thumri, Adatheka,* one or two *Choutal-s Ladra, Yat, Kashmiri, Khemta, Ekadasi, Navami.*"

Gurudev had forgotten to include in the list the following *Tal-s* which he used more than once in his songs : *Surphanktal, Adachoutal, Teodatal.* But there is no reference to some new *Tal-s* also that are used in Rabindrasangeet. However, he did not forget about the composition of his own song in the *Thumri Tal* that was almost abolished in its use by the singers of the year 1931. The reference to this *Tal* in this list is worth notice. From this it can easily be said that Gurudev had a close association with the *Thumri Tal* like the singers and composers of songs of the previous era. The drama *Chirakumar Sabha* (1893) gives direct evidence to this fact with the following song :

> *Kata kala rabe bala Bharata re*
> *Shudu dala bhata jaia pathya kare*

Gurudev composed the above song in total imitation of the national song in the *Khambaz Ragini* and *Thumri Tal* composed by Govindachandra Roy in the period of the Hindu Mela.

It has been easier to ascertain correctly the use of the *Thumri Tal* in Gurudev's song with the help of his books on music published upto the second decade of the twentieth century and with the notations of his songs. In these books, references to *raga* and *tal* were always there. But as there are no references to these in the notations of songs of the next era, it has become difficult to ascertain which one is a song of *Thumri Tal.* Moreover, as the name of this *Tal* is totally omitted from the relevant songs in the new edition of the books in which we come across a list of songs where Gurudev applied this *Tal* and whose reference is available in the old books of notations, the avenues of knowing this fact by the modern singers have been closed. They have known the songs of *Thumri tal* as those of *Kaharba Tal.* They have an idea within their mind that Gurudev had not at all composed songs of *Thumri Tal.* However, *Thumri Tal* was there in the songs of Gurudev previously and if we assess correctly, we will find that there are many such songs composed by Gurudev towards the latter part of his life as are, in fact, ones of *Thumri Tal*, which are known as ones of *Kaharba Tal* in this era, notwithstanding.

I am giving a few examples of songs I consider to be ones of *Thumri Tal*, which were composed after 1319 B.E. (1912). From this, it will be clearly revealed that Gurudev had a continual attraction for this *tal.* The songs are :

1. 'Gaanguli mor saibaleri dal'.
2. 'Ora akarane chanchal'.
3. 'Kena pantha e chanchalata'.
4. 'Subha karmapathe dharo nirbhaya gaan'.
5. 'Eso nipabane chhayabithi tale'.
6. 'Faguner nabin anande'.
7. 'Ore chitrarekhadore bandhilo ke'.
8. 'Ore grihabasi khol dwar khol'.

In fact, these songs are ones to be sung by giving strokes, like the *Thumri Tal,* at an interval of two or four accents. Its *lay* (intonation) is also rapid. There are similarities of the old 'Totak' rhyme and of the song 'Jab chhod chale Luknow nagari' by Nawab Wazed Ali Shah with the stress of rhymes of some of the songs.

If we arrange these songs of Gurudev into two divisions of *Thumri tal,* I do not think that there will be any change in their mode of singing and appreciation. If the song 'Eso nipabane' is arranged in two types of *Thumri Tal,* it will be as follows :

				+					2					
1.	E	so	I	ni	o	pa	ba	I	ne	o	o	o	I	
				+			2			0			3	
2.	E	so	I	ni	o	I	pa	ba	I	ne	o	I	o	o

In division 1, *Sam* is on the first accent and the beat, on the fifth.

In division 2, there are signs of *Sam, tal, phank* and *tal* in first, third, fifth and seventh accents respectively.

Thumri has received an honourable position as a song in the assembly of the *Ostad-s* of Northern India like *Dhrupad, Kheyal* and *Tappa* in the twentieth century. This is why the non-Bengali singers have extensively discussed on *Thumri*. That they have written the history of this song is evident from a study of the writing of Prof. G.D. Karwal of the Allahabad University. He states :

> "This (Thumri) like *Tappa,* also appeared in the nineteenth century. The word comes from *Thumak*— graceful stamp of foot. This indicates its connection with dance. It originated as an accompanying song of dance which made dance movements more understandable and impressive.
>
> "*Thumri* is *Bhao Sangit - bolpradhan* - expressive of emotions contained in the song texts. It was nurtured in the courts of the Nawab of Avadh, particularly, in the regime of Nawab Wajid Ali Shah. He was a dancer and singer of high repute.... He himself composed a number of *thumri-s* .... The style found congenial centres in Banaras, Allahabad, Patna, in addition to Lucknow, its place of birth. It was developed to excellence by Bhaiya Ganapat Rao and Moizuddin Khan.
>
> "Like *Kheyal, Thumri* is of two types- *Badi Thumri* and *Chhoti Thumri* and has two parts, *Sthaee* and *Antara*, *Badi Thumri* is in line with *Bada Kheyal* and is sung in *Vilambat laya;* and *Chhoti Thumri* follows in the footsteps of *Chhota Kheyal* and is sung in *Drut laya.* Or we might say that *Thumri* sung in *jat* or *deepchandi* theka *is Badi Thumri* and that done in tri-*tal* is *Chhoti Thumri.*
>
> "The *tan-s* of both *Kheyal* and *Tappa* are also employed, though formerly they were not used.
>
> "It is purely romantic and is suited to the singing of songs of *Bhaktiras* and *Shringar ras* -devotional and erotic texts.
>
> "*Chhoti Thumri* is either sung with dance or in *Kheyal* style, emphasising song texts but not bothering about *bol banao* and using more *tanas.*
>
> "*Badi Thumri* is usually followed by *dadra* in actual performance. *Dadra* has generally a shorter poetic text than *Thumri* and is sung in *dadra tala* whence it derives its name.

> In its demonstration Hindi or Urdu couplets or quartrains are brought in for variety and extra charm. It has the same relationship with *Thumri* and *Dhamar* has with *Dhrupada,* both, in general essentials , being the same."

From the above discussion, the matter to be noticed is that the writer did not say anything about *Thumri Tal* and *Thumri Raga,* as if these two were of no use in the Indian music. No reason has yet been established why this opinion was favoured by the researchers of the Northern India.

At present, the form and the *Tal-s* in which we hear *Thumri* songs to be sung in Bengal was first introduced by Bhaiya Saheb of Gwalior. He was a poet, singer of classical *Dhrupad, Dhamar, Kheyal* and Veena player. He could also play on the harmonium proficiently. For some reasons, he left Gwalior and learnt-singing for sometime from Sadek Ali Khan, the famous artiste of *Thumri* songs at Lucknow. He lived at Patna towards the end of the nineteenth century. Then Shyamlal Chhetri, his devoted disciple, brought him to Calcutta. In Calcutta Bhaiya Saheb Ganapat Rao's disciples were Maizuddin Khan, the reputed *Thumri* singer, and many others. A few years before his death, Ganapat Rao left Calcutta and went to the court *(Durbar)* of the Nawab of Rampur. In fact, Bhaiya Saheb Ganapat Rao and Maizuddhin Khan are the first to guides how the *Thumri* songs are sung in Bengal in this era.

Girija Chakrabarti, the famous artiste of Visnupur and learned disciple of Radhika Goswami learned *Thumri* songs of new style from Bhaiya Saheb and Maizuddin and was regarded as the best singer of *Thumri* songs in Bengal. The authoritative news that Dhurjatiprasad Mukhopadhyay published in 1335 B.E. (1928) on this matter was the following :

> "That was more than thirty-five years (1912-13) ago....... At this time Ganapat Rao and Maizuddin Khan came.Their sitting was held at the residence of Shyamlal Kshetri on Harrison Road in the garden of Dunichand opposite to Overtoon Hall. The participants there were Raja-Babu (Burman), Tinubabu, Dunibabu, Girijababu, Amiya Sanyal etc.
>
> The modern 'Lochao' *Thumri* is produced from this centre. Its exposure of ideas, *tan-kartan* and temperament are

> different from the puravi of Lucknow and Banaras. Gaharjan Malkajan and Choudhurani sisters in Calcutta and Lucknow respectively accepted this method."

Gurudev was aged in years in the era of introducing this 'Lochao' *Thumri*. Then he left his residence in Calcutta and lived most of the time in Santiniketan. He also spent a great deal of time in touring aboard. So he never received the musical environment in life, which he did in Calcutta in his boyhood, adolescent age and in early youth. Notwithstanding the impossibility of learning the *Thumri* variety of songs introduced by Ganapat Rao and Maizuddin, it is not known if he had leisure to listen to these. This is why no impression of 'Lochao' *Thumri* was left in his song. Aftr 1920, he only composed a few songs based on the *Thumri* of Lucknow like 'Sakhi aandhare ekela ghare', 'Jaoa asari eki khela' and 'Khelar sathi, vidaydwar khol'. Gurudev heard the original song from Pandit Bhimrao Shastri and Srimati Sahana Devi and set Bengali words as he desired. He made both of them sing the Bengali songs for the first time in the functions of Santiniketan and in the festival of music in Calcutta. Needless to say, as he had liked the original song, he was interested in upholding them in the Bengali language. But he himself never sang these songs, for he had no time at that age to sing after learing the original tune appropriately. He was pleased at hearing from others. Though the songs were of the patterns of *Thumri* of Lucknow or western India, these were not sung in the *tal* of this era. These were sung as songs of broken rhymes.

What is meant by the influence of *Thumri* songs in those of Gurudev was that of the songs composed in the rhyme of *Thumri tal* in Bengal in the last century. He composed many songs in the verse rhyme of this *tal.* The slow *laya* of 'Lochao' *Thumri* or Punjabi *Thumri* of the twentieth century did not yet get the opportunity to influences Gurudev.

17 AN UNKNOWN ERA OF COMPOSITION OF MUSIC IN THE LIFE OF RABINDRANATH

A few years after the demise of the revered Gurudev Rabindranath, the Visva-Bharati Publication Department received a 'Pocket Book' embossed with "1889" "R.N. Tagore" in English from Sri Samirchandra Majumder. The real owner of this little exercise-book was Srishchandra Majumder, one of the friends of Gurudev, with whose co-operation Gurudev published a book entitled "Padaratnavali" in 1922 by selecting 110 *Pad-s* from the *padavali-s* of ancient Vaisnav poets. Sri Samir Majumdar is his descendant. The exercise-book was returned to Sri Samir Majumdar after taking photographs of its every page by the Visva-Bharati Publication Department. There are about 93 songs, Hindi-broken Bengali songs and also original Hindi songs of broken ones written in Gurudev's own hand-writing in this excrise-book consisting of many pages. Moreover, there are some pencil sketches, collection of current colloquial words in the Bengali language, some newly composed nursery rhymes suitable for children, travelogue, accounts of purchase and lists of the employees in the Zamindari in different areas and their salaries are also to be found in this exerise-book. It is a store-house of diverse informations of Gurudev's nearly 14 years of life in work, poetry and music. Although the year '1889' is drawn on the cover, he started writing in this exercise-book from the Bengali year 1298 (1891). In most of its songs and poems, there are references to date and venue of composition. The authorities of the Visva-Bharati Publication Department got the opportunity of correcting references to dates of compositions of Gurudev's many songs and poetry with the help of this exercise-book. In his book "*Rabindrapratibha*" in 1960 Sri Kanai Samanta published an account of this Pocket Book for the first time by going through the copies of the photograph taken by the Visva-Bharati Publication Department.

Sri Samir Majumdar again handed over the little exercise-book entitled 'Pocket Book' to the Board of Editors of the journal, *Desh.* This time also the photograph of every page of the exercise-book was taken on behalf of the journal. By looking into those photographs, Sri Amitabha Choudhury, the well-known journalist of the *Ananda Bazar Patrika* discussed on the exercise-book from various points of view in the *Saradiya Sankhya* (Autumn issue) of the journal, *Desh* in 1377 B.E. (1970), and many readers were interested in it. Being requested by the editor of the journal to discuss on the songs of the exercise-book, I enthusiastically agreed to undertake the assignment as I knew that I would find out many unknown informations by launching upon this job.

Gurudev began writing in the exercise-book from the spot where the year and the name are written on the cover in and around 1298 B.E. (1891). It is also being seen that he has also written in the last page of the exercise-book almost at the same time. This means that he started writing from both ends of the exercise-book. The writings have gradually come face to face in the middle and have stopped. The total number of pages of the exercise-book is 269. The writings of the left side have been completed at page 110, while those of page 269 in the end have stopped at page 111 in the opposite way. He started the writings of the left side with a song, while in the beginning of the right side, there is an incomplete poem of two lines, and that, again is scratched. The condition of the first song of the left side is also nearly the same. We do not know why he scratched the whole of the song after writing the complete song. The song is : 'Sudhu jaoa asha, sudhu srote bhasa (It's only to come and go, to float on the current).

The year, date and venue of most of the self-composed songs written in the exercise-book are available. But there are no such references in case of Hindi-based Bengali songs. Every information related to the time of composition of dateless songs, the source of composition and the names of the learned artistes from whom he collected the original Hindi of Bengali broken songs, is being available through continuity of pages and some contemporary facts. The songs of the first cluster (1298-1301 BE/1891-1894) after making a list through their chronological arrangements are the following :

1. 'Sudhu jaoa aasa'
   (It's only to come and go).
2. 'Khanchar pakhi chhilo sonar khanchatite'.
   (The bird of the cage was in the golden one')
   -19 *Asad*, 1299 / July 4, 1892, Sajadpur.

3. "Amar mon manena dinarajani".
   ('Day or night my mind does not like')
4. 'Tumi natun ki tumi chirantan'.
   ('Are you new or overlasting.')
5. 'Jhara jhara varasha'.
   ('Drizzling is the rain')
6. 'Phire eso phire eso'.
   ('Return, O, return')

I have already referred that he scratched the first song of the list after writing it. The song was as follows :

Sudhu jaoa assa
Sudhu srote bhasa
Sudhu alo andhare
        Kshanik kanda hasa—
Sudhu dekha paoa sudhu chhunye jaoa
Sudhu dure jete jete kende chaoa
Sudhu nava durashay aage chale jaay
        Pichhe phele jaay michhe aasa
Hridaye hridaye aadha parichay
Aadhkhani katha shesh nahi hay—
Laje bhaye trase aadha visvase
        Sudhu aadhkhani bhalobasa
Ashesh basana laye bhanga bal,
Pranpan kaje paay bhanga phal,
Bhanga tari dhare bhase parabare
        Bhav kende mare bhanga bhasa.

[It's only to come and go
It's only to float in the current
It's only to cry and smile
        In light and darkness for a while.
It's only to meet and only to touch
It's only to go on and look aweeping.
It's only to go ahead with new hopes in vain,
        Leaving behind false aspiration.
It's half an encounter with each other's heart
Half a conversation without an end
In bashfulness fear, terror and half belief

It's only half the love.
With endless desire and broken strength
In work tireless is to receive broken results
To float on the sea with a broken boat
To live aweeping with ideas in the broken language.]

There was no date with the song. There is difference with the first draft in which at present, we are accustomed to sing the first four lines of the song. We do not come across any punctuation mark in the song.

The song was first printed in the journal "Sadhana" with notations, in the *Baisakh* (April) issue of the Bengali year 1299 (1892). It was called a "new song" in the pages of the printed song. The song, as it was printed in the journal "*Sadhana*" after slight modifications, is the following :

(Ragini : Misra Vehag — Talpherta)

Sudhu jaaoa aasa;
Sudhu srote bhasa;
Sudhu alo andhare
    Kanda hasa;
Sudhu dekha paaoa, sudhu chhunye jaaoa,
Sudhu dure jete jete kende chaaoa;
Sudhu nava durashay aage chale jaay
Pichhe phele jaay michhe aasha,

Ashesh basana laye bhanga bal,
Pranpan kaje paay bhanga phal;
Bhangatari dhare bhase parabare,
Bhab kende mare, bhanga bhasa!

Hridaye hridaye aadho parichay,
Aadhkhani katha sanga nahi hay,
Laje bhaye trase aadho visvase
Sudhu aadhkhani bhalobasa.

(Ragini : Misra Vehag—Talpherta)

It's only to come and go

It's only to float in the current
It's only to cry and smile
In light and darkness.

It's only to meet and only to touch,
It's only to go on and look aweeping;
It's only to go ahead with new hopes in vain,
Leave behind false aspirations.

With endless desire and broken strength,
In work tireless is to receive broken results.
To float on the sea with a broken boat,
To live a-weeping with ideas in broken language!

It's half an encourter with each other's heart
Half a conversation without completion
In bashfulness, fear, terror and half belief
It's only half the love.

By applying the word "Talpherta" on the top of the song, it is informed that it is composed in more than one *Tal.* In the first *kali* of the song, *aasthayee* is to be sung in three accents, in the rhyme of *Ektala.* The *tal* of the rest three *kali-s* is *Trital* in four accents. The fourth *kali* of the "Pocket Book" is turned into the third *kali.*

As the song was published in the journal "*Sadhana*" (*Baisakh*, 1299/April 1892) as a "New song", it might be assumed that the song was composed towards the end of 1298 B.E. In the book '*Ganer Bahi*' ('A Book of Songs') of 1300 B.E.(1893), by changing the *ragini* and *tal* of the song, it was named as "*Vehag-Ektala*", and the word 'pranpan' in the third *kali* was printed as 'pranpane.' When the second notation of the song was printed in the journal "*Vinavadini*" in 1304 (1897), then, by following the journal "*Sadhana*", it was written that the *ragini* is "*Misra Vehag O Talpherta*". In the book of poems of 1310 (1903) and in the volume of songs of "*Granthavali*" in 1909 its *ragini* is mentioned as "*Vehag-Ektala.*" When the third notation of this song was published in "*Sangit-prakashika*", *Bhadra*, 1316, (September 1909), its *ragini* was named as "*Misra Vehag*" and, in place of "*Talpherta*" or "*Ektala*", all the *kalis* of the song have been turned into tetra-accented *Kaoali Tal.* In this era, we sing the song accordingly. Now it is not sung in *Talpherta* or *Ektala.*

The song "Aamar man manena dinarajani" ("Day or night, my mind does not like") is without any reference to its date of composition. But through assessment of continuity of pages and other allied informations, the date of composition may probably be found out.

We know that Gurudev went to Orissa twice in 1891 and 1893 to look after their Zamindari. We correctly get the news of his tour during these two periods from the letters numbering 27-30 and from those numbering 77-88 respectively. In pages 18-30 in the "Pocket Book" under discussion, there are various descriptions of his tour to Orissa also. But no date is mentioned in connection with this tour. Gurudev had to go to Orissa once again towards the end of February, 1893. The account of expenses for journey to Orissa are written in the "Pocket Book". Gurudev himself wrote that. There is also the description of his iternerary, covering a few pages. No information with regard to his journey to Orissa this time is given anywhere. But he went to Orissa towards the middle of December, 1892. At that time, Mrinalini Devi was at Sholapur in Maharashtra with sons and daughters, under the care of Satyendranath Tagore, the 'Mejadada' of Gurudev. Towards the end of July, on receipt of the news of Mrinalini Devi's return to Calcutta, Gurudev wrote to her :

> "If you have, in the meantime, left (Sholapur), I would meet you in Calcutta. I would try if I would escort you to Orissa. That place is very healthy. I have already informed *Babamashay* (father) of my desire to a-little extent. He, too, has somewhat realised that. If I say once or twice, some results might yield, but it is nothing to hope much beforehand."

From this letter it is known that he was ready for going to Orissa. But, finally, Mrinalini Devi did not go with Gurudev. There might be some other reasons besides the permission of Maharshi Devendranath Tagore.

Gurudev has completed the poem "Jete nahi diba" at page 16 of the "Pocket Book" on *Kartick* 14, 1899 (31 October, 1892) in Calcutta. From page 18 onwards, there are different descriptions of his journey to Orissa and accounts of expenses. I am quoting how he wrote page after page from page 12.

Page18

	Cuttack	*Rupees*	—	*Anaas*
Balu's shoes	—	6	—	4
Bukshish (Tips)	—	2	—	0
My shoes	—	5	—	12
Payment to *Barkandaz* to purchase tapes etc. for registration	—	1	—	0
Desk	—	18	—	0
Repair of *Chowki*	—	1	—	0
Chati Shoes	—	1	—	8
Lock	—	1	—	8
Dhoti for bathing at Puri : 1 pair	—	2	—	0
Payment to Gafur during return from Puri	—	2	—	0
Paniwallah	—	1	—	0
Sardaipur Registration	&c	1	—	0
Bhubaneswar—*Panda*	&c	7	—	0
Mistri at Cuttack	—	5	—	0
Carriage puller Coolie at Khandagiri	—	1	—	6
Stamps	—	1	—	0
Balu (ornaments)	—	10	—	0
Palanquin	—	22	—	0
Train fare	—	1	—	4
Bakshish for two servants	—	4	—	0
Gofur	—	2	—	0

Page 19.
Sub-divisional Tax of Taluk Pandua
Tax due on 28 April.

Kathjuri : Transparent current on the edge of grey sand. Highway, low fields on two sides. Budding mangoes. Banyan, *Aswattha,* Date, cocoanut, *Valuhanta,* Bhargavi, Sardaipur. On the way, at a distance, Bhubaneswar, Dhauli inscription. Hills—broken temple atop. Fencing of *Keya, Meghdut,* the river Nag. Walking in the evening—long, clear, shadowy avenue—one or two covered carts. Paucity of passengers. Journey to Mukundapur at night—sleepy. Journey to Satyavadi in the morning. Gradual increase of passengers, carriages in rows. Satyavadi. Balu and others went. *Bhog* as a gift. Journey again. Gradual increase of number of passengers under trees beside the way. *Chati.* Big ponds.

Temple. Swamps. Scarcity of wayside trees. In the south, something like big watery areas, now and then paddy seedlings. In the west, Jagannath in the midst of a cluster of trees, sandy coast. Two or four separate houses. The blue sea. Travelling in the seacoast in the twilight.

Page 20

Bathing in the morning
Sub-divisional tax of Taluk Balia
Tax due on 28 April.

Khandagiri, Ranigumpha—picture—Pali writings—Tendency of people to inscribe ideas-scenery from above—forest. Human drawn carriage. Forest of *Kuchal* with rare leaves by the two sides of the road. The pattern of Hazaribag. Hilly roads, like serpents.

When ascended—scenery of the mountains. Causal paddy fields now and then. Big road. Stony, high and low hilly land on two sides. In front, dense cloud and blue range of mountains. Beginning of sight rain. Bunglow nearby. Broken path in the middle due to flood.

Balu	Rs. 7/- Broach	*Bakshish*	Rs. 8/-
Gafur	Rs. 2/-	Balu	Rs. 6/- shoes.
Palanquin	Rs. 18/-	Collector	Rs. 4/-
Little ship	Rs. 3/-	Boat	Re. 1/-

(Scratched with a pencil)

Page 21

He sindhu dharitri taba garbher santan
Anindya sundari, kata dirgha jug dhare
Aandhare jathare.

[O sea, the earth is the son of thy womb—
so marvellously beautiful. How for a long era
In the belly of darkness]
(only three lines, but scratched.)

Certainly I committed a great sin in my previous life. Otherwise, why was I born as a writer? When I have brought the ideas of my mind outside, I have no way out but to hear the just or unjust words of the outsiders. O the pleasant moon, if you remained lying at ease on the very juicy sea, then it might create a bit of obstructions for the poets to expose their poetic sensibilities, but the jackel at night could not go by suddenly conveying disgrace aloud by raising its mouth towards you.

When the idea of my mind was within me, then it was, as it were, my god of home, god of my desire. Now I did not know why I placed him under the banyan trees all around the way. Do all creatures realise its honour? If they do not understand, does it not remain like a statue before the eyes of the world?

Next, to the relatives and the friends, again.

Page 22

I will have to reply. Why did you write it? How did you say that? What is the meaning of that? It is also another difficult assignment. It is as if my duty to help people cross the road by my carriage I am making spade-work to cut the way.

However, with whom shall I fall out? At the time of birth, the Lord of Providence has written thus on the forehead. But in spite of any torture arising out of the mystery of birth from that senior writing of providence inflicted upon the writer, the latter remains seated by cleverly fleeing away. Again, if we write one or two words by being yielded to Him, there is no end of protest.

Page 23

Accounts of zamindari profit of the Bengali year 1295 (1888).

Page 24

Aamar mon manena! (Dina-rajani)
['My mind does not accept. (Day or night)]

Page 25

A women, seated on the altar. sketch

		Rupees	*Anaas*
Bakshish for rescuing persons		5	0
Broken Boat	_	2	0
Nitu	-	2	0
Balu	-	2	0
Duster	-	1	2
Napkin	-	1	3
		13	3

(This portion is scratched)

Pages 26, 27 and 28

The names of principal employees and their salaries of the Pargana Hayer.

Page 29

Taluk Pandua
The names of empoyees and their salaries.

Page 30

The names of employees of Taluk Balia and their salaries. A list of many words of vowels and consonants.

Page 32

The names and salaries of *Amlas* of the Trustee Department of the sub-divisions.

Pages 33-41

Gurudev composed the poem "*Pratiksha*" on three days of 16th, 20th and 27th *Agrahayan* at Rampur Boalia, Natore and Shelaidah of Rajshahi respectively. At this time, that he became seriously ill due to toothache while living at Natore is known from the letter 75 of the song "Amar mon manena" including other poems and writings from the pages of the exercise-book; it can easily be taken for consideration that the song written at page 24 was composed at a period in between 15 *Kartik* and 15 *Agrahayan*. But it has its opposite arguments.

When "*Ganer Bahi-O Valmiki Pratibha*" was published in 1299 B.E. (1892), it was stated in its preface that all the songs composed by Gurudev prior to the month of *Chaitra* (April) were included in this book. But as this song composed before *Chaitra* was not included in this book, it might naturally be assumed that the song was composed after 1299 B.E. (1892). At the time of binding this book of his own will, Gurudev separately attached to it many white sheets of paper in the end. In these pages we find many new songs of the later period, which are written by Gurudev in his own hand-writing. The song

"Amar mon manena" is also with these. But if he composed the song before the poem "*Pratiksha*" of 16 *Agrahayan* after the poem "Jete nahi diba" composed in the "Pocket Book" on 14 *Kartik,* it is natural to assume that this was not included in the *Ganer Vahi* ("The Book of Songs") by mistake. Alternately, if the journey to Orissa as described in the "Pocket Book" occurred in 1893, the song under discussion was no doubt, composed at a period after the publication of "*Ganer Vahi*".

The three songs numbering 4, 5 and 6 of the list are only referred to by the first line at page 41 in the exercise-book as follows :

Tumi nutan ki tumi chirantan;
Jhara jhara varashe.
Phire eso phire eso.

I am quoting the first song in its complete from books on poetry of 1303 B.E. (1896)

Misrabaroa
(Ohe nabin atithi,)

Tumi, nutan ki tumi chirantan?
Juge juge kotha tumi chhile sangopan:
Jatane kata ki ani bendhechhinu grihakhani
Hetha ke tomare balo karechhila nimantran
Kata asha bhalobasa gabhira hridayatale
Dheke rekhechhinu buke, kata hasi-asrujale
Ekti na kahi vani tumi ele maharani,
Kemane gopane mane karile he padarpan?

[Are you new or for ever
From age to age, hidden where you are?
With care I built this house with things in legion,
Tell me, who welcomed you here with invitation
With so much hope and love in the depth of the heart.
Did I cover in the chest, with laughter and tears,
Maharani, you came saying not a single word,
How did you step on in the mind with secret hard?]

About the song, Gurudev remarks, "I wrote a song on the occasion of *Annaprasan* (Rice taking cermony) of a girl—

"Ogo nabin atithi
Tumi nutan ki tumi
Chirantan!"

["O new guest
Are you new or
for ever?]

On April, 1931, the function related to the *namakaran (*Naming*)* and *annaprasan* (Rice taking ceremony) of Srimati Kanina, the eldest daughter of Sri Kalipada Roy, son of Professor Nepal Chandra Roy, and his wife Srimati Kamala Roy in their residence at Gurupalli, Santiniketan, Gurudev gave this song tuning anew at the special interest of Nepal Babu and others of his family and taught Amita Sen (Khuku) to sing this song in the function.

Amita sang this song in the function of that day.

The second song was :

Misramallar

Jharajhara varishe varidhara
Hay pathavasi ! Hay gatihin! Hay grihahara!
Phire vayu hahasvare, dake kare janahin asim prantare!
Rajani aandhara!
Adhira Yamuna taranga aakula akula re, timiradukula re!
Nivida nirada gagane garagara garaje saghane
Chanchalachapala chamake, nahi sashitara.

Misramallar

[Dripdrop fall the drops of rain
O wayfarer! O Motionless ! O Homeless!
The wind waits in movemet. Whom does it
Call in the bare endless field?
The night is dark
The restless *Yamuna* is wave-aspirant, shoreless,
dark with two banks,
The dense cloud roars in the sky aloud,
The lighting sparks, the moon or the
Stars are not there.]

In the letter on 29 September, 1895, Gurudev writes on the song :

> " Today that atmosphere of storm is weakend and in the morning there is mild sunlight...... The cloud is stretched throughout the sky, the wind from the east is blowing at a very great speed........... From this place, the roaring of the *Padma* at a distance is being heard. The two days yesterday and the day before yesterday— the sight was exactly like my new song :
>
> Jhara jhara varashe varidhara—
> Phire vayu hahasvare
> Janahin asim prantare—
> Adhira Padma taranga-akul—
> Nivira nirad gagane etc.
>
> [Drip drop fall the drops of rain
> The wind waits in movement
> In the bare endless field
> The restless *Padma* is wave-aspirant—
> In the sky of dense clouds etc.]

I was singing that song yesterday and the day before almost now and again."

I think that the song was composed on a rainy day in 1301 B.E. (1894) in an atmosphere as stated above.

The song 'Phire eso, phire eso" ("Return, return") is associated with the story "*Megh O Raudra*" ("The Cloud and the Sunlight") of the journal *Sadhana, Aswin-Kartik* (October-November), 1301 B.E. (1894). The writing of the story started from the middle of *Asaad* (July). But he composed the song after two months. On 29 August 1894 (14 *Bhadra,* 1301), in a letter from Calcutta, Gurudev writes about the song :

> "Today, sitting in my room in the morning, I was tuning in my new song. That the tune was very new was not true, it was somewhat *Bhairavi* of the *Kirtan* type. But singing in rhythm invites a sense of enchantment of music in the blood of the body."

The first four lines of the song included in the last chapter X of "*Megh O Raudra*" have been sung by a group of Vaishnav mendicants, while the rest of the lines of the song were sung by Sashibhusan, the hero of the story. That it is a song of the tune of *Kirtan* has also been categorically stated in this chapter. The song is written in the story in the following way :

> "A group of Vaishnav mendicants was singing with *goopi* instrument and *Khoi-karatal.*
>
> Eso eso phire eso, nath he phire eso!
> Amaar kshudhita trishita tapita chitta, badhu he, phire eso!
> Ogo nisthur, phire eso, amaar karunakomala eso!
> Ogo sajalajaladasnigdhakanta sundara phire eso!
>
> [Return, O return, my belove, return,
> Hungry, thirsty and heated is my mind,
> Return, O darling,
> O cruel, return, my pitiful and tender, come,
> O beautiful with appearance like the freshness of waterful clouds, return.]

The words of the song gradually become more feeble and weaker. They were not understood any more. But with the rhythm of the song a movement was surged in the heart of Sashibhusan. He began to muse within himself and went on, adding one line after the other by composing them, as if he could not, by any means, stop—

> Amar nitisukha phire eso, amar chiradukha phire eso—
> Amar saba-sukhadukhamanthandhana antare phire eso!
> Amar chirabanchhita eso, amar chirasanchita eso,
> Ohe chanchala, the chirantana, bhujabandhane phire eso!
> Amar bakshe phiria eso, amar chakshe phiria eso,
> Amar shayane swapane basane bhusane nikhila bhubane eso.
> Amar mukher hasite eso he
> Amar chokher salile eso,
> Amar adare amar chhalane
> Amar abhimane phire eso.
> Amar sarvasmarane eso, amar sarvabharame eso
> Amar dharama-karama-sohaga-sarama-janama-marane eso!

[Come back, my constant happiness, come back, my sorrow for ever
Come back, my treasure churned from sorrow and happiness, in my heart!
Come back my ever desired, come O closetted in my mind
Come back in my heart, come back in my eyes
Come in my sleep, dream, sitting, dress, in my universe
O Restless, O for ever, come back in clasp of hands
Come in the laughter of my mouth
Come in the tears of my eyes,
In my endearments, in trickeries of mine.
Come back in my resentment
Come in all my memories, come in all my forgettings
In my religion, work, endearments, shame, life and death, come.]

In the books of poems of 1303 (1896), the song is referred to as "*Kirtan*". This is fully a song in the pattern of *Kirtan.* The first four lines of the poem are the original song. Later, what Sashibhusan has sung by composing and adding line after line might be termed as '*aakhar*' of the original lines. To sing by adding *aakhar* is a famous coustom of *Padavali Kirtan.* In the previous era, there were many *Kirtaniya-s* (*Kirtan* players) who at the assembly of *palakirtan* achieved immense fame in the characteristics and skillfulness of adding *aakhar* at the time of singing old *Padavali-s.* Many singers devoted much more time to *aakhar* than to the original song. The same has also occurred in case of this song of Gurudev. The part of the song of Sashibhusan has been added in the pattern of *aakhar.* By this, he has been able to express the main emotion of the song very beautifully. Prior to this, Gurudev did not thus apply *aakhar* in any one of the few *kirtans* that he had composed. He made that job for the first time in this song. Moreover, it is also seen that by continually adding *aakhar* to *kirtan* songs for a pretty few years afterwards, he has sung either himself or has made others to sing. I shall make a detailed discussion on this in the appropriate place.

We are getting 25 songs written in between the period from the last week of *Bhadra* to the end of the month of *Kartik* and covering pages 42-60 at a stretch in 1302 (1895). From this number it is clearly revealed that he was deeply involved in the cadence of music during these two months of the Autumn. Evidence is also found in the letters written during this period. In a letter written from Shelaidah, on 26 September 1895, Gurudev writes :

> "I have maintained some sort of relationship with Saraswati in the discussion of music only".

On October 6, 1895, he wrote from Kusthia :

> "Now and again, I am preparing one or a half of a song and murmuring on the same, sitting on the *chowki* (divan) idly. I am picking up tunes and have been crouching myself amidst the autumn full of the reminiscence of happiness and tender in sorrow :"

The list of songs in accordance with the venue and time is as follows :

Song	Raga, date and venue
1. Utho re malin mukh (Rise, O Countenance ematiated)	— Multan 26 *Bhadra* 1302, Jorasanko (12 September, 1895)
2. Olo sai, olo sai (O friend, my friend)	— *Vibhas Khemta, 5 Aswin,* 1302 Shelaidah — Boat (22 September, 1895)
3. Madhur Madhur Dhwani baaje (The pleasing echo rings)	— *Bhupali Kaoali, 6 Aswin*, 1302 Shelaidah Boat, (23 September, 1895)
4. Bela gelo tomar path (The day ends, your path)	— *Purabi Ektala, 8 Aswin*, 1302 Shelaidah Boat, (25 September, 1895).
5. Visva-Vinarave visvajan (The world-people in the sound of the World-Veena)	— *Sankarabharan, Jhaptal,* 4 & 9 *Aswin* (21 & 26 September 1895).
6. Aha aaji mor (Aha today my)	— *Desh Pancham saoari*
7. Ke dila abar aghat (Who hurt again)	— *Kedara kaoali, Vijoya Dashami.* 12 *Aswin,* 1302 (29 September, 1895) Shelaidah.
8. Esogo nutan jivan (O new life, come)	13 *Aswin* 1302 (30 September 1895)
9. Puspavane puspa nahi (No flower in the forest of flowers)	— *Kalangda* 14 *Aswin* 1302 (1 October 1895)
10. (Aha) Jagi pohalo vibhavari [(Aha), the night dawns by awakening]	— *Ramkeli* 15 *Aswin* 1302 (2 October 1895).
11. Ohe anadi asim sunil (O, the endless beginningless blue)	— 16 *Aswin* (3 October)
12. Tomar gopan kathati (Your hidden words)	— 18 *Aswin* (5 October)

13. Chitta pipasita re (O the mind is thirsty) — 23 *Aswin* (10 October)
14. Ami chini go chini (Know I, I know) — 25 *Aswin* (12 October)
15. Amra lakshmichharar dal (We are a group of vagabonds) — 29 *Aswin* (11 October)
16. Ogo bhagyadevi pitamahi (O grand-mother, the goddess of fortune) — *Bhupal Khemta, 1 Kartik*
17. (Eki) Akulata bhubane (What a wistfulness in this world ! — 16 *Kartik* Jorasanko 1302
18. Tumi rabe nirabe (In silence you will remain) — 18 *Kartik* Jorasanko
19. Se ase dhire (Slowly she comes) — *Desh Ektala,* 21 *Kartik*
20. Ke uthe daki (Who calls out) — *Paraj,* 22, *Kartik* Jorasanko.
21. Ohe sundara mama grihe (O beautiful, in my room) — *Khmbaz Ektala,* 23, *Kartik*
22. Tumi jeona ekhani (Don't depart just now) — *Kaoali* 24 *Kartik*
23. Akula keshe ashe (She comes in ardent hair) — *Kaoali,* 25, *Kartik*
24. Hridaya chandra hridi gagane (The moon of the heart in the heart's sky) — 29 *Kartik*
25. Ki ragini bajale hridaye (What ragini you have played on in the heart) — *Sindhukanada,* 29 *Kartik*

These history of the composition of the song 'Olo sai' ('O friend') as referred to the above list is stated by Srimati Sahana Devi in her memoir as follows :

> "When the Poet lived with his family at Shelaidah, *Mashima* (Amala Das) also lived with his wife with whom *Mashima* had close intimacy. She called her (the Poet's wife) as *Kakima* (aunt). The picture of these two friends, sitting together and telling stories and making conversations, is portrayed in a song by Rabindranath. The song is : 'Olo sai, Olo sai' ('O friend, my friend')."

Written on 5 *Aswin* 1302 (22 September 1890), at Shelaidah on the boat, the song is :

(Vibhas, Khemta)

Olo sai, Olo sai!
Amar ichchha kare toder mata maner katha kai!
Chhadiye die pa dukhani
Kone base kanakani,
Kabhu hese kabhu kende
Cheye base rai.
Olo sai, Olo sai!
Toder achhe maner katha
Amar achhe kai!
Ami ki baliba, kon katha
Kon sukh, kon byatha-
Nai katha, tabu sadh
Sata katha kai.
Olo sai, Olo sai!
Toder eta ki balibar achhe
Bhebe abak hai
Ami, eka basi sandhya hale
Apni bhasi nayanjale
Karan keha sudhaile
Nirab haye rai.

[O friend, my friend!
I wish I would expose the words of the mind like you.
Stretching the two legs
Whispering by sitting in a corner
Laughing sometimes, and sometimes weeping
I remain seated a-looking.
O friend, my friend!
You have your words of the mind,
Where have I?
What shall I say, whose words,
Whose happiness, whose pain?
No words have I, yet I wish
I would speak endless words
O friend, my friend!
What a sea of words you have to tell,
I think and wonder!

> Sitting alone, when the evening comes,
> On tears I float
> When asked about the reason
> Silent I remain.]

Recently, it has been known that Mrinalini Devi went to Shelaidah on *Aswin*, 19, 1302 (6 October, 1895). So I think that whatever Srimati Sahana Devi said about the composition of the song was not possible.

Amala Devi, the *Masima* of Srimati Sahana Devi, was the sister of Deshbandhu Chittaranjan Das. Though a bit senior by age, Amala Devi called Mrinalini Devi as *Kakima* and how deep her love and respect for the latter was, is known from her letters to Indira Devi after the death of Mrinalini Devi. She writes :

> "I had no other friend like *Kakima* .. .. .. I have so many times and so many days gone and stayed with *Kakima*, after being angry with parents. The ring about which you have written is still remembered by me. Before the birth of Sami (Samindranath Tagore, Gurudev's youngest son, born 1303 B.E./1896), when we were with them at Shelaidah, I put on Kakima's finger my ring by taking it off from my finger, sitting beside the window of the boat one night. Many words of mine are entangled with that ring."
>
> "I could not ever understand well how I was related to *Kakima*. On the one hand, she was my friend never to be had any more; on the other, I had motherlike devotion to her."

Amala Devi had a very fine voice, and so she was very greatly affectionate to Gurudev. In this connection, I refer to Rathindranath. Urmila Devi has written :

> "Amala Devi went to Jorasanko very often, and sometimes stayed there for one or two months."
>
> "In those days, he (Gurudev) composed songs simultaneously with tune and words. He strolled on the big *verandah* (corridor), and as soon as the work of composing songs was finished, he cried out, Amala, O Amala, come soon and learn, I will forget just now".
>
> "The Poet's beloved greatly laughed-'Amala, have you ever seen a man who forgets the tuning given by himself'?

The Poet would immediately say, "*Chhoto Bou,* in case of an extraordinary person, everything takes place in an extra-ordinary way. You have failed to identify. Haven't you?"

In his book "*Pitrismriti*" (Reminiscence of Father) Rathindranath writes :

"During this period (1896/97 ?), Amala Devi, the sister of Chittaranjan Das, encouraged my father to compose new songs. She had great itimacy with my mother. My father had so much affection for Amala Didi that he brought her in our residence. Being introduced with musical flair, my father made arrangements for her to learn Hindi songs under Radhika Goswami. Within a few days, she was successful in learning many classical songs. The vioce of Amala Devi would easily rise and fall in climax and anticlimax respectively. Father began to compose songs suitable for her voice. I recall one or two songs composed to be sung by Amala Devi :

Chirasakha, chhedo-na more chhedo na ... .
(My friend eternal, don't leave, leave me not)
E paravase ke rabe hay.. ...
(Who will reside in this alien place ....)
Ke basile aji hridayasane Bhubaneswara probhu.... ....
(Who sits on the seat of my heart, O Lord of of the good of earth)

I think that father brought the tunings of these songs from Radhikababu. After the arrival of Amala Devi, she had to sing maximum songs in the evening soire."

Amala Devi passed away in 1919. She was then 46/47 years. At the time of the beginning of the First World War, she sang many songs in records of His Master's Voice in the name Miss Das (Ametêur), and has acclaimed a special position as the first amateur female-artiste of Rabindrasangeet. Prior to her, no female-artiste of aristocratic family is ever heard to sing Gurudev's songs in the record. It will not be irrelevant to refer to a list of Gurudev's songs sung in the records by Amala Devi.

Miss Das (Amateur)

1. Bada vismay lage- 8- 13846- *Kanadamisra*
2. Aha jagi pohalo- 8 - 13855 - *Ramkeli.*
3. Chirasakha he chhedo na - 8- 13856 - *Vehag-Kaoali.*
4. E ki akulata bhubane - 8 - 13859 - *Vahar.*
5. Ke basile aji - 8 - 13860 *Sindhu.*
6. E ki karuna karunamoy - 8 - 13861 - *Vahar.*
7. Tomar gopan kathati -8 - 13862 - *Kirtan.*
8. E bhara badar mahbhadar - 9- 13304 - *Mallar.*
9. Ayi bhubanamanomohini - 9- 13306 - *Toribhairavi.*
10. Tor apan jane chhadbe - 9- 13307 - *Baul.*
11. Maharaj, e ki saje -9 - 13308 - *Vehag.*
12. Rakho rakho re jivane - 9 - 13309 - *Shyam.*
13. Se ashe dhire - 9- 13310 - *Surat.*
14. Aro aghat saibe - 9 - 13312 - *Jhinjhit- Khambaz.*
15. Eai karechho bhalo nithur - 9- 13313 - *Imankalyan.*
16. He mor devata - 9 - 13752- *Imankalyan-Ektala.*
17. Timir duar kholo - 9- 13753 - *Ramkeli.*
18. Pratidin ami - 9 - 13759 - *Sindhukafi.*
19. Dhay jena mor - 9 - 13785 - *Misrajhinjhit.*
20. Tumi keman kare - B, 364 - *Misrakhambaz.*
21. Tumi rabe nirabe - B, 364 - *Goursarang.*

This time Amala Devi went to Shelaidah with the members of the family of Gurudev, which is known from his letters written on 16 October :

> "Though the night was deep, it was not totally silent as my two female neighbours were conversing with laughter on the boat beside me."

The "two female neighbours" as described in the letter were Mrinalini Devi and Amala Devi. That Rathindranath had said that to compose new songs it was Amala Devi who encouraged Gurudev, occurred at Shelaidah also. Here Amala Devi, by singing songs, making Gurudev hear her songs and expressing her desire to learn new songs, was able to make Gurudev compose so many songs.

Amala Devi was a spinster. Gurudev has painted a beautiful pen-picture of intimate friendship between Mrinalini Devi and her in the song "Olo sai, olo sai" ("O friend, my friend").

The initial format of the song "Visva-Vinarave" is found at pages 45, 46 and 47 of the exercise-book. He took up composing the song as *Aswin* 4, 1302, (21 September, 1895) and completed it on *Aswin* 9 (26 September). The venue of the composition was Shelaidah. This is a song broken away from a Marathi essay. Indira Devi knew the original song with its tuning and *tal.* Gurudev turned it into a descriptive song of the seasons of rains, autumn and spring, in the Bengali language, by synchronizing it with the rhyme of words of that Marathi song. The subject-matter of the original essay was different. In the 'Pocket-Book' of Gurudev, we find the song as follows :

Sankarabharan Jhanptal

Visvavinarave visvajan mohichhe,
Sthale jale navotale vane upavane
Nadi nade guha giri sagare paravare
Nitya jage saras sangit madhurima,
Nitya nrityarasabhangima;
Nava vasante nava ananda, utsav nava;
Ati manjula, ati manjula,
Suni manjula gunjana kunje,
Sunire, suni marmara pallava punje;
Pika kujana puspavane bijane;
Mriduvayu-hillola-bilola-bibhola-vishala-sarovara majhe,
Kalagit sulatita baje;
Shyamala kantara pare anila sanchare dhire re-
Kata dine kotabhasa
Dike dike kata vani
Jalatale chhalachhala,
Kathahin kata gatha
Jhara jhara rasadhara.

(4 *Aswin*/21 September)

Asadhe nava ananda, utsava nava,
Ati gambhira ati gambhira
Nil ambare dambaru baje,
Jena re, pralayankari sankari nache,
Kare garjan nirjharini saghane,
Hera kshubdha bhayala vishala nirala piyala tamala vitane
Uthe rav bhairava tane.

Pavana mallara gita gahichhe aandhara rate :
Unmadini soudamini rangabhare nritya kare ambara tale
Dike dike kata bhasa
Jhare jal jhara jhara,
Vahe jhar sansane.
Aswine nava ananda, utsav nava;
Ati nirmala ati nirmala ati nirmala ujjwala saje
Bhuvane nava saradalakshmi viraje;
Nava indulekha alake jhalake;
Ati nirmala hasa vibhasa vikasa nilambuja majhe
Sweta bhuje swetavina baje;
Uthichhe alapa mridumadhura vehag tane,
Chandrakare ullasita phullavane jhillirave tandra ane re
Dike dike kata bhasa,
Kanpe taru mara mara
Gun gun madhukara.

(9 *Aswin* / 26 September)

The song was enlisted in the list of songs for prayer at night in the next month of *Magh/* January on 11 *Magh/* 26 January. How much portion of the song was sung by altering reading is known from a study of the printed song in the journal "*Tatwavodhini Patrika*", *Phalgoon/* February, 1817 *saka/* 1302 B.E./ 1895. The changed song appeared as follows :

Brahmasangeet
(Ragini : Sankarabharan — Tal Pherta)

Visvarajalaye visvavina bajichhe;
Sthala jale nabhatale vane upavane
Nadi nade giri guha paravare
Nitya jage sarasa sangita madhurima,
Nitya nrityarasa bhangima;
Nava vasante nava ananda, utsava nava;
Ati manjula, ati manjula
Suni manjula gunjana kunje,
Pikakujana puspavane vijane;
Tava snigdha sushovana lochana-lobhana
Shyama sabhatala majhe

Kalagita sulalite baje;
Tomar niswasa-sukhaparase uchchwasa harase
Pallavita manjarita gunjarita ullasita
Sundara dhara ;
Dike dike tava vani,
Nava nava kata gatha
Aviral rasadhara.

Minor differences in reading took place during publication of the first notation of the song in the book. "*Swaralipi-Gitamala*" edited by Jyotirindranath Tagore in 1304 B. E./1897, from the song "*Visvavina*" written in the *Pocket-Book*. The song was reprinted in the book *Satagan* published by Sarala Devi in 1307 B.E./1900 with notations. Changes of words were very minor in *Satagan*. The song printed in the volume "*Gaan*" ("Songs") in the books of poetry of 1310/1903 may be called the last phase of change of reading. This song as printed in the next book in accordance with the reading of the books of poetry, stands as follows :

Sankarabharan–Misratal

Visvavinarabe visvajan mohichhe.
Sthale jale nabhatale vane upavane
Nadi nade giriguha paravare,
Nitya jage sarasa sangita madhurima,
Nitya nrityarasabhangima;–
Nava vasanta nava ananda, utsava nava,
Ati manjula, suni manjula gunjana kunje,
Suni re suni marmara pallavapunje,
Pika-kujana puspavane vijane,
Mridu vayuhillolavilola bibhola vishala sarovara majhe,
Kalagita sulalita baje!
Shyamala kantara pare anila sanchare dhire re,
Naditire saravane uthe dhwani sarasara maramara
Kata dike kata vani, nava nava kata bhas,
Jhara jhara rasadhara!
Asadhe nava ananda, utsava nava,
Ati gambhira, nil ambare dambaru baje,
Jena re pralayankari sankari nache,

Kare garjana nirjharini saghane,
Hera kshubdha bhayala vishala nirala piyalatamalavitane
Uthe rav bhairava tane!
Pavanamallargit gahichhe aandhara rati,
Unmadini soudamini rangabhare nritya kare ambaratale
Dike dike kata vani, nava nava kata bhasa,
Jharajhara rasadhare !
Aswine nava ananda, utsava nava.
Ati nirmala, ati nirmala ujjwala saje
Bhubane nava Saradlakshmi viraje,
Nava indulekha alake jhalake,
Ati nirmala hasavibhasavikasa akasanilamvara-majhe
Sweta bhuje sweta vina baje–
Uthichhe alap mridu madhura vehag tane,
Chandrakare ullasita phullavane jhillirave tandra ane re,
Dike dike kata vani, nava nava kata bhasa,
Jharajhara rasadhara.

I think that discussions with reference to the tuning and notation of this song can be made. Of the few authentic notations published so far on this song, the first we come across is the book "*Swaralipi–Gitimala*" (1304/1897) edited by Jyotirindranath Tagore. In the beginning of notations, Jyotirindranath has mentioned that the song is composed in *Sankarabharan Ragini, Jhanptal* and *Kaoali Tal.*

The word 'Visvavina' in the beginning that he has written in the notation, is :

II na na I sa na na na I sa nedha na I sa nadha na dha I pa pa I
sa na sa I na sa I ra ga ma sa I
Bi o sv a vi o na o o o ra be o bi o
sva ja na ma oo hi chhe

This means that the word 'Visva' is starting from the third accent of *Tal.* In 1307 B.E./ 1900, Sarala Devi wrote the words in division of accents in the same principle in her book "*Satagaan*". In *Sravan/ Bhadra* 1326/August/September, 1919, Dinendranath Tagore published, in notations, the portions of the songs of rains and the autumn in the books "*Ketaki*" and "*Shefali*" respectively by making a great deal of changes in division of rhymes of *Tal.* He made division of *Tal* in the following way :

```
II  na na  I na na - dhana I ᶰᵃsa  na I dha dha  pa  na  I  pa   sa  na I sa ˢᵃna ga I
    Vi  - svavi  -  o  na cr  ra   ve    o vi  o    sva     ja   na
                              ra   ga    - ma  pa    I      pa   ma maga na
                              mo   o     o  o  hi   chhe    e
```

This time, this word 'Visva' was set in the very first acenet of *tal.* As a result, the stress of words was changed.

In 1921, H.A. Poply published the song 'Visvavina' in the European method of notation in his book "*The Music of India*". He has written the notation :

> "Dr. Rabindranath Tagore was good enough to allow me to take down this song from his own singing, for which I am very grateful."

But the divisions of tuning and *Tal* as made by Mr. Poply in his notation do not tally with any one of the notations as referred to above. These are the few authentic notations published during Gurudev's lifetime.

After the publication of the notations of the two portions of the song 'Visvavina' made by Dinendranath in the books "*Ketaki*" and "*Shefali*" in 1326 B.E./ 1919, Indira Devi complained to Gurudev about deformation of tuning in the notations. In reply, Gurudev wrote to her :

> "Dinu has written the notation of 'Visvavina-rave' in the same pattern in which he has taught the boys here (in Santiniketan). He did not consider it necessary to follow the original. Just as Maithili, Vidyapati have maintained points of departure in Bengal, and we have admitted that, in the same way, there would certainly be some sort of changes in form of these alien tunings. If so, where lies the fault? Thinking over all these arguments within my mind, I would like to set him free."

The above reply made by Gurudev did not satisfy Indira Devi. She wrote a letter to Gurudev, shattering the latter's opinion through different arguments. In response, Gurudev, by shouldering the responsibilities of deformation of tuning upon himself wrote :

> "The main point is : ignorance, on the one hand. Moreover, there is idleness, I did not at all know the tuning of that song ... ... Afterwards, when the importance of application was felt, mal-synchronization was made."
> "If you ask, why Dinu committed such an act. the reason is : *'Mahajano jena gatah sa pantha'* ('The way lies where great-men tread')."

It is not known-whether Indira Devi made arguments and counter-arguments with Gurudev in this matter afterwards.

In 1363 B.E./1956, nearly fifteen years after the death of Gurudev, the authorities of the Visa-Bharati Publications Department cancelled the notation of the song 'Visvavinarave' made by Dinendranath and included in his book *"Shefali"*, and instead, published a notation made by Indira Devi. The tunings of the first five lines of both the notations of Indira Devi and Dinendranath are almost the same. Differences in tuning and rhyming are seen from the next line. Later on, in the edition of "*Ketaki*" in 1368 B.E., 1961, the notation of Dinendranath has also been included along with the new notation of Indira Devi of the portion of lines of that song. A separate and complete notation of the song 'Visvavinarave' was printed in volume XXXVI of *Swaravitan,* 1361 B.E., 1954. There is a great deal of difference between this and the complete notation by Jyotirindranath Tagore and Sarala Devi. Indira Devi certainly knew about the differences between the notation made by her and ones made by others previously. But we do not know why she made complaints against Dinendranath only on deformation of tuning. However, an erroneous problem still persists with regard to the tuning and rhyme of this song.

The time and the venue of composition of the song "Otho re malinmukh chala eibar" at page 50 are 26 *Bhadra,* 1302 (12 September, 1895) at Calcutta respectively. As the date of composition of the song written on the page immediately before this is 10 *Aswin* (2 October), I think that the exercise-book was not with Gurudev at the time of composing the song. For this, it had to be written on the exercise-book after 16 *Aswin* (2 October).

The two songs "Amra lakshmichhadar dal" and "Bhagyadevi pitamahi" have covered pages 52-54. The idea and language of these two songs are totally different from all the songs composed in between *Aswin* and *Kartik* (October and November) of this year. I think that there are special reasons for this.

While describing on the composition of the song "Amra lakshmichhadar dal" in his book "*Gharoa*", Silpacharya Abanindranath Tagore refers to the fact that a "Dramatic Club" was there in their residence. From that club, other young persons of the house and he staged and acted on the drama *Aleekbabu* by Jyotirindranath. In this, Gurudev himself participated in the character of Aleekbabu.

"In this very drama that song was sung. Rabikaka prepared it. After the acting of the drama, we all assembled on the stage and sang the last song :

> Amra sab lakshmichhadar dal
> Bhaber padmapatre jal
> Sada karachhi talamal

We also danced along with the song.

The acting of *Aleekbabu* took place in 1303-04 (1897). Sri Prabhatkumar Mukhopadhyay, the revered Rabindra-biographer, informs that the acting of *Aleekbabu* was made under the auspices of the "*Bharatiya Sangeet Samaj*" (The Indian Society for Music) established by Jyotirindranath. The *Bharatiya Sangeet Samaj* was established by Jyotirindranath in January, 1898. I do not, therefore, think that this drama was acted under the management of the *Bharatiya Sangeet Samaj.*

No information about the "Dramatic Club" as told by Abanindranath has yet been received from elsewhere. He has said that the club was established in 1888 after his marriage. It was abolished before the setting up of the *Khamkheyali Sabha (The Assembly of the Eccentrics)* on 24 *Magh* 1303 (8 February, 1896). There is no such information available even now as to prove that the acting of *Aleekbabu* was made under the auspices of the *Khamkheyali Sabha.*

About *Khamkheyali Sabha,* Abanindranath has said :

> "After this, the *'Khamkheyali Sabha'* was set up last of all. As various disturbances cropped up with the 'Dramatic Club', Rabikaka now decided to accept a few selected eccentric members, and the others would be present as invited ones. What would be its name! Rabikaka is thinking : *Kheyali*

> *Sabha.* I said : "Let it be named '*Khamkheyali*'. That's right', said Rabikaka, 'let this *Sabha* (Assembly) be named *Khamkheyali* :It was decided that a *Khas Majlish* (a grand congregation) of *Khamkheyali* would be held in the residence of every member each month, and each member would read out something in it."

"So far as I remember about the programme of the *Khas Majlish,* it was written thus. I am giving a sample : 1303/1896

> Venue—Jorasanko
> Host-in-chief—Sri Balendranath Tagore.
> Function : Recitation of *"Arasiker Swarga Prapti"* by Sri Gaganendranath. Reading out of stories entitled *'Kshudhita Pasan'* and *'Man-Bhanjan'* by Sri Rabindranath Tagore. The song of Gosainji and *Sangat* by his elder brother. Musical instruments."
> "At the time of that *Khamkheyali, 'Vaikunther Khata'* was written. It was read out in *Khamkheyali,* and was decided that we would act. Kedar became Rabikaka, Motilal Chakraborty acted in the role of the servant, my elder brother as Vaikuntha, the Maharaja of Natore in the role of Avinash and I played the role of that boy, Tinkadi."

In *Rabindrajivani (Biography of Rabindranath),* Prabhatkumar Mukhopadhyay informs that *"Vaikunther Khata"* was first acted in the year 1303/1896.

Atulprasad Sen, in his memoir, has written on the *Khamkheyali Sabha* :

> "In 1897, under his (Gurudev's) leadership, an association of music and literature was established in the name *Khamkheyali Sabha (The Assembly of the Eccentrics).* I was the youngest member of the assembly. Among the members of *Khamheyali,* there were litterateurs and well-known humorists like Dwijendralal Roy, Maharaj Jagadindranarayan, Balendranath Tagore, Jnanendranath Tagore, Abanindranath Tagore, Lokendranath Palit, etc. The procedure of activities of this assembly was a bit eccentric; there was no hard and fast rule. Its aims and objectives were : to energise humour,

to make literature lively in joy, to attract the minds of the members with different music and to appropriately satisfy the intestine at the end of the assembly. Dwijendralal Ray, the great humorist, kept this *Majlish* (congregation) of *Khamkheyali* pulsating. He made us float in the flood of laughter through singing his songs of laughter. We joined the chorus of his laughing songs. Rabindranath was the leader of the chorus ... ... Dwijendralal made us dance on the overflowing waves of laughter and Rabindranath enamoured us by creating his beautiful world of humour. Radhikanath Goswami, the famous singer, entertained us by singing classical songs adorned with *Tan* and *Lay* in the assembly of *Khamkheyali*. The talent of Rabindranath is so all-pervading that he composed songs in the ideal tuning of Mr. Goswami and the latter sang those newly composed songs in the assembly of *Khamkheyali*. Of those songs, I remember one :

Maharaj, eki saje ele hridaypur majhe,
Charantale koti sashi chandra mare

(surya mare) laje'. [In what robe, your Majesty, did you come in the palace of my heart? Crores of the moon (and the sun) die at thy feet in shame.] We were his companions. We would not be able to forget in life how the Poet entertained us by singing new and beautiful self-composed songs in that assembly. I can recall a few famous songs of those days : 'Mama jouvana-nikunje gahe pakhi, sakhi jago—jago'; 'Badhu he phire eso; mama sajala jalada snigdha kanta antare phire eso'; 'Jagi pohalo vibhavari' etc. Besides these, he would write diverse and excellent poems and essays for the assembly and read these out before us. We heard these with rapt attention. He had an extra-ordinary power of recitation. The Maharaja of Natore played on the *Vaya-Tabla* in that assembly. He was specially expert in this musical instrument. Rabindranath addressed him as 'Rajan'. Abanindranath Tagore, the world famous artist, would play on the *Esraz*. many other litterateurs would read out compositions. Of them, the poems of Balendranath Tagore pleased us most :"

The description of *Khamkheyali Sabha* that Rathindranath Tagore has left in his book *Pitrismriti* (Reminiscence of Father) is :

"In the period of my uncle, there was 'Vidvajjan Sabha' (The Assembly of Scholars), in the period of my father, that was changed into *Khamkheyali Sabha.* When *Khamkheyali Sabha* was started I was a bit grown up. So the subject-matter of this assembly is vivid in my mind. There were no rules and regulations of this assembly. It is an assembly of fifteen to twenty numbers. It was established at the encouragement of father and Baludada (Balendranath Tagore). Although there were no rules and regulations for enrolment of membership, the assembly was formed with writers, poets, artists, musicians and actors. Whatever one's erudition and intelligence might be, in order to become a member, it was considered to be a special qualification to be appreciative. Father, Baludada, Dwipudada, Gangandada, Samardada, Abandada of our family were its members. Jagadindranath, the Maharaja of Natore, along with Jagadishchandra Bose, Dwijendralal Roy, Priyanath Sen, Aukshay Babu (Senior), Aukshay Babu (Junior), Pramatha Choudhury, Pramatha Roy Chowdhury of Sanosh, Atulprasad Sen and many others whose names I cannot recall now were also associated with it. It was a customary affair of the assembly that on every month a member invited all other members in his house by turns. The assembly was held there. Though there were sufficient arrangements for dinner, it was simply an offshoot. The principal aim was to read out poems or stories, acting playlets and to sing and play on musical instruments. Whatever new poems or short stories father would write then was read out by him in the *Khamkheyali Sabha.* Many a time Maharaja Jagadindranath played on the *Paakhoaaz* with recitation of poems. He had a very sweet exposure in presentation. The rhythmic resonance of the following poems seemed exquisitely pleasing in ears with the sombre *bol* of *Paakhoaaz* :

Oi ase oi ati bhairava harase ...
Jadio sandhya asichhe manda manthare ...
Hriday amar nachere ajike ...

In *Bhadra* 1328 (September 1921), at the residence of Jorasanko, Calcutta *Varsamangal* (Invocation to Rains) was held in the northern courtyard of the *Vichitra Bhavan.* I remember even today how Gurudev recited his two poems on rains in the function of that year, and how Jagadindranath, the Maharaja of Natore, exquisitely played on the *Paakhoaaz* by harmonizing with the rhythm of these two poems. It seemed that the *bol-s* were as if speaking like poems.

Rathindranath has further said :

> "Everyone requested Dwijendralal Roy when present in the meeting, to sing songs, He sang his songs of laughter. Everyone was at the apex of laughter but Dwijubabu, with his sombre face, went on singing by playing on the table-harmonium. Atulprasad Sen had also begun to compose songs to a little extent at that time. He had also to sing now and then.
>
> "For the *Khamkheyali Sabha,* father composed one or two playlets. He probably wrote *'Bini paisar Bhoj'* by remembering Aukshay Babu (Junior). Aukshay Babu acted it alone ... ... Then *'Vaikunther Khata'* was acted. This drama was first acted in the ballroom of the residence of Gagandada.

Characters

Father	-	Avinash
Gagandada	-	Vaikuntha
Samardada	-	Kedar
Abandada	-	Tinkadi
Aukshay Babu (Junior)	-	Isan.

I said about the sitting for once. No exception to arrangements for decoration and wonderful planning for food materials each time was made in the few sittings of the *Khamkheyali Sabha* held in our house."

Khamkheyali Sabha is known to exist upto 1304 (1897) at a stretch.

The above extensive excerpt and other informations in connection with the above mentioned club and assembly were necessary on account of the doubt that arose whether the song 'Amra lakshmichhadar dal' was in fact composed in the period of the Dramatic Club. The club was abolished before the composition of this song. Instead, it was replaced by *Khamakheyali Sabha.* Whatever information we collect from the book *Ghoroa* about the ideals, aims and other descriptions of this assembly proves the fact that the song was composed as a national song for the assembly. It was not composed in the first year of the assembly, but in the second. The acting of the drama *Aleekbabu* was held within the year 1303-04 (1897). Considering all aspects of *Khamkehyali,* it seems that the song 'Amra lakshmichhadar dal' is the song of *Khamkehyali Sabha,* the drama *Aleekbabu* was acted under the sponsorship of *Khamkehyali Sabha* and at the end of acting, the actors sang it in a chorus and along with dance. The word of the song as written in the pages of the "Pocket Book" are the following :

Amra lakshmichhadar dal,
Bhaber padmapatre jal,
Amra karchhi talamal.
Moder thaka jaoya sunya haoya
Naiko phalaphal.
Nahi jani karan kaaran, nahi jani dharan dhaaran,
Nahi mani sashan baaran go–
Amra apan rokhe maner jhoke
Chhindechhi shikal.
Lakshmi tomar vahanguli dhaneputre uthun phooli,
Luthun tomar charandhuli go–
Amra skandhe laye kantha jhuli
Phirbo dharatal.
Tomar bandarete bandha ghate bojhai kara sonar pate
Anek ratna anek hate go
Amra nongar-chhenda bhanga tari
Bhesechhi kebal.
Amra ebar khunje dekhi akulete kul achhe ki,
Dwip achhe ki bhava sagare?
Jadi sukh na jote dekhbo dube
Kothay rasatal.
Amra jute sarabela karbo hatabhagar mela,
Gabo gaan khelbo khela go!
Kanthe jadi gaan na ase
Karbo kolahal.

Of late, it has been known that in this period Dwijendralal Roy formed a club named *Lakshmichhadar Dal*. Gurudev and the relatives of his house had close connection with this club even then. It is thought that the song was composed to sing in this session.

By changing the words of the song, Gurudev transformed it into the song of ghosts for the drama *Dhyan-bhanga* by Jyotirindranath Tagore. The acting of *Dhyan-bhanga* was made in *Baisakh* 1307, April 1900 under the auspices of '*Bharatiya Sangeet Samaj*' (The Indian Association for Music). The song was :

(Misra Khambaz—Ektala)

Amra bhut-pereter dal
Bhaver padmapatre jal,
Sada karchhi talamal.
Moder asa-jaoya sunya haoya, naiko phalaphal
Nahi jani dharan dhaaran, nahi sunî kahar baran,
Kebal mani bholar shashan go.
Amra apan rokhe, maner jhonke chhindechhi shikal.
Kakhan amra dhari kaya kakhan hai re gachher chhaya,
Katai mora jani maya go.
Kakhan haye jhader haoa phiri dharatal.
(Amra) Anath-bate thaki latke, pathiker ghaad deei matke,
Sunyapane jai shatke go.
(Pare) Abar ese, shmashan-dese hasi khalakhal,
Amra ebar khunje dekhi, akulete kul mele ki
Bholar khela moder sambal.
Jadi sukh na jote, dekhba dube kothay rasatal,
Amra jute sarabela karba bhut-preter mela,
Gabo gaan, khelbo khela go.
(Ar) kanthe jadi gaan na aase, karbo kolahal.

After the song 'Lakshmichhadar Dal, at page 54 of the "Pocket Book", we find :

Bhupati Khemta

Ogo bhagya devi pitamahi, mitla amar aash
Ekhan tabe aagna kara bidaay habe das!

Jibaner ei baasar rati pohay bujhi nibhe bati,
Badhur dekha naaiko, sudhu prachur parihaas!
Ekhan theme gelo baanshhi, sukie elo pusparaasi
Uthlo tomaar attahaasi kanpaye aakaash–
Chhilen jaanra aamaay ghire, gechhen je jar ghare phire,
Sudhu aachho briddha thakurani mukhe tani baash.

I think that the song was composed and sung as the closing song of the drama *Aleekbabu.* If one would assess by arranging the fourth line of the song 'Badhur dekha naaiko, sudhu prachur parihaas' side by side a statement about *Aleekbabu* by Abanindranath, one would think the same. Abanindranath remarks :

> "Formerly, it was *Aleekbabu* who returned and married Hemangini by mesmerizing father. In that place, Rabikaka, brought many people. Consequently, many characters were also created. Hemangini was kept totally in the background. Besides her, where is the girl to take part in acting? So he did not at all expose Hemangini any more."

Gurudev always loved this type of humorous function. We have also seen how, at his old age, he loved to encourage others in entertainments. In *Sravan* 1342 (August 1935) the *Adhyapakas* (Teachers) and *Karmis* (workers) of Santiniketan established a club or an association named "*Hai Hai Sangha*". In this, a group of young *Adhyapakas* and *Karmis* were associated with senior members like Silpacharya Nandalal Bose, Rathindranath Tagore etc. They twice held functions of dance, drama and music. On 7 *Bhadra* 1342 (24 August 1935) "*Hai Hai Sangha*" arranged a variety function named *Bharasa Mangal* at Singha-Sadana. In this performance, a group of *Adhyapakas* and *Karmis* who never danced before, showed the dance in imitation of Gurudev's song "Baaki ami rakhbo na kichhui". Moreover, two made a duet dance with the song "Ay tabe sahachari" in the dresses of a male and a female. To sing in this function Gurudev at that time composed a few comic songs : "Amra na gaoar dal re", "Paye padi, shon bhai gaiye" and "O bhai kanai, kare janai".

Besides these, he also gave tunings to Sukumar Ray's poem "Gaan dharechhen Bhismalochan Sharma" to sing it in the function.

The song at page 57 is "ke uthe daki mama baksha-nide thaki". He composed the song at Jorasanko on 22 *Kartik* 1302 (12 November,

1895). As there are differences between the initial form and the current one of the song, I am quoting both. In his first composition of the song, Gurudev made a great deal of scratches.

(Paraz)

Ke uthe daki
Mama vakshanide thaki
Karun madhur adhir tane
Viraha-vidhur pakhi.
Stimita pavan kunjabhavan
Timiravrita supta bhuvan.
Ke he ekanta ? Hridayaprante
Jagichhe ekaki.
Kahare chahe ki gaan gahe!
Nidravihin ki duhkha dahe!
Ghumao re asanta
Ki karili sara dinanta,
Ami je sranta vedanaklanta
Tandralasa aanki!

(22 *Kartik,* 12 November, Jorasanko)

The present reading is also written at this page, but it is completely scratched e.g.:

"Nivida chhaya gahana maya
Pallava ghana nirjana van
Santa pavane kunjabhavane
ke jage ekaki
Jamini vibhora nidraghanaghora
Ghana tamalshakha nidranjanamakha—
Stimitatara chetana hara
Pandu gagana, tandramagana—
Chandra sranta dikbhranta
Nidralasa-aankhi."

The songs of 1302 B.E., 1895 have been completed at page 60 of the "Pocket Book".

The next pages covering 63-67 are dealt with 14 Hindi break-away Bengali religious songs with original Hindi songs. There are four Hindi songs which Gurudev did not utilize for composition of Bengali songs. There is no date of composition with these songs. There are dates of composition with a few songs. If we arrange the songs one after the other and prepare a list, we will find that of the songs composed in 1303 (1896), some are self-composed, some Hindi break-away Bengali songs with original Hindi words, some Hindi songs which are not broken in Bengali and two Vedic songs. For example :

Self-composed songs :

1. Ujjwal kara he aazi e anandarati—, 9 *Baisakh* 1303, (22 April 1896)
2. Azi kon dhan hate visve amare—, 14, *Sravan* 1303 (30 July, 1896)
3. Ke jaay amritadhamjatri—, 29 *Bhadra* 1303, (15 September, 1896)
4. Amar satya mithya sakali—*Desh-Ektala.*
5. Ar kata dure achhe se—
6. Santa ha re mama chitta nirakul—
7. Ayee bhuvanamanomohini—*Pous* 1303, (December, 1896).

Hindi break-away Bengali songs and original Hindi songs

1. Sitala tava pada chhaya, taapaharan.
   Vanguri mori moor genyee zin chhunyo.
2. Nishidin jagia aachha nath he.
   Thakuria anchara more chhadi de.
3. Azi hridi aasane tomare kari.
   Pyari tere pavana pakaro, sav meli.
4. Tomahin kate jeevan he prabhu,
   Tum vina kaiso rahgi te piyu.
5. Hridya avaran khule gelo.
   Nasire ma varan koelia.
6. Madhur rupe virajo he visvaraj–
7. Azi mama man chahe jeevan–
   Phooli van ghana mor aay vasant ri.
8. Harashe jago aazi, jaago re.
   Hasas jaago lal, lal lay kanara.
9. Santi kara varishan niraba dhare,
   Sambhuharapada jugadhyana vakhani natharanga.

10. Sundara vahe ananda mandanila,
    Sankara Siva Pinaka Gangadhara.

Hindi songs not translated into Bengali.

1. Komal vele, eri jahan, mora.
2. Kanganva mori ladere ati.
3. Raj dularka vanara aailo.
4. Tu kahan payo nayee ho aparampar.
5. Sudur dure aayori so mura mura.

Vedic songs

1. *Srinvantu visve amritasya putra aa je dhamani.*
2. *Sangachchhadvang sangvadadvang Sangvo manangshi jaanatam.*

This type of Hindi break-away Bengali songs composed before 1303 (1896) are not to be found in the "Pocket Book".

Sri Prabhatkumar Mukhopadhyay has informed that the song "Ujjval kara he aazi e anandarati" in the list was composed by Gurudev on the occasion of the marriage between Nalini Devi and Suhrid Choudhury. This ceremony took place on 14 *Baisakh* 1303 (27 April 1896).

Gurudev composed the song "ke jaay amritadhamjatri" to sing in the 'upasana' (prayer) on the day of the passing away of Rammohan Roy. The song is composed on 29 *Bhadra* (15 September).

It is known that Rammohan Roy passed away within a few days after brief illness from fever on 27 September, 1833 at Bristol, England. According to the Bengali year, it was in the month of *Aswin.* Right from the Santiniketan Vidyalaya period the song has been sung on the commemorative meeting of Rammohan Roy and it is even now sung.

On the song "Ayee bhuvanamanomohini", Sri Mukhopadhyay writes :

> "In December 1896, at Beadon Square, Calcutta, Rabindranath sang 'Vandemataram' in his own tuning at the 12th session of the Congress Invitation of the guests at the residence of Jorasanko. Rabindranath sang his newly composed song—"Ayee bhuvanamanomohini".

On this session, Rathindranath writes in his book "*Pitrismriti*" :

> The Congress session in Calcutta was held a year before the Natore Conference (1896). The British Government did not allow anywhere to hold political meetings towards the *Maidan* (Brigade Parade Ground). It was decided that the pandal of the Congress would be erected at Beadon Square. Beadon Square was very near to our residence. So in our residence, too, there was a pretty hue and cry with regard to the arrangements for the Congress. Father was assigned to arrange for songs. Rehearsals were going on. Father gave tunings to Bankimchandra's 'Vandemataram'. In the beginning of the Congress Session, father sang this song alone. Saraladidi played on the Organ... ... In the Congress of 1896, "Vandemataram" was first sung."

From the above two excerpts, it is known that Gurudev and many of the members of his family were associated with the arrangements for the Congress this time. And, in this connection, the leaders of other provinces had an opportunity to come in close contact with Gurudev and everyone of the members of his family. All the leaders were invited at the residence of Jorasanko. Gurudev sang the song "Ayee bhuvana-manomohini" before the audience in that reception. The pattern of application of the words of the song is worth observation. The invocation of *Bharatmata* has been made with the help of Sanskrit words from the beginning to the end. There is almost no colloquial word. The song is composed in *Misra Tori-Bhairavi Ragini* and *Trital.* It is clearly understood that the song was composed keeping in the mind the thought that the non-Bengali leaders might easily appreciate its idea and form. Atulprasad Sen has remarked about the composition of the song as follows :

> "Nearly thirty years ago, the Congress Session was once held in Calcutta. Many distinguished representatives came from different provinces of India. Rabindranath invited them in his residence at Jorasanko. The alien people did not know Bengali, at least they did not understand easy colloquial Bengali but many of them knew Sanskrit. So he composed a unique profusely Sanskrit-mixed *Bharat-Sangeet*. He himself taught many of us this song. I remember we sang this song in

> the thunderous voice and with percussion instsruments. All of us—male and female—had to put on white dresses. Rabindranath himself was our leader. We sang : 'Ayee bhuvanamanomohini.'

The initial form of the song was :

Ayee bhuvanamanomohini.
Ayee nirmala-suryakarojjwala dharani
Ayee Janakajanani-janani.
Neela sindhujaladhouta charanatala
Anila-vikampita shyamala anchala,
Santa lalata tomara Himacahala
(Ayee) subhratushara-kiritini.
Prathama prabhata udaya tava gagane
Prathama samarava tava tapovane,
Prathama pracharita tava vana-bhavane
Jnanadharma kala kavyakahini.
Chira kalyanamayee tumi dhanya,
Desha videshe vitarichha anna,
Jahnavi yamuna vigalita karuna
Punya piyusha stanyavahini.

(*Pous*, 1303, December, 1896)

In the next two pages after this song, the two Vedic hymns are there one after the other.

The first is :

Srinvantu visve amritasya putra aa je dhamani
Divyani tasthuh vedahmetang purusang mahantang
Adityavaranang tamasah parasthat
Tameva viditvatimrityumeti nanyah pantha vidyate-ayanaya
Etajnegang nityamevatmasangsthang,
Natah parag veditavyang hi kinchit.
Sangprapyai namrisayo jnanatriptah
Kritatmano vitaraaga prasantah
Te sarvagang sarvatah prapya dhira
Yuktatmananah sarvamevavisanti
Tameva viditvati mrityu .. .. ..

Vignanatma saha devaischasarvai
Pranabhutani sangpratisthanti yatra
Tadaksharang vedayate yastu soumya
Sasarvagnah sarvamevavivesa.
Yaschayamashminnakashe tejomayohamritamayah purushah
Sarvanubhuh. Yaschayamashminnakashe tejomayohamritamayah
Purusah sarvanubhu, Tameva viditvati ......

In later periods some lines of this hymn are omitted and one or two lines are added. The second hymn is :

Sanggachchhadhvang sangvadadhvang sangva managshi janatam
Devabhangan yathapurve sanginanana upasate
Samano mantrah samitih samani
Somanang manah saha chittamedham
Samanang mantrang abhimantraye vah
Samaniva aakuthi samana hridayani vah
Santanamastu voh mano yatha vah susahasati.

There are differences of lines from the procedure of singing this hymn at present. That this hymn was sung as an inaugural song in the "*Sanjeevani Sabha*" to enkindle the sense of nationalism in Gurudev in his adolescent age is known to us through his *Jeevansmriti* and from the autobiography of Jyotirindranath Tagore. It is not known if it was sung in the Congress Session this year. But when the Congress Session was held in Calcutta in 1917 at the Wellington Square, then this hymn was sung on the first day, of its inaugural function along with 'Vandemataram' and 'Desh desh nandita kari'.

Probably, both the hymns were sung in the Congress Session at Beadon Square-or the two hymns were presented before the leaders in the invitation meeting along with "Ayee bhuvanmanomohini" at the Jorasanko residence. Gurudev wrote the two hymns in his exercise-book to meet the necessities of adding tunes anew.

Just after the two hymns, the names of many reputed persons of Calcutta in those days along with those of the residents of the Tagore family at Jorasanko covering three pages are written. I assume that it is a list of the persons to attend the reception-meeting for the national leaders. The names of relatives in the beginning are :

Badadada, Dwipu, Aru, Mohini, Jogini, Ramani, Nitu, Sudhi, Mejadada, Suren, Bibi.
Hitu, Ashu, myself, D.N. Chatterjee, Lakshijal, Sobhona, Jyotidada,
Dada,
Badadidi, Satya, Nitya,
Nadidi, Sarala, Hiran, Jyotsna,
Sejadidi, Chhotadidi, Sukumar, Aswini, Nalini Banerjee, Gagan, Jyoti, Niru, Sesendra, Rajani.

The names of External invitees :

Tripura	Gurudas Banerjee
Badathakur	Hirendranath Dutta
Santosh	Sahitya Parishat
Natore	Mrinalini
Cooch Behar	Poet Ghosh Brothers
Sucharu	
Dighapatia	Girindramohini
(name scratched)	
Jagadish Basu	Harishchandra Neogy (name scratched)
Dwijendral Roy	Baradacharan Mitra
Ghosh & Kar	Upendrakishore Ray Choudhury
Our pleaders	Pradip
(names scratched)	
Prematosh Babu	Aukshay Baral
Trivedi	Vijay Majumder
B.L. Gupta	Devendranath Sen Bijnor
C.R. Das Amala	(Gaganchandra Roy)
Mrs. S.R. Das	Nagendranath Gupta
K.N. Roy Esq.	Chandranath Basu
L. Palit	Nabinchandra Sen
Rajnarain Bose	Aukshay Maitra
Shrish Majumder	Lahorini
Priyanath Sen	Uma Das
R.C. Dutta	Priya

Prabodh
Prabhat Kumar
Sibnath Sastri
Haraprasad Sastri

The Raja of Purnea (name scratched)
Kamelswari & Co. (name scratched)
Dinendrakumar
Ramanimohan Ghosh
Dinesh Ch. Sen
Prematosh Bose, 115 Amherst St.
Babu Hemchandra Sen
Babu Surendranath Maitra
Kalimohan Ghosal
Mahendrachandra Home
Abhoysankar Majumdar
Atulananda Dutta
Kulada Ranjan Roy

I am now submitting a few remarkable informations with reference to the songs of the Congress Session of this time :

> The storm of movement of protest that arose in the circle of intelligentsia in the different regions of India as a consequence to imposition of preventive detention rule upon Miss Annie Besant and her associates by the Government of Madras in 1917 for their movement of the 'Home Rule League' was also flanked by the educated people of the then Bengal. Sri Prabhat Kumar Mukhopadhyay states on the movement of protest in Bengal in his book *Rabindrajibani (The Biography of Rabindranath)* :
>
> "In Calcutta, the Town Hall was proposed for requisition to hold a protest-meeting against the internship of Besant. The Government of Bengal informed the authorities of the hall that they could not provide any one with government or semi-government buildings to protest against the activities of the Provincial Government. No public meeting could be held in the Town Hall. Then Rabindranath wrote '*Kartar Ichchhay Karma*' and at first read out in the Rammohan Library Hall on August 4, 1917. But even though efforts were made to hold the meeting in a more spacious hall, no space was available. At last J.F. Madan, the owner of the Alfred Theatre, arranged for the lecture.
>
> At this moment of excitement, the Poet wrote the song 'Desha desha nandita kari'. What an excitement at the Vichitra

> Bhavan we saw! What a movement of the leaders! What a discussion and secret strategies! "The meeting held on 11 August 1917 (at the Alfred Theatre) was presided over by Bhupendranath Basu. The Maharaja of Natore, Jagadindranath played on the *Paakhoaaz* and the group of 'Vichitra' sang the song 'Desha desha nandita kari'."

In his memoir, Amal Hom has written about the composition of this essay and the song 'Desha desha nandita kari' :

> "1917, The demand for self-rule has become strong throughout the country. The whole of India from one end to the other is swept away by the movement for 'Home Rule for India' under leadership of Annie Besant. The British Government interned Mrs. Besant... ... ... Arrangements are going on to hold a protest-meeting. Ronaldse, the Governor, informed that no meeting would be allowed to be held. Surendranath, Chittaranjan and others went for deputation to the Governor. After a great deal of requests, the permission to hold the meeting was obtained. Meanwhile, Rabindranath came to Calcutta with his historically famous address '*Kartar Ichchhay Karma*! ... ... One day Pandit Madanmohan Malaviya came to meet Rabindranath... ... ... He requested the Poet to compose a song on the occasion of this renaissance of the country."
>
> "On the very next day, that song—the famous one—was composed : 'Desha desha nandita kari mandrita tava bheri'..."
>
> "It was decided that the song would be sung in the meeting of the reading out of the essay '*Kartar Ichchhay Karma*."
>
> "Rehearsals of songs started in the assembly hall of 'Vichitra'—the red building of Jorasanko. Jagadindranath, the Maharaja of Natore, sat in 'Sangat' with his *Paakhoaaz*. Dinendranath came from Santiniketan with his associates, and here, too, a few of us assembled.
>
> "That the song was first sung at Rammohan Library on the day of the reading out of the essay is referred to in *The Calcutta Municipal Gazette,* Tagore Memorial Special Supplement, September, 1941. The following is referred : "Composed, at the request of Pandit Malaviya, his famous national song 'Desh desha nandita kari mandrita taba veri',

> which is sung for the first time at the meeting at Rammohan Library."

September 5, The Government of Madras liberated Mrs. Besant from internship. She came to Calcutta. The Calcuttans greeted her with enthusiasm.

The Congress Session to be held in Calcutta towards the end of December was already fixed. On October 4, Mrs. Besant was elected in the session of the reception committee in Calcutta to preside over the Annual Conference of the Congress. At that time, arrangements for Gurudev's drama *Dakghar (The Post Office)* were going on under the auspices of the '*Vichitra*' association of Jorasanko. Acting started on October 10, after erecting the stage to the western corner of the 'Vichitra' hall. Sri Prabhatkumar Mukhopadhyay, the biographer of Rabindranath, states :

> "Acting took place on two days in Vichitra : once for the members of Vichitra and the next day for the distinguished guests. Of the audience on the last day there were Annie Besant, Lokmanya Tilak, Madan Mohan Malaviya and Mohandas Karamchand Gandhi."
>
> But Sri Prabhatchandra Gupta has written in the journal "*Geetavitan Vaarsiki*" published in 1350 (1943) : "The drama, *(Dakghar)* has been acted at least seven times consecutively upto December".
>
> On October 25, 1917 Gurudev informs Mr. Pearson in a letter : "We staged *Dakghar (The Post Office)* in our Bichitra Hall, gave five performances and felt happier each time we did it."

Rathindranath Tagore writes in his memoirs :

> "After every show when I wanted to put down the stage, demand was made for another repeat performance and thus Amal's three-walled cottage remained a fixture in the Bichitra Hall for many weeks. I believe the seventh and last performance was given for the entertainment of the delegates of the Indian National Congress then being held in Calcutta. After the session of the Congress all the distinguished members including the grand old Lady-President, Pandit

> Madan Mohan Malaviya, Mahatma Gandhi, Gokhale and Lokmanya Tilak came to the play at our house."

In the drama *Dakghar* published by Visva-Bharati the following is stated :

> "It seems that the re-acting of *Dakghar* was held towards the end of December, 1917, and in the beginning of January, 1918. This is because on December 26-29, 1917 the Annual Conference of the Indian National Congress was held in Calcutta. It is known that by inviting leaders like Lokmanya Tilak, Mrs. Besant, Gandhiji, Malaviyaji etc. a special show has been arranged on that day."

In its September 1941 issue of *The Calcutta Municipal Gazette,* the following is stated on the acting of this drama :

> "*Dakghar* (Post Office) is staged by the Poet at the Vichitra Club Hall, ... the performance being witnessed by Gandhiji, Tilak Maharaj, Malaviyaji, Mrs. Besant and other prominent Congress leaders."

We come across the same news in *The Visva-Bharati Quarterly* published in October next. It is to be found in the part "The Tagore Chronicle" in the "Tagore Birthday Number" :

> "The *Dakghar (Post Office)* is staged by the Poet at the Vichitra Club Hall, the audience including Gandhiji, Lokamanya Tilak, Mrs. Besant, Malaviyaji and eminent personalities."

From the above news it can be assumed in general that the acting of *Dakghar* was held five nights in the month of October and the acting of the seventh and the eighth nights were held after the Congress Session.

Sri Prabodhchandra Sen, in one of his essays, states about the songs of the Congress Session, 1917 :

> "It is necessary to give an account of the four songs of the three days of the Congress and the poem "India's Prayer'."

"The inauguration of the first day (16 December) was made as usual with the song 'Vandemataram' under the direction of Srimati Amala Das. Besides that, some more songs were sung. Of those, the song 'Desha desha nandita kari' is specially remarkable.

Before the beginning of activities of the first day, Rabindranath read out his poem" India's Prayer'.

On the second day, Sarala Devi's 'Namo Hindustan' (Hindustan, I salute thee) and on the third day, 'Janagana-mana-adhinayak' were sung."

In *The Calcutta Municipal Gazette,* the first day's session of the Congress in 1917 is described as follows :

> "On the opening day he receives a great ovation and reads 'India's Prayer' (a poem) immediately after singing Bande-Mataram."

In the 'Tagore Birthday Number' of *The Visva Bharati Quarterly,* the following is stated :

> "The Poet attends the Congress Session on the first day, receiving a great ovation, and recites the poem 'India's Prayer'."

In the appendix of '*Chithipatra*' (Letters), Volume VI, published by Visva-Bharati it is stated : "After the singing of the Vedic hymn *Sanggachchhaddvang sangvadadvang* and *Vande-Mataram* and reading out of letters wishing success of the session by Bepin Chandra Pal, "Gurudev recited 'India's Prayer' at the call of the President of the Reception Committee."

The real information related to the songs of the Congress in 1917 at Wellington Square, Calcutta is available from a 16-page printed booklet. Six Bengali songs with their English renderings boosting national ideas along with a hymn from the *Rigveda* were printed in it for the advantage of the members coming from different provinces of India to join the Congress, to have an understanding of the central ideas of the songs. Its publisher was the Congress Office and it was printed at the Kuntalin Press. The following matter was in the first page :

"Thirty-Second Indian National Congress
Songs
(with translations)
Calcutta
1917
Two annas"

From the second page, the list of the few songs, with translations, as printed consecutively is as follows :

Translator

1. *Sanggachchhadvam Sangvadadvam...*Rigveda ... not mentioned
2. *Vandemataram ...*Bankimchandra ... Aurobindo
3. *Desha desha nandita kari...*Rabindranath Tagore ... Rabindranath
4. *Atita gouravavahini...*Sarala Devi ... Indira Devi
5. *Je din sunil jaladhi...* Dwijendralal Roy ...
6. *Mile save Bharatasanatan...* Satyendranath Tagore...
7. *Janaganamana adhinayak...* Rabindranath Tagore ...

From the above list of songs published by the Congress Reception Committee and from the above news, it is assumed that on the day of inauguration of the Session the hymns of the Rigveda *Vandemataram, Desha desha nandita kari* were sung along with the recitation of the poem 'India's Prayer'. On the second day, the two songs 'Atita gouravavahini' and 'Je din sunil jaladhi haite' were sung, and, on the third 'Mile save Bharatsantan' and 'Jana gana mana adhinayaka' were sung. The responsibilities for directing these songs were Sarala Devi, Indira Devi and Dinendranath.

The word 'chorus' was printed with the English translations of four songs, from the fourth one 'Atita gouravavahini' to the seventh song 'Jana gana mana adhinayaka' as set forth in the above list, of their lines of refrain. For example, the word 'chorus' was printed beside the English translations of lines having words like Banga, Bihar, Ayodhya, Utkal, Madras, Maratha etc. of the song 'Atita gouravavahini'. The word 'chorus' in Bengali and 'chorus' above its line in English were written beside the two lines with words like 'Dhanya hailo dharani tomar' of the song "Je din sunil jaladhi haite" by Dwijendralal Roy. The word 'chorus' was on the head of the English rendering of the line 'Gaao Bharater joy' of the song "Mile save Bharat

Santan". In the song "Jana gana mana adhinayaka" the 'chorus' was on English translation of the last two lines of every *kali.* Perhaps thinking over this choric method of music, Indira Devi wrote in her book *Rabindra Sangeeter Trivenisangam* published in 1316 (1909) :

> "He (Gurudev) has followed to sing a foreign chorus, every exciting song or a refrain after every *kali* of a song, e.g., 'Jaya jaya jaya he' of the song, "Jana gana mana adhinayaka" or 'Jaya jaya narottama' of the song "Matrimandir punya-angana" etc.

The song 'Jana gana mana adhinayaka' composed by Gurudev is of five *kalis* in total. But in the Congress Session of this time only three *kali-s* that is the first, the third and the fifth *kali-s* were sung. In its two *kali-s* (stanzas), changes of two words are noticed. For example, the expression 'aikya vidhayaka' of the third stanza has replaced 'Jana gana mangala dayaka' of the refrain of the first *kali.* In the same way, the word 'patha-parichayak' replaced the word 'aikyavidhayaka' of the third *kali.* Besides these, the word 'Punjab' of the second line in the beginning of the song was changed and printed as 'punjub'. Sri Prabodhchandra Sen remarks on the English translation of this song :

> "From this very time the journal of the song to win over the national mind starts and this course of journey has to some extent become easy through its translation into English. Within a very short time after the above-mentioned Congress Session, the English version of the song made by the Poet was published in the journal *The Modern Review* (February, 1912)."

But from the booklet of songs it is being known that the first English translation of the song was made by Indira Devi at the time of the Congress Session. So the origin of winning over national mind by the song was made through this first translation by Indira Devi. We can unhesitatingly accept the fact that her translation was recommended by Gurudev.

Although the English translation of the song "Desha desha nandita kari" was printed in the booklet, there are exact references, like other songs, to the name of the translator. But the name of Gurudev is there below the translation as a composer. After the composition of the song in August, it was first published in the journal *The Modern Review* under the caption 'The Day is Come' as its English translation. The name of Gurudev was below the translation. So we can take it for granted that the translation in the booklet of the Congress was made by Gurudev alone.

Of the list of other songs of this year, the songs included in the list of Hindi break-away Bengali songs with original Hindi ones are the following :

> Vanguri mori moor genyi jin chhunyo,
> *Imankalyan-Ektala*-Mid-movement.
> Pyeri tere pavana pakaro, sav meli.
> *Vehag-Dhamar Vilamvit.*
> Tum vina kaiso rahgi to piyu.
> *Vagesri-Adatheka*-Mid-movement.
> Phooli vana ghana mor aay vasanti ri.
> *Vahar-Choutal-Drut* movement.
> Sambhu harapada yugadhyana vakhani natharanga.
> *Tilakkamod-Surfakta*-Mid-movement.
> Sankara Siva Pinaki Gangadhara.
> *Imankalyan-Surfakta*-mid movement.

These songs, along with notations, are printed in the book "*Sangeetmanjari*" published by Ramprasanna Bandyopadhyay, the eminent musician of Visnupur in 1314 (1907). So it can be unhesitatingly said that in 1309 (1896) Gurudev did not get the chance to have these songs from "*Sangeetmanjari*". He got these songs collected from generation to generation by the *Ostadi* families of Visnupur, from Radhikaprasad Goswami, the classmate of Ramprasanna and famous teacher of music.

Radhikaprasad was born in 1270 (1863). Jagatchand Goswami, his father, was an eminent *Mridanga* player. Of the four sons of Jagatchand, the first one, Krittivas, learnt how to play on a *Mridanga* from his father. The third and the fourth sons Radhika Goswami and Nakuleswar or Nakulchandra Goswami were experts in vocal and instrumental music. Before his death, Nakulchandra was appointed to the work of teaching music for sometime at Santiniketan. Radhika Babu started learning music in his boyhood and was a student of Anantalal Bandyopadhyay, the father of Ramprasanna, for 15 years. For the next ten years, he was engaged in the persuit and collection of music. At the age of 25, he came to Calcutta and was appointed to the post of a singer of the *Adi Brahma Samaj.* At that time, he came in contact with the members of the family of Gurudev. In 1303 (1896), Radhika Babu sang songs in a session of *Khamkheyali Sabha,* and Krittivas Goswami, his elder brother, played on the *Mridanga* as his accompanist. This is stated by Abanindranath Tagore, in his book "*Gharoa*". In 1304 (1897) he was appointed to the post of *Sangeetacharya* (Principal of Music) of the *Bharat Sangeet Samaj* founded by Jyotirindranath Tagore. He held this post upto *Falgoon* 1304 (March 1898). After the death of Maharshi Devendranath Tagore in 1311 (February 13, 1905), the Trustees of *Adi Brahma Samaj* formed the executive committee of the *Samaj.* Its *Acharya* and President was Dwijendranath Tagore and Secretary, Gurudev Rabindranath. Of the musicians, there were Radhikaprasad Goswami and Shyamsundar Misra. The percussionist also was Krishnadhan Bandyopadhyay. In 1323 (1816), at the invitation of Manindrachandra Nandy, the Maharaja of Kashimbazar, Radhika Babu was appointed to the post of Professor and Head of the musical institution there. He served this school for 18 years. He died in *Magh* 1331 (February 1825). Three years before his death, he was teacher in the *Durvar* of Bhupendranath Ghosh, the Zemindar of Calcutta.

Some informations on the life and work of Radhika Babu in relation to the Tagores of Jorasanko are to be found in Rathindranath Tagore's book, "*Pitrismriti*" where he writes :

> "In those days, songs and music continued all the time at our residence. In the *Vaithakkhana* (outer room), Dwipendranath (the father of Dinendranath) thronged the session with the *Ostad.* The renowned *Ostads* of those days would always come to sing in this sitting. Radhika Goswami was a regular singer of Dhrupad.
>
> "Learning about her (Amala Das) ability to sing, father sent her to Radhika Goswami to learn Hindi songs. She learnt *Ostadi* songs within a short period.
>
> "I suppose, father took the tunings of these songs from Radhika Babu.
>
> "*Maghotsav* was the biggest incident of the year at our residence. This function was held in a great pomp so long as Maharshi was alive. The arrangements for the ceremony, especially the rehearsal of songs would start from a month ago. Father had to compose new songs every year. When tunings were set on songs, father taught Radhika Babu or

> any other singer. Then Dwipudada would take up the responsibility of continuing rehearsals ... Father would not sing any song at the time he worshipped by sitting on the altar. He divided some songs to be sung in solo among elder sisters. Two or three songs were exclusively meant for Amala didi so long as she was there."

Rathindranath has written that Gurudev composed new songs every year for *Maghotsav.* This is correct. It is clearly understood from a study of the list of songs for worship in the evening in the *Maghotsav* of the *Brahma Samaj* in 1818 *Saka* (1303 B.E., 1897) that most of the songs of this time was sung in the *Maghostav* of 1303 (1897).

The Vedic Song
Srinvantu visve amritasya putrah aa je dhamani divyani tastuh
Brahmasangeet

1. Sunadara vahe ananda mandarila—*Imankalayan—Sur Faaktal.*
2. Seetal tava padachhaya—*Imankalyan-Ektala*
3. Aazi kon dhan hate—*Kedara-Chowtal*
4. Aar kata dure aachhe she—*Hamvir-Teora*
5. Aazi mama man chahe—*Vahar-Choutal*
6. Harashe jago aazi—*Hamvir-Dhamar*
7. E ki karuna, karunamoy—*Vahar-Adatheka*
8. Amaar satya mithya sakali—*Desh-Ektala*
9. Azi hridi Asane tomare kabi—*Vehag-Dhamar*
10. Ke jaay amritadhamayatri—*Vehag-Choutal*

At the time of composing Bengali songs by following Hindi ones, Gurudev would note the Hindi songs first in his exercise-book. Then he would tell the singer to go on singing again and again. Then observing the rhyme of words and method of pronunciation along with the tuning of the original song, he would go on writing the Bengali words in accordance with his own ideas. At the end of composition of words he would hand over that matter to the singer and tell him to sing that song by synchronizing it with the tuning and *tal* of the Hindi song. The Bengali songs are written in two ways in the exercise-book. There are some in which he wrote the Hindi songs first and, below these, he put the break-away songs. The songs of this group are :

1. Vaanguri mori moor geyni
2. Haras jago lal, lal
3. Sambhu harapada yugadhyana
4. Sankara siva pinaki

He wrote the words of the Bengali songs upon those of the Hindi songs. These songs are :

1. Phooli vana ghana mor aay vasant ri
2. Tum vina kaiso rahgi te piyu
3. Nayeere ma varana koyelin
4. Thakuria anchaya more chhadi de
5. Pyari tere pavana pakaro

The following are samples of how he wrote Bengali words upon Hindi ones :

Azi mama mana chahe jeevana vandhure
1. Phooli vana ghana mor aay vasanta ri
2. Azi hridi dasane tomare
Pyari tere pavana pakaro
Nishidin jagiya aachha natha he
3. Thankuria anchara moro chhadi de.

At page 70 along with the Hindi and break-away songs, there is a six-line song "Jaago re aazi jaago re tanher sathe" below the Hindi song "Tu kanha pare nayee ho". The Bengali song is totally scratched. The song is :

"Jaago re aazi jaago re tanhar sathe
Sei nitya jagrata premabhare ekaki ananda nirmala antare
Bhakti Yogasane
Nirnimesha premanetra jaagichhe jar nityakal nirvikar
Dike dike loke loke gagane gagane
Adho urdhe nityakal
Sarvajeevane deha prane nisvas prasvase jaagichhen nayane nayane sayane swapane."

There is no doubt that the song is a break-away one from the Hindi song. Although the Bengali song "Madhura rupe virazo he visvarup" at page 67 is a break-away one, the original Hindi song is not written. The Hindi song was "Kounorup vane ho."

Most of the Hindi songs that Gurudev collected from Radhikaprasad Goswami and wrote in his exercise-book were either collected or composed by the teachers of music of the previous era. In it, there were some personal collections of Radhika Goswami also. For this reason, most of the songs with notations are found in the book "*Sangeetmanjari*" published by Ramprasanna Bandyopadhyay, the classmate of Radhikaprasad, in *Vaisakh*, 1321 (May 1914). There are some songs which are to be found in "*Sangeetchandrika*" published by Gopeswar Bandyopadhyay before the year 1917. But variations in reading are seen between the same song collected by Gurudev from Radhika Goswami and printed in other books. From this it is clearly revealed that changes of words took place in the mouths of singers. Gurudev wrote the songs exactly as he had heard from the mouth of Radhikaprasad. Afterwards, when Ramprasanna Bandyopadhyay or Gopeswar Bandyopadhyay published the same song in their books, the influence of their pronunciations was seen. To clarify this point, the following few songs are quoted as samples from the exercise-book of Gurudev, the book on music and the journal on music as stated above :

1. **The Exercise-Book of Gurudev 1303 (1896)**

Vaanguri mori moor geyni zin chhunyo
E langrava karki kalayi dolan laag
Nidar daraye thani daaryeri
Sangkilu gayee sav, duramur mu sak gayee
Sarke pharke je ha.

"*Sangeetmanjari*" 1314 (1907).

(Mid-movement) *Imankalyan, Ektala.*

Asthayee

Vaanguri mori more gayee, jine chhunya langrava
Karke kalayeen dazan lagi nidar daraz thani nidar eri.

Antara

Sangke lagayee, sav durmur mushkaye gayeen,
Sarke faraki ha.

2. **Gurudev's Exercise-Book, 1303 (1896)**

Pyari tere pavana pakaron, sav meli
Kheliye ho fage
Vuria valma chiha brazame
Taruni kon birage.
Yatahi gurukul lajna borta
Savki badhta me, ke anuraga
Eki fagoona duze piharna
Tije kant sohaga

***Sangeetmanjari* 1314, (1907)**
(Vilamvit) Vehag, Dhamar.
Asthayee

Pyari tere payan pakar sav mili kheliye ho faag.

Antara

Vuria valma chinhen brazme, taruni kone biraag.

Sanchari

Yatahin gurukul lazan bolot, savki vadhat me ke anuraag.

Abhog

Ekhin fagoon duze brazvan tize kant sohag.

Of the Hindi songs in the exercise-book, there are a few songs of Jadubhatta, a scholar in music. The songs are also found in "*Sangeet-Manjari*" and "*Sangeetchandrika*".

1. **Gurudev's Exercise-Book 1303 (1896).**

Sambhu Siv Mahesh adi Trilochan
Bhavabhay Hara Bhavesh Dinanatha
Jatajuta Pinaka bhasma rundamala
Garala gale dhara Hara uda Baghambar.
Nachata chandrabhala bombom ghana baza
Ati apurva Hara gunagaoa Tripuresha
Vira chandra narapati prakash kara natha
Su adhara dhare samadhur tan sachi sundara.

***Sangeet Prakashika, Magh* 1303 (February, 1903)**
Chhayanat-Surfaktal

Sambhu Siva Mahesha adi Trilochana bhava-bhay-hara-Bhavesha
Dinanatha daanava-dalana Dineswara
Jatajuta Pinaki bhasma rundamala garala gare dhara hara Odhe baghamvara
Nachata chandrabhala bom bom ghene ghene baze ati apurva
Haraguna gaoyata Tripureswara
Virachandra narapati prakash kara nath su-adhare dhare
Sumadhur tan Sanchi sundar.

***Sangeetmanjari*, 1314 B.E. (1907)**
(Mid-movement) Chhayanat, Surfaaktal

Asthayee

Sambhu Hara Mahesha, adi Trilochan
Bhava bhava hara Bhavesha, Dinanath, Danavadalana Dinesha vara

Antara

Jatajuta Pinaki bhasmarundamala
Garala gare rava hara, uda baghamvara.

Sanchari

Nachata chandrabhala, bom bom vaze ghana ghana,
Ati apurva hariguna gavata Tripuresha.
Virachandra narapati prakasha karana, so adhara dhare
Sumadhura tan sachi sundara.

Gurudev's Exercise-Book, 1303 (1896)

Sambhu harapada jugadhyana vakhni natharanga
Teri kirtan dinayna, gaaota janasamaja
Joy Tripuranath dayal Virachandra
Gunijana pratipalaka data.

***Sangeetmanjari* (1314 (1907)**
(Mid-movement) Tilak kamod, Surfaaktal

Asthayee

Sambhu harapada juga dhyani, vakhani nath ranga
Teri kirtan dinrayna, gavata janasamaja

Antara

Jayati Tripuranath dayalvirachandra gunigan pratipalak
Tu saman data kahi nahi ho raj.

Those two are the invocations by Jadubhatta to Virchandra Manikya, the king of Tripura, and for this, the name of Maharaja Virchandra has got its place in it. Jadubhatta composed these two songs while he was appointed as one of the courtsingers of the *Rajdurvar* (Royal court) of Tripura. Being pleased with the qualities of Jadubhatta, Maharaj Virchandra adorned him with the title "Tanraj".

We know that in 1875 Jadubhatta was appointed as a singer in the residence of Maharshi Devendranath Tagore and of the *Adi Brahma Samaj.* At that time Jyotirindranath Tagore founded a free institution of Music for pupils at the house of the *Adi Brahma Samaj.*

Jadubhatta imparted instructions on vocal and instrumental music there from 7-30 p.m. to 10 p.m. on all days except Sundays and

Wednesdays. But he could not continue the work for a long time. He went to Agartala as a singer of the Royal Court of Tripura. Maharaj Virchandra was then the king of Tripura. He resigned from 1862 to 1896. A few days before 1885, Jadubhatta left Agartala and being ill, returned to Visnupur. He died there at the age of 45. Jadubhatta received the title "Ranganath" from the king of Panchakot of the district of Bankura. As he had a great attraction for this title, he often used the two words "Ranganath" or "Nathranga" as a *bhanita* exposer of his songs. He has retained both these two exposers in the songs stated above.

Gurudev composed "Madhura rupe viraja he Visvaraj" by breaking away another song of Jadubhatta. It is a song of two *Kali-s* (stanzas) The original Hindi song is not written in the exercise-book. But the song is available in the book "*Sangeetmanjari*" as a song of four *Kali-s* (stanzas) in total.

The song of Gurudev as written in the exercise book :

Madhura rupe viraja he visvaraj
Shovan sabha nirakhi manaprana bhule
Nirava nishi sundar vimal nilamvar
Suchiruchir chandrakala charan mule.

The original Hindi song as printed in *Sangeetmanjari* 1314 (1907).

(Madhya-gati) Tilak-kamod, Jhaanptal

Asthayee

Kavana rupa vani ho rajadhiraj
Azu nai nirakhi ranganatha gaave.

Antara

Tyaji aguruchandana, bibhuti anga bhukhana,
Jata mukuta kaisi vani aave.

The Second Antara

Kaisi mukhamandala, jhalasa sruti kundala,
Bhai chandrabhate mrigachhala paave.

The third Antara

Varazivara amvara, pahana vaghamvara
Shishapura gangadhara dharasi dhave.

The two Hindi songs of the *ragini*-s *Bhairavi* and *Lalit* with an exposer of Tansen have been found in the exercise-book. In taking up the work of translating the song of the *Bhairavi ragini* into Bengali, Gurudev only wrote the line "Ananda ushakale mangala rabi" on his first line. There is nothing upon the rest of the lines. With the help of the book "*Triveni Sangam*" by revered Indira Devi, it is being known that it is a *Dhrupad* song of *Surfaaktal* and by breaking this, Gurudev composed the song "Ananda tumi swami mangala tumi". We can assume the line "Ananda ushakale mangala rabi" as the initial form of that song. The song "Ananda tumi swami mangala tumi" is found in the group of songs of the year 1309 (1902). The Hindi song composed is by Tansen and available in the exercise-book :

Bhairavi

Omkara mahadeva sankara tuma
Sakala kala purana karata aasha.
Nih chahi dharata dhyana, sumarana kara mana,
Dekhata darshana gayee prasha
Hara dukha dwandwa, shohata jata ganga
Rundamala para shoha vaghamvara vasa,
Tansen sevaka bhavata mama inchha
Phala puve hoyaka, lasa nivasa,

This song is not yet available in the well-known books of the *Ostad-s* of Vishnupur. It seems that only Radhikaprasad knew the song.

Gurudev composed the song "Pantha ekhan kena alasita anga" by breaking the second song of *lalit ragini.* The original song is printed with notations in the first volume of *Sangeet-Chandrika* published by Gopeswar Bandyopadhyay before the year 1917. The Hindi song with exposure of Tansen and with Gurudev's hand-writing was the following :

Lalit

Range jugata so gaye vajaye
Tala mana sura sangata aaye
Duguna triguna chouguna so bheda vajaye
Sav loga data pramana so aave
Apana mukhta guni kaha ve
Tala mana sura gera na pave
Tana Sena kaho ve guniyana
Chhatrapati Akavara saye vujhaye

***Sangeetchandrika* : Volume I**

Lalit-Surfaaktal

Asthayee	—	Ranga dhugata son gave vazave Tala mana sura sangata aave
Antara	—	Dwiguna triguna chouguna so bheda vatave, Jav laag dat praman dekhave.
Sanchari	—	Apna mukh ten guni kahave Tala mana ke vevara pave.
Abhog	—	Tan Sen kahe hoye guniyana Chhatrapati Akavara ko rijhave.

In most of the songs in the exercise-book of Gurudev, the names or "exposure" of the composers are not available. There are many songs of this type in *Sangeet-Manjari* and *Sangeet-Chandrika* also. We do not know its reasons.

From the exercise-book, it is known that Gurudev composed many songs of the criteria of love and a few ones of those of seasons of during the period from the last week of *Bhadra* (September) to the middle date of *Aswin* (October) of 1304 (1897) at Patisar. The date and venue of composition of most of these songs are referred below. Towards the end of the list, we get some songs of the criterion *Pooja* (worship). These few songs are break-away ones from Hindi. But, like other songs, there is no reference to time and place of composition. Though there is no such reference, it has been possible to find out, in general, the time of these songs through other informations.

The list of songs of 1304 (1897)

1. Kena dhare rakha o je jave chale.
2. Vritha geyechhi vahu gaan. (*Misrakanada,* 28 *Bhadra,* 1304)
3. Kena vazao kankana kanakana.
4. Heri navina shyamala ghana—(6 *Aswin, Ichhamati,* Storm & rain).
5. Ebar chalinu tave (6 *Aswin* 1304 *Ichhamati*).
6. Jamini na jete jagale na (7 *Aswin* 1304 The river *Yamuna*).
7. (Bandhu) Kiser tare asru jhare (7 *Aswin* 1304, The river *Varala*).
8. Ami kebali swapana karechhi. (*Vehag, Jhaaptal,* 8 *Aswin* 1304 *Valeswari*).
9. Bhalobeshe sakhi komala jatane. (8 *Aswin,* 1304*).* Sahajadpur).
10. Tumi sandhyar meghamala (*Imankalyan,* 9 *Aswin* 1304, *Chalanvil,* Rain and storm).
11. Jadi varana kara tave (*Chhayanat* 9 *Aswin* 1304, *Chalanbil*) (Storm taking place twice or thrice in a day. The boat tilting).
12. Ami chahite esechhi (*Kalangda,* 10 *Aswin.* The river *Nagar*)
13. Sakhi pratidin haay (*Aleya,* 10 *Aswin,* The river Nagar) (Cloud and rain, Saturday, *Amabasya)*
14. Vidhi dagar aankhi jadi (*Bhairavi, Jhaaptal,* 10 *Aswin.* The river *Nagar*). (Inside the paddy field).
15. Badhu michhe raag korona (*Vaaroan, Multan,* 10 *Aswin,* Patisar)
16. Ogo kangal aamare (12 *Aswin,* Patisar)
17. Eki satya, sakali satya (13 *Aswin,* on the railway).

Songs without dates :

1. Nitya satye chintan kora re
2. Ke balile aazi
3. Uthi chala sudin aila
4. Laha laha tuli laha he.

From this list it is clearly understood that Gurudev had composed 15 songs out of his own inspiration in this year also like *Aswin* 1302. At that time Amala Devi came and lived at Shelaidah. She encouraged Gurudev in composing new songs by singing and hearing how to sing.

No specific information on whether she was at Shelaidah with her sons, daughters and other members of her family this time is being available. But some hints are available from a statement by Rathindranath Tagore in his book "*Pitrismriti*" in this matter.

Rathindranath states :

> "When father was rapt in music amidst intervals in his writings, he brought Amala Didi from Calcutta. By day she was busy in working with mother ... ... Whe evening came, everyone assembled to hear songs, leaving all other jobs. The boatmen took the jollyboat by attaching it with the *Bazra.* I hurried in having my meal and sat on that boat after crossing over the window. Surendada was ready with *Esraz* in his hands. The jollyboat was unfastened, taken to the mid-stream and was anchored there. Then singing started. Father and Amala Didi would go on singing one after the other by turns ...... Those nights seem like dreams now. But even today when I hear songs like—
>
> Bela gelo tomar path cheye ......
> Tumi sandyar meghamala, tumi amar sadher sandhana
>
> I remember those nights ......"

The second song was composed at the locality of *Chalanbil* of *Zemindari* in *Aswin* 1304 (October 1897). The first song is a pretty old one of a few years. From the description and the song as stated above it can be said that in *Aswin* 1304 Mrinalini Devi, Amala Devi, Surendranath Tagore and Gurudev's sons and daughters—every one was with Gurudev at Patisar. Probably, it was Amala Devi's very presence that encouraged Gurudev this time also to compose songs.

"Vritha geyechhi vahu gaan"—a song that Gurudev started writing as follows and then scaratched it, is :

Virtha geyechhi vahu gaan
Kotha sanpechhi mana pran
Haila diva avasaan.
Nirava nisha dhire dhire
Andhare dash dik ghire,
Mahasagar valutire
Dhu dhu kariche e shmashan.

He wrote the song upto this, scratched it and wrote in the next page by correcting it as follows :

(Misra Kanada)

Geyechhi vritha vahu gaan.
Sanpechhi kotha mana pran!
Tumi ta ghume nimagan
Ami jagia anukhan,
Alase tumi achetan
Amare dahe apaman.
Jatri save tari khule
Gela sudur upakule
Mahasagar tatamule
Dhu dhu karichhe e shmashan!
Kahar pane chaha kavi
Ekaki vasi mlan chhabi
Astachale gela ravi
Haila diva avasan.

Gurudev composed 'Kena vaajao kaankana kata chhala bhare' towards the beginning of the month of *Aswin.* We come across a very important statement in connection with this song. Gurudev writes :

> "In my early age, I have endeavoured to express the ideas of my mind through songs. I hope I have come over this afterwards. The songs of mature age are not meant for expressing ideas but for giving forms. The allied poetry is also an expotent of form. Whatever is being expressed in 'Kena vaajaao kaankana kana-kana kata chhala bhari' is the play of forms of imagination."

To elucidate this play of form which is necessary, Gurudev writes elsewhere :

> "Most ideas are old to us. And the characteristics of our mind are that as we have not the ability to feel the complete beauty and *rasa* of old accustomed things, so when a poet attracts our mind through incorporation of new language, rhythm and a new approach to speaking in old ideas, then

we can appreciate the original *rasa* of the thing anew. Then the expression eternally heard rings in the ears and the mind in new music. A principal work of the poet is to retain the world always lively. The greenness of trees, the blue of the sky, the golden colour in the evening—all these would have become ematiated by now through dust if the poet would not go on throwing imagination upon it all the time. As the mind of man is ripened quickly through heat of thoughts, the function of the poet through poetry is to drench the mind with the nectar of imagination and to keep it lively and fresh endlessly. He does not give anything new. He only tries to keep the mind anew."

The initial form of the songs is :

Kena vaazaao kaankana kanakana kata chhala bhare,
Ogo ghare phire chala kanaka kalashe jala bhare,
Kena jale dheu tuli chhalaki chhalaki (Kara khela chhala chhalare)
Kena-chaha khane khane twarita nayane kar tare kata chhala bhare.
Hera yamuna velaay aalase helaay gela vela
Jata hasi bhara dheu kare kanakani kalasware.
Hera nadi-parapaare gagana kinare meghamela,
Chahe hasia hasia gopane tomari mukha pare kata chhala bhare.

The two expressions 'Kara khela' and 'Chhala chhala' as above are both scratched. But during publication of the next book, the expression 'Kara khela' has been retained. The line 'Heri navin shyamala ghana nil gagane' has been corrected and written in the book as 'Heria shyamala ghana nil gagane'. The song as written in the exercise-book is :

Heri navin shyamala ghana nil gagane,
Sei sajala kajala aankhi padilo mane.
Sei adhara karuna makha minati vedana aanka
Nirave chahiya thaka viday-khane;
Heri navin shyamala ghane nil gagane.
Azi jhara jhara jhare jal vijuli hane

Vane pavana matia othe pagala gaane.
Mama gaopana paranapute konkhane vyatha fute
Kar kotha veje othe hridaya kone!
Hari navin shyamala ghana nil gagane.

The first line of the song was written as follows :

"Heri saghana meghamala gagana kone,"
"Heri saghana niradamala gagana kone!"

Later on he scratched both.

The song "Bandhu kiser tare asru jhare" composed in *Vibhash* and ***Ektala*** is in the exercise-book as a song of six *Kali-s* (lines), but in the next book of music it is printed in sixteen *Kali-s*. The rest ten *Kali-s* are added at the time of publication of the book of poems *"Kalpana"*. The unity of ideas between this song and the one "(Ogo) Bhagyadevi pitamahi mitla tava ash" composed in 1303 (1896) is worth notice. It is not known to anyone today in which tuning the song was sung. The song as written in the exercise-book is :

(Bandhu) Kisertareasru jhare kiser ashe dirghaswash!
Hasyamukhe adristere karva mora parihas.
Riktarakta sarvahara
Visve sarvajayee tara,
Bhagyalaksmi garvamayeer nayko tara kritadas!
Amra sukher sfita vuker chhayar tale nahi chari
Amra dukher vakramukher chakra dekhe bhay na kari
Bhanga dhake jathasadhya
Bajiye jabe joyvadya
Chhinna aashar dhwaja tule bhinna karva nilakash!
He alakshmi rukshakeshi tumi devi achanchala
Saral tomar ritiniti nahi jana chhalakala
Amra varaputra taba
Jaha dive tahai laba,
Diba tomar dhanyadhwani mathay vahi sarvanash.

Of the above mentioned list, the reasons for composition of the song 'Sakhi pratidin haay' numbering 10 as stated by Indira Devi in her memoirs may be referred :

> "As I have been born as a Bengalee girl and as I have crossed twenty far ahead as the terminal point of being old in a comparatively modern era and have achieved half-foreign liberation for women long days ago, so to keep to historical truth I cannot but confess that I had no want of a partner of life before my marriage. The most 'thrilling' previous groom was a totally unknown man who had been standing for many days on the other side of our gate, beneath a tree in the field to have a look at me. Later on, I came to know his name and I have heard that his sister came to propose on behalf of him, but it is needless to say that none of us approved this proposal. Rabikaka composed the song "Sakhi pratidin haay ese fire jaay" on this state of affairs."

The rest of the songs of this criterion has in each more or less variations of reading, but I do not think this to be elaborately analysed. Four out of the five songs without dates that we get after the song "Eki satya sakali satya" composed during the railway journey on *Aswin* 13 are Hindi break-away songs of the criterion of *'Pooja'* (worship) and the fifth one is that of *'Swadesh'* (own country). The first one is 'Nitya satyachintana karo he vimala hridaye'. Maharaja Anand Kishore, the music lover Zamindar of Bihar, composed the original Hindi song. The song is to be found in the second volume of *Sangeet-Chandrika* by Gopeswar Bandyopadhyay. Gurudev wrote the Hindi song first in the pages of his exercise-book and then wrote the Bengali equivalent of each word upon each line of the song. The first line of the Hindi song as written in the exercise-book is 'Kali nam chintan karore mere mon'. He composed "Ke basile aazi hridayasane bhuvaneswara prabhu" by breaking away the Punjabi *tappa* of Sharimia. The song is very much known to the audience of this era. The Punjabi *tappa* is included in the *Falgoon* 1334 (March, 1929) issue of *Sangeet-Vijnan Patrika*. The first line of the song is : "Ve pari jan tande tande par". The song is not included in the exercise-book. The first line of the third break-away song is : "Uthi chala sudin aila ananda sougandha uchchhasila". He has written the whole song below the Hindi one without writing the words of the song upon those of the Hindi song. The Hindi song as written in the exercise-book is :

> "Uthi chal sudinnachatari ali
> Hun aayi to Helen.

Lalan teri aarati karti tua
Sundar natangar nari."

The song is printed with its notation in *Sangeet-Prakashika : Asadh,* 1312 (July, 1905). Some changes in words of the song as published in the journal have taken place—

"Uthi chal sudhi nachata ri ali hu
Aito Helen.
Lalan teri aarati karata tua
Sundar natanagar,
Sudhi nachaturi Ali hu
Aito Helen."

This sons as printed in *Sangeet-Manjari* published by Ramprasanna Bandyopadhyay, the teacher of music of Vishnupur, in 1314 (1907) with notations at page 304 is :

(Mid-movement) *Kedara, Surfaaktal*

Asthayee

Uti chale sudin nachatare ali hu
Ayin to Heline.

Antara

Lalan teri aarati karti tua
Sundara nata nagar nari sudin nachata re
Ali hu
Aayin to Heline.

The fourth song of the exercise-book :

"Laha laha tuli laha he bhumital hate
Dhulimlan e paran, rakha tare kripachokhe
Rakha tare sneha karatale
Rakha tare aloke, rakho tare amrite
Rakha tare niyata kalyane."

This is also a Hindi break-away song but the original song is not there in the exercise-book. After a minor change, this song is being sung in the *Maghotsav* of 1304 (1897) :

(Ragini-Adana Tal-Kaoali)

"Laha laha tuli laha he bhumital hate dhulimlan e paran,
Rakha taba kripachokhe, rakha taba sneha karatale,
Rakha tare aloke, rakha tare amrite,
Rakha tare niyata kalyane, rakha tare kripa chokhe,
Rakha tare sneha karatale."

From a study of the list of songs for evening prayer in *Maghotsava* of the *Tatvavodhini Patrika* of 1819 *Saka* (1304 B.E., 1897) Gurudev composed all these break-away songs as above by thinking over this prayer.

The songs for the *Maghotsava* of 1304 (1898) :

1. Uthi chala sudin aila—*Kedara, Ektala.*
2. Eso he eso varenya sumahan—*Misrasurat, Surfaaktal.*
3. Bhaktahridvikasha praanavimochana—*Chhayanat, Surfaaktal.*
4. Ke vasile aazi—*Sindhu, Adatheka.*
5. Sudhasagar tire he—*Sahana, Dhamar.*
6. Nitya satya chintan kara re—*Adana, Jhaanptal.*
7. Laha laha tuli laha he—*Adana, Kaoali.*
8. Vahe nirantar antanta anada—*Lachchhasar, Jhaanptal.*

The second song in the list is not written by Gurudev. The song "Sudha sagar tire he" is not in the exercise-book. This is also a Hindi break-away song. The original song is in the book *Sangeet-Manjari.* Its first line is : "Ayo fagoon barho maan, wanda ko chhayla dole gokul ki dagar". The fourth song "Ke vasile aazi hridayasane" was made to sing by Amala Das in the prayer. Radhika Goswami taught her.

"Ke aase chale jaay" is the last song of the year 1304 (1897) as found in the exercise-book. It has no date in it, but in the *"Tatvavodhini Patrika" Falgoon* 1304 (March 1898) the song is first published with notations. In the first *kali* of the song as found in the exercise-book of Gurudev, there is the following :

"Ke ese jaay fire
Akula nayaner nire"

The lines of the fourth *Kali*

"Punya kutire visanna
Ke bale saajaaiya anna
Sneher upahar
Ruche na mukhe aar,"

A slight change in these two *Kali-s* is noticed in the journal *Vinavadini.* The first kali :

"Ke ese jaay phire phire, akula nayana-nire".

The fourth *Kali :*

"Punya kutire visanna, ke basi sajaiya anna
Se sneha-upahar ruche na mukhe aar"

Changes of words in these take place once more in the collection of poems : volume "Songs" :

The first *kali* :

"Ke ese jaay phire phire akula nayaner nire ?"

The fourth *kali :*

"Virala kutire visanna ke base sajaiya anna ?"

"Tari amar hathat dube jaay/ kon khane re kon pasaner gaay" follows after the above in the exercise-book. This song was composed for the novel *"Chirakumar Sabha"* of 1307 (1900). Bepin of the novel is singing the song before "Rasik". The following translation of a Sanskrit *Sloka* has also been found in this exercise-book :

"Kunjakutirer snighda alinder par
Kalindi kamalgandha bahibe sundar,
Mudita nayaka lina taba ankatale,
Basanti subas uthe elana kuntale;
Tahar kariba seva, se din ki habe,
Kisalay pakhakhani dolaiba jabe?"

After minor corrections, the *sloka* is printed in the novel as :

"Kunjakutirer snighda alinder par
Kalindi kamalgandha chhutibe sundar;
Lina rabe madirakshi taba ankatale,
Bahibe basantibas vyakul kuntale
Tahare kariba seva kabe habe haay
Kisalay pakhakhani dalaibo gaay ?"

Just after the Bengali translation, three sanskrit *slokas* have been found in the exercise-book :

1. "Nivistah palyanke mridulatara tulidhavalite
Anandang purnendu pratimmupadhanang pramudito
nidhyayagre"
2. "Vahanti sindurang pravala kavari bhara timira
Dwisang vrindairvandi kritamiva navinarka kiranang
Tanatu kshemang na stava vadana soundarya lahari
Parivaha srotah saraniriva simanta saranih."
3. "Smitajyotsnajalang tava vadana chandrasya pivatang
Chakoranag asidati ramataya chanchujarima."

Probably, Gurudev collected these *slokas* for *"Chirakumar Sabha"* of 1307 (1900), but he did not utilize these.

Just after the song "Tari amar hathat dube jaay" the following is written :

"Duiti hridaye ekti asan
Patia basa he hridayanatha."

In *Baisakh* 1307, (April, 1900), this song has been printed and published in *"Kalpana"* in the name *'Vivahamangal'*. This song has been said to be of the year 1304 (1897) in the Visva-Bharati edition of

Rabindra-Rachanavali and in the birth centenary edition of the Government of West Bengal. But there is no information on the composition of the song related to the occasion of the marriage of the person concerned. As this song is just after the song of *"Chirakumar Sabha"* and as the marriage ceremony of Kritindranath Tagore, Gurudev's own brother's son, in the month of *Asadh* (July) is scheduled, the song might also be of the year 1307 (1900). Besides these, from the book *"Gaaner Vahi"* by revered Indira Devi in 1299 as preserved in the Rabindra Sadan, it is seen that the song *Vivaha-mangal* of *Kalpana* is not there in the songs written by Gurudev from 1300-1304 (1893-1897) in a separate paper in his own hand. The sense of doubt still creeps until sufficient informations with regard to the composer and the time of composition of this song are available.

As I have referred to earlier, of the Hindi break-away Bengali songs till now available, there is not a single one in which the date of composition is given. But it is seen that almost all these songs written nearer the pages of other songs with dates have been inserted in the list of songs of prayer of the *Maghotsav* of the same year. The composition of songs for *Maghotsav* and activities in connexion with its preparation would start from nearly a month ago. Every year Gurudev would compose Bengali songs by breaking away Hindi ones in need of the function and, on the day of function, the *Ostad-s* of Hindi songs would sing most of these songs. The main singer of this group was Radhika Goswami. That Gurudev deeply respected him as a learned musician is known from his own written statement :

> "Radhika Goswami had not only collection of songs and knowledge of the forms of *raga-ragini-s* but he could also instil a special *rasa* into the song. That was more than mastery."

In this era, Radhika Goswami was the principal assistant to Gurudev in the composition of Hindi break-away Bengali songs.

From 1305 to 1308 (1898-1901), besides the above two songs "Tari amar hathat" and "Duity hridaye ekti asan", there is no other song in Gurudev's exercise-book. For this reason, it is not possible to assert, by going through this exercise-book, how many Hindi break-away Bengali songs Gurudev composed with the assistance of Radhikababu during these four years. But he composed a pretty few songs and a list is also available from the programme of activities of songs for *Maghotsav* from 1305-1308. Gurudev composed the Bengali songs of the patterns of Hindi *Dhrupad, Dhamar, Kheyal* and *Tappa* sung in *Maghotsav* by breaking-away Hindi songs received from Radhikababu. The trend of composing songs of this type through joint endeavour remained uninterrupted upto 1311 (1904).

The list of songs for *Maghotsav* as published in the *"Tatvabodhini Patrika"* from 1305 (1898) :

1820 *Saka* / 1305 B.E. (1898)

Songs for morning prayer :

1. Vimal anande jaga re—*Bahaduri Todi, Dhima Tetala.*
2. Pipasa hay nahi mitila—*Bhairabi, Kaoali.*
3. Tumi Kachhe nai bale—*Kirtan.*
4. Nayana tomare paayna dekhite—*Kirtan.*

"In the evening, Srijukta Babu Rabindranath Tagore *Mahasay* sang Vedic songs in a sweet voice."

Songs of the evening prayer :

1. Taba raj-singhasan birajita,—*Imankalyan, Choutal.*
2. Din phurala he sangsari,—*Bhimpalasri, Adatheka.*
3. Madhura rupe viraja he,—*Tilakkamod, Jhaanptal.*
4. Chirasakha chhedona,—*Vehag, Kaoli.*
5. Majhe majhe taba dekha paai,—*Kirtan.*
6. Ohe jeebanaballabha.—*Kirtan.*

The first two of the list of songs for the morning are break-away songs. The first song was a record of the His Master's Voice and was sung by Radhikaprasad Goswami. The first song of the list of the function in the evening was not of Gurudev. The next three are break-away songs. The song "Madhura rupe" was first broken away in 1303 (1896). It is in the exercise-book. In the *Maghotsav* of this year, Radhikababu made Amala Devi sing the song "Chirasakha chhedona". The song "Ohe jeevana ballabha" of the tuning of *Kirtan* was composed on 8 *Baisakh,* 1301 (21 April, 1894). Sri Prabhatkumar Mukhopadhyay says that Gurudev composed this *kirtan* in memory of the death of Kadamvari Devi (8 *Baisakh,* 1291, 21 April 1884).

1821 *Saka,* 1306 B.E. (1899)

Songs for the morning :

1. Tomari name nayan melinu—*Ashabhairon, Teoda.*
2. Azi shubha subhra prate—*Deogandhar, Choutal.*
3. Raksha karo he—*Choutal.*
4. Sada thako anande—*Khat, Jhaanptal.*
5. Jani he jave prabhat habe—*Bhairavi, Jhaanptal.*
6. (Azi) pranami tomare—*Vibhas, Ektala.*

Songs for the evening prayer :

1. Mahavisve mahakase—*Imankalyan, Teoda.*
2. Diner vichaar karo—*Puravi, Ektala.*
3. Tomari gehe palichha snehe—*Khambaz, Ektala.*
4. Hridi mandir dware—*Kedar, Dhamar.*
5. Azi e bharat lazzita he—*Bhupali, Kaoali.*
6. Tomari sevak karo he—*Chhayanat, Choutal.*
7. Sukhahin nishidin—*Gourmallar, Kaoali.*
8. Din jaay re din jaay—*Piloo, Madhyaman.*
9. Prabhu khelechhi anek—*Desh, Ektala.*
10. Ke janita tumi daakibe—*Kirtan.*
11. Vani taba dhaay ananta—*Adara, Choutal.*
12. Kemane rakhibi tora—*Sindhuda, Jhaanptal.*
13. Bhuvan haite bhuvanbasi—*Vadhhanssarang, Ektala.*
14. Bhay hate taba abhay—*Vehag, Choutal.*
15. Ichchha habe jabe—*Kalangda, Thungri.*
16. Premanande rakha purna—*Sindhu, Ektala.*
17. Ami sangsare mon—*Kirtan.*

The Song "Diner vichar karo" (Number 2) is not Gurudev's.

1822 *Saka,* 1307 B.E. (1900)

Songs for the evening prayer :

1. Hridayashashi hridi-gagane—*Imankalyan, Teoda.*
2. Pratidin taba gaathaa—*Jilfbaroan, Surfaaktal.*
3. Tomari ragini Jeevan—*Iman, Teoda.*
4. Mahanande hero go tare—*Tilakkamod, Teoda.*

5. Sakha he mama hridaye—*Chhayanat, Ektala.*
6. Pratidin ami he—*Kaafi, Jhaanptal.*

1823 *Saka,* 1308 B.E. (1901)

Songs for the morning prayer :

1. More daaki laye jaao—*Ramkeli, Teoda.*
2. Bal daao more bal daao—*Bhairavi, Ektala.*

Songs for the evening prayer :

1. Mora satyer pare mon—*Bhupnarayan, Ektala.*
2. Amar vichar tumi karo—*Kedara, Teoda.*
3. Safal karo he prabhu—*Mallar, Kaoali.*
4. Ami ki bale karibo—*Sindhubaroan, Jhaanptal.*
5. Daka more aazi e—*Paraj, Kaoali.*
6. Ami jenesune tabu—*Kirtan.*

"The Vedic song that was sung on the prayer at night on 11 *Magh* was : Tamisvaranang paramang mahesvarang."

The first song for the evening prayer of *Maghotsav* 1308 (1901) was composed and sung at Santiniketan on 7 *Pous* (22 December), some-time after the foundation day of the Brahmacharya Vidyalaya.

From a study of the list of songs for *Maghotsav* from 1303 (1896) till now, we will see that Gurudev used the *ragini-s* of the morning at the time of composing songs for the morning prayer. For example : *Bahduritodi, Bhairavi, Ashabhairon, Deogandhar, Asoari, Khat, Vibhas,* and *Ramkeli.*

The *ragini-s* of the evening and night are in the songs for prayer in the evening and at night :

> *Sankarabharan, Jhinjhit, Imankalyan, Kedar, Hamvir, Vahar, Desh, Vehag, Misrasurat, Chhayanat, Sindhu, Sahana, Adana, Alachchhasar, Bhimpalasri, Tilakkamod, Puravi, Khambaz, Bhupali, Gourmallar, Piloo, Sindhuda, Vadhhanssarang, Jilfbaroan.*

As an exception, only one song of *Kalanda ragini* and *Thumri tal* in the evening prayer of 1306 (1899) is available.

In Hindi songs, a system of singing *raga-ragini-s* by dividing the day and the night into different *prahar-s* (group/cluster of hours) has been going on for a long time. Gurudev, also, did not ignore this principle in case of his songs. Considering the songs for the morning and the evening prayers, he has been carrying out this principle with sincerity from the era of the beginning of composition of songs of the criterion of *pooja* (worship).

The "Trital" is nowhere in the songs of *Maghotsav* in which Gurudev applied a few *tal*-s. The reason is : the *tal* which we now use as *trital* in the *Kheyal* songs of *Madhya-lay* was known as *Kaoali* through its rhyme in Bengal in the nineteenth century. For this very reason, the name *Kaoali* has been retained instead of Trital in Gurudev's *Kheyal* break-away Bengali songs of *Madhya lay.*

The following are the seven songs of the tuning of *Kirtan* that we find in the above-mentioned list of songs for *Maghotsav :*

1. Tumi kaachhe nai bale hera sakha tai.
2. Nayana tomare paay na dekhite.
3. Majhe majhe taba dekha paai.
4. Ohe jeevan ballabha.
5. Ke janita tumi daakibe.
6. Ami sangsare mon diechhinu.
7. Ami jenesune tabu bhule thaki.

Although there are variations in tuning in those songs, these are composed in the rhyme of *Ektala,* but the remarkable fact is that Gurudev added letters in each of these and made these sing in the *Maghotsav.* We are first introduced with this type of endeavour in the song "Eso eso phire eso, badhu he phire eso" of the story *"Megh o Roudra"* in 1301 (1894). We have already discussed how he extended the words of the song by adding letters in the pattern of how to sing. Prior to that, he did not compose a single *Kirtan* with letters added. Four years after the song "Eso eso phire eso", that is, in the year 1305 (1898), he was seen to be involved in composing this type of song once again with renewed vigour. In all, there were four *Kirtan* songs this year, in 1306 (1899) two, and in 1308 (1901) one. Afterwards, he never composed this type of *Kirtan* songs.

The song "Nayana tomare paay na dekhite" as included in the above-mentioned list, was sung in the *Maghotsav* of 1293 (1887). The song "Ohe jeevana ballabha" was composed on 8 *Baisakh* 1301 (21 April 1894) and two songs "Ami jenesune tabu bhule thaki" and "Majhe majhe taba dekha paai" were first composed in 1291 B.E.,

1806 *Saka* (1884). At the time of their first composition, there were no *aakhar*-s. These were made to sing by inserting *aakhar-s* first in this era.

Perhaps the reason for Gurudev's enthusiam in composing *Kirtan* songs with *aakhar-s* in this era was the participating *Kirtanwallas* in the ceremony of the auspicious day of zamindari at Shelaidah. That Gurudev listened to their songs is revealed in his letter written to Mrinalini Devi in 1301 (1884). He wrote to her about the ceremony :

> "The auspicious day was celebrated yesterday with an aroma of songs and music and prayer etc. In the evening a group of *Kirtanwallas* came in the Kachhari (Zemindari Office). I heard their *Kirtan-s* upto 11 p.m."

From the above it is clear that he would listen to *Kirtan* songs patiently.

From a news of the prayer on 13 *Magh* 1306 (28 January, 1900) we also come to know that Gurudev sang his own songs of the tuning of *Kirtan* in functions at Jorasanko. In the *Tatvavodhini Patrika* the following is relevant :

> "After prayer, Srijukta Rabindrababu started his newly composed pleasant *Kirtan :* 'Ami sukh bale dukh cheyechhinu, tumi dukh bale sukh diyechha (Sangsare mon diyechhinu). A few singers of the *Adi Brahma Samaj* participated in this *Kritan* and *Mridanga Karatal* (percussion instruments) began to follow. The revered Srijukta Babu Hitendranath Tagore played on the harmonium and made the beauty of music and *Kirtan* more pleasant."

From this, it is supposed that Gurudev's songs of the *Kirtan* type were sung in the ceremonies of the house by adding *Dohar, Khol,* and *Karatal* like the *Kirtanvallas.*

In Santiniketan, the Brahmacharya Vidyalaya was established on 7 *Pous* 1308 (22 December, 1901). In 1309 (1902) Gurudev escorted Mrinalini Devi there after the summer vacation. Mrinlini Devi was seen as the mother of the Ashram family beside Gurudev. But she became ill just after her arrival here. She was escorted to Calcutta in the month of *Bhadra* (September) for treatment. But it was futile. She passed away on 7 *Agrahayan* (22 November). Towards the end of the month, Gurudev came back to the Vidyalaya with his sons and daughters. He has left an account of how he had borne the pains of the death of Mrinalini Devi in the poems of his poetic creation *"Smaran"*. Most of these poems were first written by him in this exercise-book under our discussion. The date of composition is written after each of these poems. How deeply the mind of Gurudev was grief-stricken, with the pains of Mrinalini Devi's death, from 29 *Agrahayan* to 1 *Magh* can be understood from these poems. This is also evident from his letter written on 18 *Agrahayan* to Dineshchandra Sen :

"Dear Sir,

If the bereavement that God has prized me with becomes meaningless what a mess like this can happen! I accepted this with my head bowed down. She who, by her own life, kept me continually helpful, would also make the rest of my life successful by death also. Her auspicious memory would always be my guide to my all good deeds and strengthen me".

Even in this mental condition, Gurudev had to go to Calcutta in need of the imminent *Maghotsav* from Santiniketan. As the responsibility for composing songs suited to this ceremony was principally entrusted to him, he composed many songs anew for the prayer in the morning and in the evening of *Maghotsav* this time also. But in the songs of this time are expressed a grave appeal to pacify the restless mind out of the deep pains of death. He has tried to cross over the deep darkness of sorrow that has plunged into his mind.

The list of songs for *Maghotsav* 1824 *Saka,* 1309 B.E. (1902).

Songs for the morning prayer :

1. Pantha kena alasita anga—*Lalit, Surfaakta.*
2. Swapan jadi bhangile rajani prabhate—*Ramkeli, Ektala.*
3. Monomohan gahan jamini seshe—*Ashavari, Jhaanptal.*
4. Achhe dukkha, aachhe mrityu—*Vibhas, Ektal.*
5. Dukkha rate he nath ke dakile—*Sarfarda, Ada.*
6. Ananda tumi swami mangala tumi—*Bhairavi, Surfaakta.*
7. Sangsar jabe mon kede lay—*Bhairavi, Jhaanptal.*
8. Jadi e amar hridaya duar—*Sindhu-Bhairavi, Jhaanptal.*
9. Tomar pataka jare dao—*Bhairavi, Thumri.*

Songs for prayer at night :

1. Ghate vase aachhi anmana—*Puravi, Ektal.*
2. Sangsare tumi rakhile—*Imankalyan, Jhaanptal.*

3. Alpa laiya thaki tai—*Chhayanat, Ektala.*
4. E Bharate rakha nitya prabhu—*Surat, Choutal.*
5. Duare dao more rakhiya—*Suratmallar, Ekadashi.*
6. Mandire mama ke asile—*Adana, Ektala.*
7. Bajao tumi kabi—*Vahar, Surfaakta.*
8. Sunya hate phiri he—*Kaafi, Surfaakta.*
9. Nivira ghana aandhare—*Sahana, Navatal.*
10. Amare kara jeevan daan—*Sankaraa, Choutal.*
11. Tomara asime pranamana—*Vehag, Kaoali.*
12. Gabhira rajani namila hridaye—*Paraj, Rupkada.*
13. Santa ha re mama chitta—*Jhinjhit, Thumri*

'Sangsar jabe man', 'Jadi e amar', 'Tomar pataka', 'Ghate vase aachhi', 'Sangsare tumi rakhile', 'Alpa laiya thaki tai' and 'Tomar ashime'—these seven songs of the list have already been printed in the book of poems *Naivedya* in 1308 (1901). The two songs 'Santa ha re mama chitta' and 'Pantha ekhan kena alasita' were composed in 1303 (1890) and 1304 (1897) respectively.

The new songs he composed for the *Maghotsav* of this time :

1. Swapan jadi bhangile.
2. Achhe duhkha aachhe mrityu.
3. Duhkha rate he nath ke.
4. Ananda tumi swami.
5. Duare dao more rakhia.
6. Mandire mama ke.
7. Nivida ghana aandhare.
8. Gabhira rajani namila hridaye.
9. Monpran kadia lao he nath.

The song numbering 9 was not made to be sung. Altogether five songs of the above list are break-away ones from Hindi.

1. Swapan jadi bhangile.

(Hindi)

Achhe duhkha aachhe mrityu.
Maruke gayee ri
Dhint langarba
Chailata rakha.
Var chhute haar tute
Karki karki chhurian su.

3. Duhkha rate he.

(Hindi)

Rangarat mat aaye piya
Baat kahta it aaye piya
Azhun sahe nid piya
Naina ratnaae
Chaal chalta it raat aachhe piya.

4. Ananda tumi swami

(Hindi)

Omkar Mahadev sankar tum.

(Discussion on this song has been previously made)

6. Mandire mamake

(Hindi)

Sundaro lago haay piyaba
Chapala chapala chokhana lakhana
Dur dur mur mur phiri muchkani vani.
Latki chalni mukut sukan
Bhrukuti kutil alak jhalak
Halkani kudal kapalni ani ani.

This song is included in Gopeswar Bandhopadhyay's *Sangeet-Chandrika* Vol. II. But words are not the same everywhere.

9. Manpran kadia lao he

(Hindi)

Hasi hasi garoa lagbe, kahain moko-
Basari bajabe mere jiyako lobhabe pyare.
Sukh se kati sachi rayan shyam sanga
Ot prata jia chhin le jabe pyare.

'Duare dao more rakhiya' and 'Nivir ghana aandhare' of this list are specially remarkable songs from the point of *tal,* because the *tal* of these songs are totally new and Gurudev's own creation. The name of the *Tal* of the first song has been given *'Ekadashi'*. The *Tal* is of 11 accents in total and is divided into 3:2:2:4 division of accents. The second one is of *'Navatal'*. It is divided altogether in 9 accents, and its division of accents is 3:2:2:2. Gurudev did not, meanwhile, make any attempt to compose his own songs in new *Tal-s.* The unusual *tal, 'Rupkada'* was for the first time introduced by him in the song 'Gabhira rajani'.

The song 'Achhe duhkha aachhe mrityu' is at present very much known. But that the song was composed out of the emotions of the pains of Mrinalini Devi's death is first known this time through the "Pocket-Book." The first *kali* of the song as found in the exercise-book was :

"Mrityu shokduhkha pare shubhra rage.
Achhe duhkha aachhe mrityu
Viraha dahana lage.
Tabu ananda jage he."

In the middle line there was—'Vasanta kusum vikase anata raage'. In the last line is 'Ei purnatar paye kavi sthan maage'.

The song 'Gabhira rajani namila hridaye' was scratched by him twice and was completed in the third time. In the first time, it was :

"Asim mangale milile madhuri
Khela hala samadhaan.
Chapala chanchala lahari lila
Atale hala abasaan."

This is the *Sanchari kali* of the song. By scratching it, he wrote for the second time :

"Madhura sandhya namila hridaye
Ar kolahal nai
Rahi rahi sudhu sudur sindhur
Dhwani sunibare paai.
Sab akangsha chitte aase fire
Gabhir aandhare ghanay bahire
Ekti dip sudhu hera re antare
Nibhrite jvale ek thain".

This was also cancelled. He wrote for the third time :

"Gabhir rajani namila hridaye
Ar kolahal nai".

There is no difference between the rest of the *Kali-s* and the printed lines in the present book. The word 'gabhir' was, though written in the exercise-book, scratched.

So long we knew that Gurudev has expressed his emotion of pains out of the death of Mrinalini Devi in the poems of the book *Smaran* only, but as he did not express that the revelation of that pain was also made in the tunings of songs, the exact dates of composition of the songs like 'Achhe duhkha aachhe mrityu, 'Duhkha rate, he nath ke', 'Ananda tumi swami', 'Nivira ghana aandhare', 'Gabhira rajani namila' etc. were not so long identified. If an analysis of the songs of *Maghotsav* of 1309 (1902) at the backdrop of the death of Mrinalini Devi is made well, it becomes easy to understand the real purpose of the prayer at the time. Gurudev wanted to reach the world of joy through the pangs of death.

The song 'Joy hok tabe jay' is just after the songs of *Maghotsav*. In introduction to this song written to Acharya Jagadishchandra Bose and published by Visva-Bharati in the collection of letters of Gurudev, *'Chithipatra'* Vol. VI, the following is stated :

> "The 'Bharat-Sangeet Samaj' arranged a 'Saraswat Sammalan' (Meeting of Scholars) to convey welcome to Jagadishchandra (19 *Magh* 1309, 2 February, 1903) ... ... Rabindranath Tagore composed the song 'Joy hok taba joy' for the function."

"The song is published with the editorial comment as follows in the journal *Bharati (Falgoon,* 1309, March 1903) under the caption *'Vandana' :*

> "This year, during the time of the meeting of scholars, Vignanacharya Jagadishchandra Bose has been awarded honour and offerings by the different societies and communities of Calcutta. This song is composed on that occasion."

Then the songs of wedding follow. These were composed sometimes before 22 *Jaistha* 1309 (5 June, 1903).

As there are no dates in these two songs, it is not being correctly stated for whose relatives' marriage those were composed. However, it is known that, the day of marriage of Surendranath Tagore, Gurudev's very affectionate, son of the elder brother, was on 14 *Asaad* 1310 (18 May 1903). It seems that prior to this marriage, Gurudev composed these two songs in the month of *Jaistha,* May. The two songs are : 'Je taranikhani bhasale dujane' and "Dujane jethay milichhe sethay". After these, there are no songs besides poems pages after pages in the exercise-book. After a pretty few months, exactly in *Jaistha* and *Asaad,* 1311, eight songs with their references to date and venue of composition were available :

1.	Mon tumi nath labe hare.	20 *Jaistha* 1311. Santiniketan. (3 June, 1903)
2.	Daandaao amar aankhir aage.	22 *Jaistha* 1311. Santiniketan. (5 June 1903)
3.	Azi jata tara taba aakashe.	24 *Jaistha* 1311. Santiniketan (7 June 1903)
4.	Garab mama harechho, Prabhu.	25 *Jaistha* 1311 (8 June 1903)
5.	Sabar majhare tomare.	26 *Jaistha* 1311 (9 June 1903)
6.	Je keho moro diyechho sukh.	26 *Jaistha* 1311 (10 June 1903)
7.	Ki sur baze amar prane.	23 *Asaad,* 1311. Majaffarpur (7 July, 1903)
8.	Tumi je amare chaao.	23 *Asaad* 1311 (7 July 1903)

It seems that the period of publication of the volume *'Gaan'* (songs) of poetical works edited by Mohitchandra Sen has created a complexity with the period of composition of these eight songs. That the volume, a collection of songs, were printed in 1310 (1903) is also referred below the name and address of the printer. But these eight songs of 1311 (1904) were printed in pages 323-331 of the book. Let me discuss why this discrepancy arose.

In a notice of a monthly journal, *Samalochani* (Number 8), published in 1310 (1903) it was informed that the book of poems is divided into 8 volumes and its 7th and the 9th volumes are collections of songs and dramas respectively. But the next announcement in the 9th issue of the journal is : "The books are being completed mainly in nine volumes. Eight volumes have been published. The volume on songs will be published within the month *Chaitra* (April)." The same announcement on the volume of songs was also there in the next tenth and the eleventh numbers of the journal. From this it is easily assumed that the different volumes of the book of poems could not be printed, in accordance with numbers, one after the other. At least exception to this was made in case of the volume on songs. Though it was stated that it would be published in the month of *Chaitra* (April), it was actually not made so. It will have to be assumed that it was printed sometime in the month of *Asaad* 1311 (July 1904). Otherwise these songs can, under no circumstances, have their places in this book of poems.

On 6 *Magh,* 1311 (20 January 1905) Maharshi Devendranath Tagore passed away at Jorasanko.

Naturally, all the members of the family were shocked at this death. Under such mental condition, Gurudev could not compose new songs more than one. He retained five songs from those of the month of *Jaistha* (June) last, took two from *Naivedya* of 1308 (1901) and the two songs more were written by others. This time Gurudev broke away from Hindi. In total, there were ten songs. These are :

1826 *Saka,* 1311 B.E. (1904)
Songs for the evening prayer :

1. Saktirup hera taar (a break-away song)—*Iman, Choutal.*
2. (Amar) mon tumi nath labe hare—*Chhayanat, Jhaanptal.*
3. Garab mama harechha, Prabhu—*Deshmallar, Dhamar.*
4. Nisithasayane bheve rakhi—*Vagesri, Teoda.*
5. Sakala garva dur kari diba—*Adana, Ektala.*
6. Je keha more diyechha—*Kaafi, Teoda.*
7. Oi je dekha jaay (other's song)—*Kaafikanada, Kaoali.*
8. E ki emoher chhalana (other's song)—*Kaafi kanad, Kaoali.*
9. Daandao amar aankhir—*Vehag, Teoda.*
10. Azi jata tara taba—*Lum-Khambaz, Thumri.*

After the death of Maharshi Devendranath Tagore, a big joint family for a long time was shattered. The big congregation of *Ostadi Sangeet* (Classical music) at Jorasanko came to an end. Gurudev got greater opportunities to pay attention to the activities to the education of the students of Santiniketan Vidyalaya. Simultaneously, the emotion of composing songs by Gurudev began to flow henceforth in a new trend. The Nature of Santiniketan received a special position in songs composed at present. Gurudev abandoned the avenue of composing Bengali songs by breaking-away Hindi ones in need of the functions in Santiniketan and Calcutta and started going on totally independently. Consequently, new ideas and new forms full of the emotions of *rasa* appeared in the songs of the criterion of *pooja* (worship).

18 RABINDRANATH : A DEVOTEE TO THE CLASSICAL INDIAN MUSIC

Gurudev Rabindranath published his first poetical work *Kabikahini* in book-form in 1876. He was then only fifteen or sixteen years. By expressing his deep devotion to the *raga-raginis* of the Indian music in a certain place of this poetical work, he said :

"Vasanta surabhita bataser sathe
Mishia mishia ei saral ragini.
Ekek ragini aachhe karile sraban
Mane hay aamari ta praner ragini–
Sei raginir mata amar e pran,
Amar praner mata jena se ragini
Kakhana ba mane hay puratan kaal
Ei raginir mata aachila madhur".

[With air fragnant of the spring.
This *ragini* simple is in continual unison.
A *ragini* is there if one does hear
Seems as if the *ragini* of one's heart
My heart is alike that very one.
That *ragini* is alike my heart.
The time of yore sometimes it seems
Was pleasant like this *ragini.*]

Living in the lively environment of the classical Indian music at the house of Jorasanko, how the feelings of *rasa* of *raga-ragini*-s in this music easily acclaimed a place in the mind of Gurudev is understood very clearly from the above lines. Although it is not fully revealed, yet it is understood that, like a blooming flower, its real meaning will be revealed one day. It actually happened so. In his old age, he said :

> "Our learned persons said by attuning in *Bhairavi Todi* that it was a song for the morning. But is there any replica of the various echoes of newly awakened family of the morning? Not a least even. Then, what was the meaning of calling *Bhairavi Todi* as the *ragini* of the morning? That indicates that the learned persons have heard with all their hearts the inherent music of all sounds and silence in the morning. Any effort to synchronize this song with any external part will be a failure.
>
> "In our country, the *ragini-s* of morning, noon, afternoon, midnight and rains and spring have been composed.
>
> "That a deeper expression is there behind outer expression is being expressed by *Todi Kanada* of our own country.
>
> "We know what an underscribable earnestness of beauty *raginis* instil in our mind. For this, as soon as a comparison is made between the fifth *ragini* and Radhika, an undirected but ever-known pleasant idea arises in our mind, which could not have been possible with any affluence of description."

From the above quotations, it is at least understood that Gurudev has mentioned about a definite system of singing *raga-ragini-s* by day or night, at different cluster of hours and seasons in classical Indian songs and he has also said that the scholars of the classical music of our country are the exponents and disseminators of this system. Besides this, we have also received invaluable directions from him about the way to appreciate the real *rasa* of the Indian *raga-ragini-s* in the mind.

In finding out the reasons, in Gurudev's mind for the use of *raga-raginis-s* in accordance with time in the Indian music, whatever is known in course of discussion on the history of evaluation of the *raga-ragini-s* of the Indian music is very suprising. In this essay through an exhaustive discussion with illustrations on the above, we would try to understand how Gurudev was influenced by it.

When the eminent singers and instrumentalists of the Indian classical Hindi songs would sing *Aalaap, Dhrupad, Dhamar* and *Kheyal* of a particular *raga-ragini* at Gurudev's residence in Calcutta, they would always sing by carrying out the specific rule of *ragini-s* meant for the clusters of hours of the day. They would sing the *ragini-s* of the day after sunrise but would not sing the *ragini-s* of the day after sunset. Then they would sing *ragini-s* meant for the night.

In this era, even now, eminent singers and instrumentalists try to obey this system with sincertiy.

This rule of serving *raga-ragini-s* in connection with definite time by day or at night is a very old system associated with the Indian classical music. But, in writing, we first come across the specific reference to this system of singing in a book in Sanskrit entitled *Sangeet-Makaranḍa.* 'Narad' composed this book. But he is not the Narad as described in the *Purana* or the *Upapurana.* The researchers are of opinion that he is a totally different man. They say that the book was composed in a period between the eighth and the eleventh centuries. Whatever is said in *Sangeet-Makaranda* about the *raga-s* or *ragini-s* to be sung in accordance with time is :

Sangeetadhyaye tritiyah padah
Abhah suryangshah.
Gandhare devagandhare dhannasi saindhabi totha.
Narayani gurjari cha bangal pat manjari. 10
Lalitandola Srika sourastreyajuya Sakshikey.
Mahiarh samvedi cha vasantan suddhabhairavah. 11
Velaveli cha bhupalah Somaragastathaiva cha.
Ete ragastu gatavyah pratahkalo visheshatan. 12
Sankarabharanah purva valahamsastathaiva cha.
Deshi monohari chaiva Saveri doumvuli tatha. 13
Kambhoji gopikambhoji kaishiki madhumadhavi.
Vahulidvyang mukhari cha tatha mangala koushika. 14
Ete ragavisheshastu madhyanhe parikirtitih.
Suddhanata cha Salange nati suddhavaratike. 15
Goulo malava Gourashha Sriragaschahri tatha.
Tatha ramakriti rajji chhaya sarvavaratila. 16
Varatika dravatika deshi nagavaratika.
Karnatahaya gouriti ityate chandramangshajah. 17
Varatika tatha suddha dravadiraga sangkshika.
Frahanapara gatarya mahlari mahuri tatha. 21
Andoli cha ramakriti chhayanta cha rangaka.
Madhyanhatparate yeme gouderagani yoni cha. 22
Krimopori gatavya suddhasalanganatika.
Etang kalavidhing Snatva gayedyah sa sukhi bhaveta. 23
Ragavela praganera raganang hingsaka bhavet.
Yah Srinoti Sa daridri ayanarshyati sarvada. 24

Devata vishje gitang punyanama pravardhanam.
Adhyatmikena yogena sarvapapa prasasanam. 25
Vivaha samaye dana devatastuti sangyute.
Avela raga markanya na deso bhairaving vina. 26

Whatever we understand from these *slokas* of *Sangeet-Makaranda* is :

> Gandhar, Devgandhar, Dhannasi, Saindhavi, Narayani, Gurjari, Bangal, Patamanjari, Lalit, Andol, Srika, Sourastra, Jayasakshik, Mahlar, Samvedi, Vasant, Suddha-Bhairav, Velauali, Bhupal and Som etc.—these *ragas* will have to be sung specially in the morning.

Sankarabharan, Purva, Valhangsha, Deshi, Monshari, Saveri, Doumuli, Kamvoji, Gopikamvoji, Kaisiki, Madhumadhavi, Vahulidray, Mukhari, Mangal, Koushika—these *raga-s* will have to be sung at noon.

Suddhanata, Salango, Nati, Suddhavaratika, Goula, Malav, Soud, Srirag, Ahri, Ramkriti, Rajji, Chhaya, Sarvavaratika, Karnat, Gouri—these *raga-s* are born out of the parts of the moon, that is, these should be sung in the evening.

Varatika, Suddha, Dravadi, Sangkshika will have to be sung on clusters of hours. Mahlar, Madhavi, Andoli, Ramkriti, Chhayanat, Rangaka will have to be sung in the subsequent hours afternoon. All the *Guoda ragas* like Suddhsalang, Natika will have to be sung after the third cluster of hours.

One who sings by obeying the rules of time like this becomes happy.

It is harmful for the *raga-s* to be sung untimely. One who hears becomes poor and destroys his longevity. The songs on gods are boosters to virtue. For spiritual reasons, these are destroyers of all sins. It does not become an offence if other *raga-s* except *Bhairavai* are sung in an unscheduled period, at the time of marriage, gift, and worship of gods.

In 1131, Someswar II composed a book on music entitled *Manasollas* or *Abhilasartha Chintamani ragini-s* for specific seasons as follows :

> Srirago raginijuktah sisire giyate vudhai
> Vasanta sasahayastu vasantatou pragiyate.

Vairabha sasahayastu ritau grisme praglyate
Panchamastu tatha geyo ragiraya sahasarade.
Maigharage raginitiryukte varsashu giyate.
Nettanarayan rago ragiya loha hemaka.

Its meaning, in general, is : *Srirag* and the *ragini-s* of the same type are sung in the winter. *Vasant* and its allied *ragini-s*, Bhairab and its allied *ragini-s Pancham* and its allied one *Magharaga* and its allied *ragas, natorarayan* and the related *raga-s* are to be sung in the spring summer, autumn, rains and in the late autumn respectively.

In 1610, Somnath the writer of books of music, has directed in 29 lines on the way of singing the *raga-ragini-s* in accordance with time in the following way :

Dhanasrirmalavasristha raktahangsho vasantakah
Deshakhyo deshakari cha bhupali prasabhastatha,
Madhyamadih kollohaso vangali bhairavastatha,
Narayana vibhasascha pratargeya ime vudhai.
Gurjari revaguptischa koumari kajjalitatha,
Sankarabharana stodi sourathi ramakrittatha
Nadanama kriyarago velaveli kudavika,
Gunakari jayasrischa tathaiva sivavallabha.
Ete ragah pragiyante prathama pracharottaram
Hangsakhyo dipaka ragah kamvedi kankanastatha.
Sarango devaganthari rago devagirih para.
Erovatoharjuno rago ratnavali tatha param,
Asavari cha hindole monohararastathaiva cha.
Vaijayanti tatha ragah sarvaschaiva varatikah.
Ete raga pragiyante dvitiya praharottaram.
Ghantaragastatha dhakkah sriragah kokilah punah
Soudamini kurangascha triveni cha suralava.
Purvi vihamgade ragoh samanta kudnudastatha.
Vadahanagshah pahadi cha chakradharastathaivacha.
Kalyanakhyavarali cha majjubhasa tata param.
Singharava statha ragastathaina patamanjari.
Sarve goulastatha natah kalpatarustathaivacha.
Ete ragah pragiyante tritiya praharottaram.
Saindhave magharagascha malahari panchamastatha.
Nilamvari mukhara cha bhairav lalitasthitha.
Meghanadastatha deshirago mangalakeshakah.

Godaragascha mallars ragah anandabhairavi.
Sankaranandamanavyou rajdhani cha sarvari.
Saveriraga ityetah sarvadah cha sukhapradah.

The meaning of the above is :

Dhanasri, Malavasri, Ṛaktahangsa, Vasantak, Desh, Deshkari, Bhupali, Prasabh, Madhyamadi, Kolahas, Vangali, Bhairav, Narayan and Vibhas will have to be sung in the morning.

Gurjari, Revagupti, Koumari, Kajjali, Sankara-bharan, Todi, Sourathi, Ramkarit, Nadramkriyā, Velaveli, Kudavika, Gunokari, Jaaysri, Siva-vallabh—these *raga-s* will have to be sung after the first cluster of hours.

Hansa, Dipak, Kamvedi, Kangkom, Sarang, Devgandhari, Devagiri, Eravat, Arjun, Ratnavali, Asavari, Hindol, Monohar, Vaijayanti, Varatika,—these *raga-s* have to be sung after the second cluster of hours.

Ghanta, Dhakka, Srinag, Kokil, Soudamini, Kurang, Triveni, Suralay, Purvi, Vihangada, Samant, Kumud, Vadahangaha, Pahari, Chakradhar, Kalyan, Varali, Majjubhasa, Singharav, Patamanjari, Soul of all types, Nat of all varieties. Kalpataru etc.—these *raga-s* will have to be sung after the third cluster of hours.

Saindhava, Megh, Malhari, Pancham, Nilamvari, Mukhari, Bhairavi, Lalit, Meghnad, Deshi, Mangalkeshak, Gor, Mallar, Anandabhairavi, Sankarandada, Manav, Rajdhani, Sarvari, Saveri—these *ragini-s* always bring forth happiness.

In between 1564 and 1647 the book *Sangeetdarpan* was composed by Chatur Damodar Misra. The rules and regulations of using *raga-ragini-s* in accordance with time as informed by him through this book are the following :

Atharag Vela

Madhumadhavi cha deshakhya bhupali bhairavi tatha,
Velavali cha malhari vangali samgurjari,
Dhanasri Malavsrischa megharagascha panchamah.
Deshakaro bhairavascha lalibascha vasantakah.
Ete ragah pragiyante prataràrambha nityashah.

Surjari koushikaschaiva saveri patamanjari.
Reva gunakari chiva bhairavi vamakaryapi.
Sasrathi cha tatha geya prathama praharottaram.
Vairabi todikachaiva kamodi cha kudayika.
Gandhari nagsavdicha tatha deshi vishesatah.
Sankarabharano jheno dvitiya praharatparam.
Sriragomâlavakhyascha gouri trivan sangjnakah.
Natakalyan sangjnascha salanga nattakangtatha.
Sarve natascha kedari karnatyabhirika tatha.
Valahangshi pahadi cha tritiya prharatparam.
Ardharatravadhirgeya raga ete sukhapradah.
Yathoktakala evaite geyah purva vidhanatah.
Rajatnaya sadageya natukalang vicharayet.

Itirag Vela

Sriraga raginiyuktah sisire giyate vudhai,
Vasantah sa svahayistu vasantatou pragiyate.
Bhairavah sa svahayestu ritou grisme pragiyate.
Panchamastutatha geyo raginya saha sarade.
Megharago raginivih yuktovarsha sugiyate
Natanarayanrago ragina saha hemake.
Yathechchhaya va gatavyah sarvatrishu sukhapradah.
Iti rituvela. Iti Somesvara matam.

The above refers to the following as meaning :

Madhumadhabi, Deshi, Bhupali, Bhairavi, Velavali, Mollari, Vangali, Samgurjari, Dhansri, Malavsri, Megharaag, Pancham, Deshkar, Bhairav, Lalit, Vasant *raga-ragini-s* are always started from the morning and sung.

Gurjari, Koushik, Saveri, Patamanjari, Reva, Gunakari, Bhairavi, Ramkari, Sarathi, *raga-ragini-s* will have to be sung after the first *prahar* of the day.

Vairathi, Hodika, Kamodi, Adaika, Gandhari, Nagasabdi, Deshi, Sankarabharan, *raga-ragini-s* should be sung after the second *prahar* of the day.

Srirag, Malavrag, Gouri, Trivani, Nat-kalyan, Natsalang and all kinds of Nat, Kedari, Karnati, Abhiri, Pahadi, *raga-ragini*-s are to be sung after the third *prahar* of the day.

These *raga-ragini-s* that give us happiness can be sung upto midnight. One would sing this song in the above mentioned time as prescribed earlier. But, in accordance with the order of the king, these can be sung at any time. There is no calculation of period or time then.

With all the *ragini-s,* Srirag, vasanta-raga and other *raga-s* as its followers, Pancham and its follower *raga-s*, Megharag and *ragas* following it, the Natanarayan with its *raginis* will have to be-sung in winter, spring, autumn, rains and early autumn respectively. But any *raga-ragini* can be sung in every season at all times provided that it brings forth happiness.

Chatur Damodar Misra informs that he has accepted this principle of singing *raga-ragini-s* in accordance with time and seasons from the book of Someswara.

In the sixteenth century, we are acquainted with the specific principle of using *raga-ragini-s*, in accordance with time, with the Dhrupad song through the Dhrupad songs of the saint poets of the party of Vallabhacharya the founder of the Vaisnava *Pustimarg Sadhana* of that era. In this respect, what is said in Hindi by Sri Udaysankar Shastri of Agra and researcher of the present era can be rendered as follows :

> In the second decade of the sixteenth century, after the death of Vallabhacharya, the famous *Vaisnav* devotee of North India and exponent of *Pustimarg,* his son, Viththalnathji was promoted to the post of the *Acharya.* He made elaborate arrangements for the service towards Krishna. For this, he arranged regular ceremonial service and service of the festivals of the years. He decided three parts of *seva* (service) : *Sringar, Bhog,* and *Raag.* He formed a group of singers consisting of eight disciples out of whom Kumbhandas, Surdas, Krishnanddas and Paramananddas belonged to his father and the rest four—Govindswami, Chhitswami, Chaturbhujdas and Nanddas of his own party to negotiate with the *ragas* appropriately. He named it *Astachhaap.* This party of *Astachhaap* were assigned to sing kirtan in accordance with the thoughts of activities favourable to *Astadarshan* (Eight views) of the Lord Srinath with *ragas* convenient to time and season and with the help of *tal,* tuning and instruments. The two stages of *Seva are : Nityotsav Seva*

(Regular ceremonial service) from morning till evening and the *Varsotsav Seva* (The service for the annual ceremonies) of twelve months and six seasons. In the *Nityotsav Seva,* there are *Astapraharik Darshan* (Eight-fold views of cluster of hours) e.g. Mangla, Sringar, Gval, Rajbhog, Utthapan, Sandhyabhog, Arati and Shayan. Both the ceremonies continue with *Astadarshan.* Arrangements are there in accordance with ideas and *rasa* in the fitness to time.

For each *Darshan* or *Jhanki,* a head *Kirtaniya* assisted by eight singers and percussionists were there. However, in the *Jhaki* of Rajbhog, probably all *kirtan* performers sing together.

The other devotees in that era in Vrindavan e.g. Swami Haridas, Hariram Vyas, Hitoaharivangsha and their disciples also sang their *padas* by tuning their *ragas* in accordance with time. The time of eight *Jhaki* for the regular service of the Vallabha community was well fixed and the *pada* and the arrangements for its *raga,* too, is specified. Surdas and other *Kirtaniyas* sang *Kirtan* song at the *Jhaki* of the regular service of Srinathji in accordance with that arrangement. That tradition is going on till now. The time and *raga* of each of those eight *Jhakis* are as follows :

1. *Mangala :* 5-30 am. 6.30 am.; *Lalit, Bhairav, Vibhas.*
2. *Sringar :* 7:00 am. - 8 am.; *Vilaol, Gunkali, Ramkali.*
3. *Gval :* 8:30 am. - 9:30 am.; *Ramkali, Devgandhar, Todi, Ashavari.*
4. Raaj-bhog : 10:00 am. 12:00 Noon; *Asavari, Sarang.*
5. *Utthan :* 3:30 pm. - 5 pm.; *Dhanasri, Bhimpalasri.*
6. *Sandyabhog :* 4:30 pm. - 5:00 pm; *Gouri, Purvi, Puria.*
7. *Sandhya-Arati :* 5:30 pm. - 6:30 pm.; *Sri, Jaisri.*
8. *Shayan :* 7:00 pm. - 8:00 pm. *Iman, Kamod, Vehag, Kedara.*

In 1660, Lochan Pandit of Mithila published a book of music entiled *Ragatarangini.* In this book he has written on the time of singing a few *ragas* that were in vogue in those days, in the chapter "Arvachin Ragasamaja". The original *slokes* of the book are :

Arvachin Ragasumayah

Brahma muhurte gatavyo Bhairavo ragasattamah

Arunadavelayang geyo Ramkeli punah.
Pratarvelavali geyo purvahnne Subhogohapi cha.
Purvahnne yati gaettangTodimati monoharam.
Sankaradou Baradicha geya gayaka nayakai
Diva tritiya prahare gatavyasavari janai.
Kaafi madhyahnnasamaye Sarangohpi cha giyate.
Aparanhe Nati Jneyastadvat gattu Malavam.
Aparanhavasane va sayannhe Sati Jati va.
Sayangkalastu Kalou vai Gouriragasya bhutale.
Nishamukhe tu Kalyanah Kedarastu mahanishi.
Dvitiya prahare ratrou Karnatah sarvas-angmatah
Aparahnnepi Sourastrah prabhate Sangvegahpicha
Panchamo meghasanchare Mallaraḥ parikirtitah.

The meaning of the above is :

> The *Bhairav raag* is to be sung in the very early morning—*Brahma-muhurta. Ramkeli* is to be sung with the rising of the sun, *Vela-vali* in the morning and in the *Purvahna, Subhag.* At the time of passing of *purvahna, Todi,* is to be sung. *Sankara* and *Baradi* will be sung in the third cluster of hours-prahar of the day. *Savari and Kaafi* will be sung at noon. *Nati* and *Malav* should be sung at the end of the afternoon or at the time of the end of the evening. *Gouri-raag* should be sung in the morning, and *Kalyan* in the opening of night. At dead night *Kedar* should be sung. *Karnat* is agreed by all to be sung in the second cluster of hours at night. *Adara* should be sung in the third cluster of hours of night. *Sourastra* is sung in the afternoon. *Pancham* is sung in the morning and at dusk. *Mallar* is to be sung with the spread of clouds.

Sri Rajyeswar Mitra informed through his book *"Mughal Bharater Sangeet Chinta"* (Musical thoughts of the Mughal India) that during the reign of Aurangzeb, a scholar in music named Fakirullah composed a book of music titled *"Raagdarpan"*. In this book there is a list of appropriate *ragas* to be sung in the appropriate time. This book was composed in 1666. According to researchers, this is a translation of the book *Mankutuhal* written by Mansing Tomar, the king of Gwalior (1486-1514). The translation was made in the Persian language. As a specimen, I am quoting from the list of using Indian *raaga-raagini-s* in accordance with clusters of hours, as collected by Rajyeswar Mitra from this book.

Period of Singing		*Name(s) of the Raaga-raagini(s)*
Early morning		*Bhairon, Vangal, Maadh, Harakh, Vaisakhi, Lalat, Vibhas, Gond, Madhmat, Saont.*
Morning		*Vasant, Patmanjari, Todi, Gurjari, Mallari, Gondmallar, Sankarabharan, Hamir, Nat.*
After sunset	:	*Kanhoda, Salanghat, Tarqyan (Evan).*
Evening	:	*Sri, Sindhu, Puria, Madhmat, Abhiri, Kedara, Gouri, Shyam, Rujhvi-Jayjayanti, Mouna-dhyan, Gharashyam, Vadhi.*
At the end of the day	:	*Multani, Tori, Maas, Jayati, Gouri, Chhayant.*
At the first cluster of hours of the day	:	*Pancham.*
Second cluster of hours day	:	*Deskhar.*
Fourth cluster of hours day	:	*Deogidi, Tilangi, Puria.*
4:00 am.	:	*Karnat.*
Second cluster of hours day	:	*Sarang.*
Afternoon	:	*Gour.*
At any time	:	*Ramkari* or *Ramkeli, Deshi.*

The list of songs to be sung in accordance with clusters of hours as Sri Rajyeswar Mitra has upheld in his book "*Mughal Bharater Sangeet Chinta*" from the book *Tufatul Hind* composed by Mirza Khan, a Muslim scholar of music in 1675, includes the following :

Raaga-raaginis		*Period to be sung*		
Bhairon	:	Autumn	:	Morning.
Maalkosh	:	Dew-fall	:	Late night.
Hindol	:	Spring	:	First cluster of the day.
Dipak	:	Summer	:	Mid-day.
Sri	:	Winter	:	Day-last part.
Megh	:	Rainy season	:	Night-last part.
Bhairavi	:	Early autumn	:	Morning

Raaga-raaginis	*Period to be sung*	
Vadari	: Autumn	: End of the day.
Madhmadh	: Autumn	: Morning.
Sinduvi	: Autumn	: End of the day.
Vangaal	: Autumn	: End of the day.
Todi	: Dew-fall	: After the first clusters of hours by day.
Goudi	: Dew-fall	: At the end of the day.
Gunkari	: Autumn	: Morning.
Khamvavati	: Dew-fall	: After mid-day.
Kakav	: Dew-fall	: Late night.
Ramkari	: Spring	: First part of the day.
Lalit	: Spring	: Morning.
Deshi	: Summer	: Second cluster of hours by day.
Kamod	: Summer	: Second cluster of hours by day.
Nat	: Summer	: At the end of the day.
Kedar	: Summer	: Mid-night.
Kanhada (Kanda)	: Summer	: First cluster of hours at night.
Malasri	: Winter	: Second cluster of hours by day.
Maroa	: Winter	: Last cluster of hours by day.
Dhanasri	; Winter	: Second cluster of hours by day.
Vasant	; Spring	: Mid-day.
Mallar	: Rainy Season	: Mid-night.
Gurjari	: Rainy Season	: First part of the day.
Bhupali	: Rainy Season	: First part of the night.
Deshkar	: Rainy Season	: Late night.

In 1610, 'Aahovela', a scholar of music, composed *Sangeet-parijat,* a book on music. From the list of *raag-raagini-s* that he has given to be used it is being known that he has either quoted or followed the opinion of Somnath from his (Somnath's) book *Raagavirodh* composed in 1610. From this it may naturally be assumed that Somnath and Aahovela were certainly grown up in the education of a special *Sangeet-gharana* (School of music). For the conveninence of readers, I am quoting the lines of *Sangeet-parijat* by Aahovela in order to compare with *Raagavirodh :*

Dhanasrirmalavasrischa raktahangsha vasantakah.
Deshkahyo deshkari cha bhupali prasavastatha.
Madhyamadi kollahaso vangali bhairavastatha.
Narayani vibhasascha pratargeya ime vudhai.
Gurjari revaguptischa koumari kajjali tatha
Sankarabharana sthodi sorath raamkrittatha
Nadaramakriyarago velavali kudavika.
Gunkari cha jayasrischa tathaiva sivavallabha.
Ete ragah pragiyante dvitiya praharottam.
Hansakhyo dipak raagah kamvodi kankanasatatha.
Sarango devagandharo rago devagirih para.
Eravatorjune rago ratnavali tatah param.
Asavari cha hindolo monoharastathaiva cha.
Vaijayanti tatha ragah sarvascheva varatikah
Ete ragah pragiyante dvitiya praharottaram
Ghataragastatha dhakkah sriragah kokilah punah.
Soudamini kuranagascha triveni cha suralayah.
Purvi vihangado ragah samanta kumudastatha
Vadahansah pahadi cha chakradhara stathaiva cha.
Kalyanakhyavarali cha majuubhasa tatha param.
Singharavastatha raagastathaiva patamanjari.
Sarve goulastatha natah kalpatarustathaiva cha.
ete ragah pragiyante tritiya praharottaram.
Saindhavi megharagascha mallari panchamastatha.
Meghanadasatatha deshi rago magala koshakah.
Goundaragascha mallaro raga anandabhairavi.
Sankarananda manavou raajdhani cha savari.
Saveriraagaityetah sarvada cha cukhapradah.

The list of the *raaga-raagini-s*, controlled in clusters of hours and the seasons, of the classical songs of North India that we have got till now continued for near about nine centuries at a stretch. The remarkable thing in it is that the directions to sing *raaga-raagini-s* in accordance with clusters of hours, that we have come across in different books are not the same everywhere. There are ample differences. But all writers are of opinion that the *raaga-raagini-s* must be sung by following the clusters of hours and the seasons. Just as they have emphasized on carrying out these directions, so some of them have also said about the situation when these directions may not be obeyed.

The rules of singing above-mentioned *raag-raagini-s* composed by the Hindu and the Muslim scholars of music were not only limited to them but there are also sufficient evidences that the influence of these rules fell upon the Karnatic music of South India and the songs of the Bengalees of Eastern India. Let us direct our attention towards that.

The Karnatic music of South India is another branch of classical Indian music. Captain C.R. Day, an Englishman, composed a book about this music, titled *The Music and Musical Instruments of Southern India and the Deccan.* It was published in 1891. He has extensively discussed on the South Indian Music in those days. In the fourth chapter of his book, the list of using the *raag-raagini-s* in Karnatic music according to clusters of hours, which he has referred to, is quoted below. He remarks :

> "In all the Sanskrit treaties a system seems to have been laid down by which the different *ragas* are apportioned to certain seasons of the year and hours of the day."

In modern times this system, as far as the hours of the day are concerned, is still carried out, and no musician, unless specially ordered, will sing any *raga* out of the proper time of the day apportioned for it.

The reason given for this is, according to Willard, that musicians declare that the times and season, allotted to each are those at which the divinities are at leisure to attend at the place where their favourite tune is sung, and to inspire the performer with due warmth in his execution. Superstition seems to have given birth to this absurd custom and it still exercises a strong hold upon all professional musicians, principally from the fact that it has been handed down from time immemorial; therefore it would be considered improper to make any change. Even in educated circles among the Hindus it would be thought a display of ignorance to call for a particular *raga,* unless for special reason, at an improper season.

The modern custom which plays down this hard and fast law seems to differ widely from that of all the ancient authorities, the names of the *ragas* now apportioned to the different periods of the day being quite at variance with the directions contained in Sanskrit, indeed, the writer of each treaties seems to have had a classification of his own distinct from that of other authorities. At the present time, musicians divide the twenty-four hours of the day into four periods, each of which is sub-divided into two parts.

The following table shows at a glance the hours appointed for the performance of the popular *ragas* according to the Karnatic system.

By referring to the rule of the use of *raag-raagini-s* in accordance with the cluster of hours he has said :

Time	*Raaga-raagini-s to be sung*
6:00 am. - 9:00 am.	*Bhupali, Kurangi, Sahuli, Kamkriya, Vilhari, Malhari, Mukhari, Yamuna, Raghupti.*
9:00 am. - 12:00 Noon	*Bhairavi, Meghranagi, Saranga, Bhalati, Madhyamarati, Deshi, Kariamvari, Mangal-pushika.*
12 Noon - 3:00 pm.	*Purvi, Sankarabharan, Gurjari, Kaafi, Kalyani, Deshi, Mohan, Sriraag.*
3:00 am. - 6:00 pm.	*Vasant, Narayani, Hindoli, Sourastra, Todi, Ramali, Gouri, Vadali, Pantuvarali, Puvani, Malav.*
6:00 pm. - 9:00 pm.	*Lalit, Velevali, Kamvoji, Saveri, Viagada, Punanga, Nat, Gundakriya, Monohari.*
9:00 pm. - 12 Mid-night	*Bhangala, Saveri, Ahini, Mangal-koushik, Kedar.*
12 Mid-night - 3:00 am.	*Vauli, Yogini, Chitravela, Karnata, Surati, Mangeri.*
3:00 am. - 6:00 am.	*Deshakshi, Devgandhari, Bhandi, Dhanyashi, Marwa, Devkriya, Mondali, Gouri.*

It is not heard that the learned persons in Karnatic music of this era have any appreciable faith in this rule.

Palakirtan or *Lilakirtan* is originated through arrangement of the *Padavalis* of the different *Padàvali* composers of Bengal. It has a history. I am making an attempt to narrate it in brief.

By going through the biography of Chaitanyadev we can know that Chaitanyadev heard the songs composed by the Vaishnav *Padavalikars* of his contemporary period or before him, and he was the person who introduced *namsangkirtan.* But we do not encounter any correct information that he would listen to *Palagaans* on manifold *Vrindavanlila* of Radhakrishna. The first introduction of *Palagaan* in the Bengali language was made much later after his death.

Sri Narottam Das, a devotee of Chaitanyadev, was born a year before the death of the latter in 1533. He was the son of Krishnananda Dutta, the Landlord of Gopalpur of Rajshahi, North Bengal. In his youth, being fascinated by the *Goudiya Vaishnav* religion, he left home towards the end of the sixteenth century. He went straight to Vrindavan. He received his initiation there from a *Guru* (master) named Lokenath

Goswami, spent days in meditation, prayer and reading treaties for nearly twelve years at a stretch. The time of his living at Vrindavan was the era of the Vaishnav *Pustimarg* meditators established by Vallabhacharya.

After the death of Vallabhacharya, his son, Viththalnath was posted to the position of the *Acharya* of this religious community and first introduced with the help of eight Vaishnav poets and devotee-singers a kind of *Pala* song with various *raaga-raagini-s* in accordance with clusters of hours and seasons in the temple of Vrindavan. Of these persons Surdas, the blind poet and singer, was the principal one. They introduced a kind of *Palagaan* (song by turns) in *Brajabuli,* following Srikrishna's manifold *Lilas.*

The life of Narottam at Vrindavan was spent in such a forceful environment of music. He succeeded there in the study of treaties and in meditation and prayer, returned to his country and established his seat of meditation—*Sadhanashram,* at Khetri, a village under Rajshahi. No more did he return to the residence of Zemindari.

Towards the end of the sixteenth century, at the time of setting up a new temple, Narottam arranged for a huge conference of *Kirtan* songs of the new pattern. He sent invitations to the then all Vaishnav meditators to attend this ceremony of music. He composed a pretty few *pala* or Lilakirtan by following Radhakrishna's *Vrindavanalila* in order to entertain the group of devotees attending the *Kirtan* ceremony. The community of the Vaishnav devotees named this song introduced by Narottam as *Garanhati* because the village Khetri was under a *pargana* named Garerhat in that era. With enthusiasm stemmed out of this new pattern of song, more *Palagaan-s* were gradually created. The names of the *Palagaan-s* so long had are as follows :

> *Janmalila, Nandotsava,' Valyalila, Gosthalila, Radhakunja, Milan Suryapuja, Jalakriya, Pashakriya, Daanlila, Subalmilan, Uttargostha Nrityarash, Maharash, Vasantalila, Vasantirashlila, Holilila, Holi's Nrityarash, Jhulan, Kunjabhanga, Nishantalila, Purvaraag, Rupanuraag, Abhisaar, Apekshanuraag, Kalahantarita, Vasak-sajja, Utkanthita, Khandita, Vipralavdha, Maan, Viraha, or Maathur, and Vangshivadan* etc.

A Vaishnav devotee remarks : "The experts do not recommend some *pala-s* of some *kirtan-s* to be sung beyond the scheduled period of time. For example, there is no way to sing beyond the scheduled day or within the stipulated few days for *Jhulan, Nandotsav, Holi, Vasant, Fooldol,* etc. In comparison to other songs, freedom in case of *Kirtan* songs is a great deal limited. *Gostha* or *Kunjabhanga* at night, and *Uttargostha* or *Rashlila* are not sung. *Khandita* cannot be held without morning. There is a system to sing *Kunjabhanga* very early in the morning. There are some persons who do not listen to *Kalahantarita, Maan* etc. if sung in the afternoon or in the evening. The gradation of a *Pala* is determined in accordance with that of *Lila.* Perhaps this principle is not always maintained. But in the Vaishnav community enough care is seen to keep to this principle. Another reason for this is that, as *Pala-s* are determined according to time, the *raaga-raagini-s* of the songs have also been arranged accordingly. It can be said for example that the affluence of *Bhairav, Gouri* and *Vehag* is seen in each of *Kunjabhanga, Uttargosthi and Raash* respectively.

Narottam lived together with the *Astachhapi* community of Vrindavan for many years, attained diverse knowledge about their songs, came back to his own country and was able to apply that knowledge to his newly introduced *palagaan.* It is, of course, true that when *Kirtan* songs of the patterns of *Manoharshahi, Raneti* or *Mandarini* and *Jharkhandi* after the demise of Narottam, the pattern of singing in the *Garanhati* style and the application of *raaga-raagini-s* in accordance with time as introduced by Narottam underwent extensive change. The influence of regional simple tuning and *Tal* in these songs were seen. Gradually, the *Kirtaniyas* began to forget the classical way of singing in the Garanhati pattern. Today, it has really become very different to have its exact identity.

At that time, Narottam made another remarkable activity. It is the change in the pattern of singing *Namkirtan* or *Sangkirtan.* About *Namkirtan* of four hours, eight hours and twenty-four hours, a devoted Vaishnav remarks :

> "This *Namgaan* is made in different *raaga-raagini-s* and in different rhythm or *tal. Bhairav, Bhairavi* in the morning, *Vagesri* at noon, *Puravi, Imankalyan* in the evening, *Vehag* at night—names are made in this way by turns. ... The assembly of *raaga-raagini-s* in *Namsangkirtan* is, to a great extent, under the *Vaithaki* and Hindusthani system."

Narottam thus formed *Namkirtan* at the time of *Kirtan-Mahotsav* of Khetri. A few years ago, I had heard singing *Namkirtan* of this pattern at Navadwip. "In *Kirtan* every *pala* is a part poetry. The *Kirtan* singer selects different *pada-s* of different *padakartas* (composers of *padas*) and arranges in the form of *pala.*" In the very beginning of the soiree of this type of *palakirtan,* one is to "sing *Gourchandrika* (inaugural song) and make *lila-gaan* of Radhakrishna." This *Gourchandrika* "is like a *mantra* to attract Srigouranga Mahaprabhu in *Kirtan.*" "If the Gourachandrika is not sung in the systematic *Kirtan,* there is no rule to make *lila-gaan* of Radhakrishna." In *palakirtan,* singers are to select a favourable *Gourachandrika* in keeping with the original idea or *rasa* of the *pala* and sing before the beginning of the *pala.* The aim of this song is not to invoke Gourangadev and convey respect and devotion only. Narottam introduced *Gourchandrika* songs indicating invocation to Chaitanya in the assembly of ideas or *rasa-s* similar to various *lila-s.* He gave it the place in the *lila-kirtan* of Bengal like songs signifying *Mahajan-nama* (the names of great persons) introduced by the Vaishnav devotees of Vrindavan and sung before the *pala-gaan.*

A discussion of the history of the musical life of Narottam, a devotee of Chaitanya, clearly reveals the fact that it was due to his endeavour that our *Naam-kirtan, Lila-kirtan* or *Pala-kirtan* enriched. Specially, the system of using *raaga-raagini-s* like the Vaishnav *pala-gaan-s* introduced in the middle era at Vrindavan in the *Guranhati* method of singing, influenced Narottam and he arranged the *pala-kirtan* of Bengal accordingly.

Ramnidhi Gupta first introduced *Tappa* song in the Bengali language. He was known as Nidhubabu. Born in 1741 at the village Chapta near Triveni, he had his education in Calcutta. He was educated in Bengali, English and Persian languages. In 1776, he joined the service in the department of revenue in the town Chhapra of Bihar. He had to stay there for twelve years. As he had devotion to the classical Indian music, he regularly received his training in *Dhrupad-Kheyal* and *Tappa* songs from a renowned Muslim *Ostad* there during leisure hours. In 1794 he left the service there, came to Calcutta and started living permanently. Here, before his death in 1245 B.E. (1838), he composed more than five hundred *Tappa* songs in the Bengali language with *raaga-raagini-s* and *tal-s* of the classical Indian music. He was really a good singer and so he made to listen to those songs by singing himself and taught the group of *Akhrai* songs created by him in that era. Being invited, he never presented the audience with his songs. If any one wanted to hear his song, one irrespective of being rich or poor would come to his assembly—*aasar* to hear. In 1244 B.E. (1837). he published a collection of his songs named *Geetratna* (A Gem of Music). In introduction, he remarks : "In this book, songs according to musicology and imagined by scholars in music in various *raagini-s* were published. Besides these, ... *raaga-s* like *Bhairavi* and the like were classified systematically after ascertaining the time of those *raaga-s* and *raagini-s* in the appendix."

The following is a specimen selected from the huge list of the time-schedule of *raaga-raagini-s* he prepared.

Raaga-raagini-s		*Time-schedule*
Adana	...	After 1:30 am.
Iman	...	after evening
Kalangda	...	At dawn
Kanada	...	At 1:00 am.
Kaafi	...	In the afternoon
Kedar	...	After 1:30 am.
Khat	...	After 1:30 am.
Khambaz	...	After dusk
Gour	...	Day and night
Goudi	...	Evening
Chhayanat	...	After four *Dandas* at night
Jayjayanti	...	After 1:00 am.
Jhinjhit	...	Day and night
Todi	...	After 1:00 pm.
Paraj	...	Midnight
Purabi	...	Last hours of the day
Vibhas	...	Morning
Vageshwari	...	After four *Dandas* at night
Vehag	...	1:30 am.
Vehar	...	Day and night
Varoa	...	The whole night
Bhairav	...	At 4 *Dandas* at night
Bhairavi	...	In autumn at dawn
Malkosh	...	At 2:00 am.
Multani	...	At 2:30 pm.
Lalit	...	Morning
Sankarabharan	...	After 1:30 am.
Sohini	...	After 1:30 am.

Sindhu	...	After 1:30 am.
Hamir	...	At 4 *Dandas* at night

In the second decade of the nieteenth century (1819), in the Bengali year 1225, Radhamohan Sen, a resident of Calcutta, composer of *Tappa* songs in the Bengali language, good singer and music-critic, composed a big book titled *Sangeet-taranga.* This is written in the Bengali *Payaar* rhyme. While introducing this book by Radhamohan, a researcher has said, "This book is a neat collection from manifold ancient books on music in Sanskrit, Persian and numerous other languages."

In this book, a well-scheduled harmony of all the opinions in vogue—Someswar, Hanuman, Kalanath, Bharat, Naam-puran etc. on theories of music in this part of the world covering different countries upto Hindustan and extending upto Calcutta where Bengal ends—has been shown. "For this, without saying his own words on ascertaining time-schedule for *raagas,* whatever he has come across from a perusal of *Sangeet Parijat* opinion, *Naad-puran* opinion, and *Toftal-chhend,* he has stated the same in his book in, of course, his own language. I am quoting a few specimens of how he has expressed in Bengali poetry :

Raaga-raagini-s		Time-schedule
Bhairavi	:	*Sarat ritur ushare gaay.* (To be sugn in autumn at dawn)
Puravi	:	*Dibasher Shesh ushate gabe* (To be sung in the last hours of dawn)
Sahana	:	*Yaminir pratham prahar gata hay Takhani janibe ai gaaner samay* (The first cluster of hours passes. Just then is the time for this song.)
Meghmallar (Mallari)	:	*Eke Varasha nishi-tate ghoratara Upasthit haila pray dwitiya prahar* (The rainy night with darkness deep. The second cluster of hours does appear)
Kanada	:	*Echari prahar rati* (This the fourth cluster of hours at night)

Vehag	:	–
Bhairav (Bhairon)	:	*Chhay danda nishi thakite gabe.* *Arun udaye sankadha pare.* (To be sung at six *dandas* at night to get the true spirit in sunrise.)
Lalat (Lalit)	:	*Rajani-prabhat samaye gabe* (To be sung in the morning)
Pancham	:	*Nishi sheshe chari dande gabe gunakar.* (*Gunakar* will sing after the end of night at four *dandas*.)
Vibhas	:	*Dui danda rajani thakite gabe gaan.* (Sing before two *dandas* before the end of the night).
Kedar	:	*Nishi madhye gabe gaan sadananda mane.* (Sing the song within night in an all-time joyful mind)
Ramkeli	:	*Ushakale ramkelire gaay* (Ramkeli is sung at dawn)
Iman	:	*Rajanir pratham prahare gabe gaan* (Sing in the first cluster of hours at night)
Kalyan	:	*Rajanir pratham prahare gabe geet* (Sing in the first cluster of hours at night)
Nasant	:	*Nishir tritiya yamete gaan* *Vasanta ritute sada vidhan* (To be sung in the third cluster of hours at night. To be sung all the time in spring)
Dipak	:	*Gaaner prabhave murtiman hutasan* *Hutasane pude parvater tarugan* *Hu hu sabde jwale agni davanal praay* (Like fire the song reacts. The trees of the mountain does in fire burn. Fire burns like one amid forest)
Chhayanat	:	*Chari danda nishi pare karibek gaan* (Sing after four *dandas* at night)
Sohini	:	*Dwitiya prahar yamini gate*

		Kariben gaan vidhan-mate (Sing after the second cluster of hours at night in accordance with the rule)
Gour-Sarang	:	*Tritiya-prahare gaan adesh* (To be sung in the third cluster of hours)
Sarang	:	*Diba asta danda pare* (To be sung after eight *dandas* by day)
Bhupali	:	*Nisite ek pa'r parete gaay* (To be sung at night after one cluster of hours)
Paraj	:	*Madhya rate paraj raagini kaila gaan* *(Paraj raagini* was sung at midnight)
Dhansri	;	*Sesh dibate gaibe* (Sing in the fag end of day)
Todi	:	*Dibar pratham prahare gaay* (To be sung in the first cluster of hours by day)
Kalangda	:	*Ushakale ei anuragere gaaibe* (Sing this *raaga* at dawn)
Kaafi	:	*Ki nishi ki diba-gaaibe sakale* (Sing all by day or night)
Thumri raagini	:	*Gaaner samay nishi kimba dibabhag* (The time to sing is night or day)
Malkoush (Malkosh)	:	*Gaan-bidhi yaminir aadya yam tabat.* (The rule of singing is the initial cluster of hours at night).
Ashavari	:	*Dibasher pratham prahar haile gata.* (To be sung after the first cluster of hours by day).
Gouri	:	*Gaan tulya dila yaminir mukhe.* (To be sung on the eve of night).
Natmallar	:	*Varasa ritute gaan sarvada niyam.* (The rule is to always sing in the rainy season).
Vahar	:	*Vasanta ritute sada gaaner koushal.* (To always sing in the spring).
Bhimpalasri	:	*Tritiya prahare gaabe.* (Sing in the third clsuter of hours).

Yogia	:	*Divadya-yamardha samaye gaabe.* (To be sung in the first half of the day
Vagesri	:	*Samasta divasete gaaner prakaran.* (To be sung at any time by day).
Sri	:	*Dinamane dui danda thakite gaaila.* (To be sung before the remaining two *dandas* by day).
Jayjayanti	:	*Pratham prahar nishi gate* *Janiben gaaner samay ei mati.* (After the first cluster of hours of night.) The time to sung this, know, please).
Adana	:	*Yaminir pratham prahare gita hay.* (Is sung in the first cluster of hours at night).

The names of the six *raaga-raaginis* suitable for the six seasons of the year in accordance with the opinions of Somesvar have also been referred to by him. He has written :

Names of the seasons		*Raaga-raagini-s*
Winter	:	*Sriraag.*
Spring	:	*Vasant.*
Summer	:	*Bhairav.*
Early Autumn	:	*Pancham.*
Rains	:	*Megh.*
Late Autumn	:	*Natnarayan.*

But he has said that there is no need for assessment of time to sing these songs.

The kings of Vishnupur in West Bengal were great lovers of music. When we see that towards the end of the eighteenth century, a Dhrupad singer from Delhi, Bahadur Khan, a descendent of Tansen came at Vishnupur along with a *Paakhoaaz* player named Pir Box and were accorded honour as teachers of music in the royal court, we notice their special devotion towards practice in the Indian classical music. A ring inspired by the king, as a group of young Hindu persons of Vishnupur accepted their discipleship. From then onwards till the end of the nineteenth and the beginning of the first two decades of the twentieth centuries Vishnupur was considered to be holding a very important position in the world of the classical music of Bengal. Kshetramohan Goswami, one of the eminent scholars in this school of music, came from Vishnupur to Calcutta and was placed as the master of music—*Sangeet guru*—in the courts of Jatindramohan Tagore, the rich landlord and his brother, Sourindramohan Tagore. With the direction and enthusiasm of these rich brothers, Kshetramohan went on accomplishing various activities in connection with the dissemination and spread of classical music. He was the innovator of Bengali notations of the new method and was also a writer of a few books. The history that he has delineated in connection with the evolution of music in his book even now pleases the researchers of music in this era. He has given in this book a list of the use of *raaga-raagini-s* in accordance with time made by the learned persons of music in that era. I am quoting the list as printed in the book :

Calculation of time	*Sanskrit Ra-raagini*	*Modern raaga-raagini-s*
From *Morning* 1 *Danda* Upto 5 *Dandas*	*Bhairav, Bharavi, Kangali, Ramkeli, Yogia, Khat, Asavari, Gandhar, Bhatiari.*	
From 6 *Dandas*	*Vibhas, Devogiri, Kutubha.*	*Sefarda, Sukhal, Velaol.*
Upto 10 *Dandas*	*Alahia, Velavali, Patmanjari.*	
From 11 *Dandas*	*Sindhura, Sindhu, Kaafisindhu,*	*Darvari, Todi, Lohar.*
Upto 15 *Dandas*	*Suddh Todi, Kaati Todi, Lakshmi Todi, Gurjari Todi, Mudra Todi, Khat Todi.*	*Todi, Sukhrai Todi, Nachari Todi, Joanpuri Todi, Bahaduri Todi.*
From 16 *Dandas*	*Vrindavani Sarang, Madhumadhavi.*	*Mian's Sarang.*
Upto 20 *Dandas*	*Sarang, Samanta Sarang, Goud Sarang, Vadahans Sarang, Suddh Sarang.*	
From 21 *Dandas* Upto 24 *Dandas*	*Bhimpalasri, Rajvijay. Dhani, Dhavalsri.*	*Multani, Varoa, Piloo, Mali Goura.*
From 25 *Dandas* Upto 28 *Dandas*	*Dhanasri, Malasri. Puria-Dhanasri, Puravi, Varati, Ahiri.*	
From 29 *Dandas* Upto Evening	*Srirag, Chitragouri, Trivani, Maroa (Malav), Saajgiri.*	
From Night 1 *Danda* Upto 5 *Dandas*	*Haamviri, Shyam, Kedari, Chhayanat, Kaamodi.*	

From 6 *Dandas*	*Kalyan, Suddhraj, Buria,*	*Iman, Imankalyan,*
Upto 10 *Dandas*	*Jayjayanti, Bhupali.*	*Imamkpuria.*
From 11 *Dandas*	*Suddh Kanada, Nayaki,*	*Hosain-i-Kanada*
Upto 15 *Dandas*	*Kanada, Koushiki, Kanada,*	*Adana, Sahana.*
	Mudra Kanada, Vagisvari Kanada,	
	Kanada, Khamvavati or Khamvar, Paraj,	
	Kalingda or *Kalangda.*	
From 16 *Dandas*	*Vehag, Vihanga Vehag, Vihangada* or	
	Vehagda, Devvehag, Arun Vehag,	
	Sankirna, Smapurna, Sankara, Sankarabharan,	
	Rativahi or *Raini.*	
From 21 *Dandas*	*Natnarayan, Kedar Nat*	
Upto 25 *Dandas*		
From 26 *Dandas*	*Maalkosh, Hindol,*	
Upto 29 *Dandas*	*Sohini.*	
At 30 *Dandas*	*Lalit.*	

A few invaluable words that Kshetramohan has said with reference to the above is worth remark here. For instance :

> "When the day and the night will be equally divided then this rule will be applicable, but shortening or lengthening of time-division as above will also be made with the increase and decrease of day and night."
>
> "If the disciples sing the *raagas* at a time other than the one as stipulated by the writers of books on music, it does not become an offence."
>
> "(*Raaga-raagini-s*) that should be sung in functions and in auspicious activities—*Bhairav, Kalyan, Bhupali, Shyam, Hamvir, Adana, Sahana.*"
>
> "One can sing the *Raaga-s* of *Tappa* in different seasons, and in different *rasas* ...... of everytime. The rules for the seasons etc. should not be taken into consideration. All types of *raaga-s* can be sung unhindered at every time in response to the orders of the king or in the battle-field also."
>
> "According to Someswar, there are rules for singing *Sriraag, Vasant, Bhairav, Pancham, Megh* and *Natanarayan raaga-s* in winter, spring, summer, autumn, rains, and in late autumn respectively. It is not necessary to assess time-divisions like forenoon etc. in order to sing these *raagini-s* according to seasons."

From the period of the first publication of *Sangeetsaar* in the seventh decade of the nineteenth century upto the first two decades of the twentieth century we come across so many books on music in Bengali in which we get a clear account of the fact that the learned scholars of music in Bengal were very conscious of the rules of application of *raaga-raagini-s* in time. The Bengalees have endeavoured to carry out this rule of many centuries with sincerity. How references were made in connection with the use of *raaga-raagini-s* in the later authentic books by following *Sangeetsaar* may be explained through the following example taken from a single book :

Sachitra Visvasangeet
Raaga-s and Raagini-s

From Morning upto 5 *Dandas* :

Bhairav, Bhairavi, Vaangali, Ramkeli, Yogia, Khat, Asavari, Gaandhar, Bhatiari.

From 6 *Dandas* by day upto 15 *Dandas* :

Vibhas, Devgiri, Kukubh, Aladia, Velavuli, Pathmanjari Sefarda, Sukla-Velaol.

From 11 *Dandas* by day upto 15 *Dandas* :

Sindhura, Sindhu, Kaati Sindhu, Suddh Todi, Kaafi Todi, Lakshmi Todi, Gurjari Mudra, Gujari Todi, Khat Todi, Suddh Gujjari and modern other *raagini-s.*

From 16 *Dandas* upto 20 *Dandas* by day :

Vrindvani Sarang, Madhumat Sarang, Pathhangsika Sarang and Suddh Sasrang.

From 21 *Dandas* to 24 *Dandas* by day :

Bhimpalasri, Multani, Rajvijay, Dhani, Dhavalsri and other modern *ragini-s.*

From 25 *Dandas* to 28 *Dandas* by day :

Dhanasri, Malsi, Puriadhanasri, Puravi, Varati and *Ahiri.*

From 29 *Dandas* by day upto the evening :

Sriraag, Chitragsuri, Trivani, Malav or *Maroa, Sritanka, Sargiri* or *Saajgiri.*

From 1 *Danda* to 5 *Dandas* at night :

Hamvir, Shyam, Kedari, Chhayanat, Kamodi.

From 6 *Dandas* to 10 *Dandas* at night :

Kalyan, Suddhraag, Puria, Jayjayanti, Bhupali and other modern *raagini-s* e.g., *Iman, Imankalyan, Imanpuria.*

From 11 *Dandas* to 15 *Dandas* at night :

Suddhkanada, Nayaki Kanada, Koushiki Kanada, Nagaddhani Kanada, Mudra Kanada, Vagisvari Kanada, Khambaz, Paraj, Kalangda or *Kalingada* and modern *Hossain-i-Kanada* and *Adana, Sahana.*

From 16 *Dandas* to 20 *Dandas* at night :

Vihag, Vihanga Vihag, Vehagada or *Vihangada, Devvihag, Arunvihag, Sankirna, Sampurna, Tanka, Sankura,* and *Sankarabharan.*

From 21 *Dandas* to 25 *Dandas* at night :

Natanarayan, Kedarnat.

From 26 *Dandas* to 29 *Dandas* at night :

Maalkosh, Hindol, Sohini.

At 30 *Dandas* at night :
Lalit

The Publisher of *Sachitra Visvasangeet* has given this list by mainly following the book "*Sangeetsaar*" and making minor changes.

Ramprasanna Bandyopadhyay of Vishnupur wrote a book entitled *Sangeet Manjari* in the first decade of the twentieth century i.e., in 1314 B.E. This is a book of notations of songs like *Dhrupad Dhamar. Kheyal* and *Tappa* along with a description of *raagas*. The following is a specimen of the detailed list of the *raaga-s* and *raagini-s*. They sang or they knew to be sung at the stipulated clusters of hours by day or at night :

Day : 1st Cluster of hours :
Bhairav, Ramkali, Yogiya, Kalingda, Bhairavi, Vibhas.
Day : 2nd Cluster of hours :
Asavari, Gourasarang, Alahiya.
Day : 3rd Cluster of hours :
Bhimpalasri, Varoan.
Day : 4th Cluster of hours :
Multani, Purani, Dhanasri, Gouri.
Night : 1st Cluster of hours :
Kalyan, Imankalyan, Kedara, Chhayanat, Natamallar, Bhupali, Durvari Kanda.
Night : 2nd Cluster of hours :
Nayeki Kanada, Sahana, Sindhu, Vahar, Desh, Jayjayanti, Khamvaz, Jhinjheti, Mallar, Vasant, Maalkosh, Pancham, Paraj, Piloo, Vehag, Lalit.

Gurudev was born in the midst of a living environment of classical Indian music of his house. He had learnt from his childhood different types of songs like *Alaap, Dhrupad, Kheyal, Tappa* etc. of the renowned *Dhrupad* singers of that era. Moreover, when his father and his elders composed songs in Bengali, suitable for these regular ceremonial prayers, they would set tunes in different famous or infamous *raaga-raagini-s* current in those days on those songs with the help of the scholars of Hindi *Dhrupad, Kheyal* and *Tappa* songs. These songs are now called by us Hindi break-away songs or break-away songs. Gurudev had also heard and sung these songs from childhood. Naturally, these songs were composed by considering the prayers for the morning and the evening. The learned persons added tunes in relevant *raaga-raagini-s*. This means that the prayer songs of the morning and the evening were attuned with the *raaga-raagini-s* of the morning/day and the evening/night respectively.

When Gurudev had composed songs in need of morning and evening prayers at their residence at Jorasanko and Santiniketan, he had also followed the avenues of the elders. From this point of view, he had sincerely carried out the regulations of the use of the *raaga-raagini-s* of the Indian music. He did not ignore it. But the devotion to use *raaga-raagini-s* in accordance with time revealed in Gurudev in such a different way as we have not paid sufficient attention to that. It is his relevant mention of time or season of any *raaga-raagini* in his poems, songs, essays and dramas. A more or less exhaustive account of this follows :

From a study of this list of the names of *raaga-raagini-s* and their timely applications it will be seen that there is an influence of the use of *raaga-raagini-s* in accordance with the time of the classical Indian music of Vishnupur.

Agamani and *Saarigaan* are at the very beginning of the list. The names of these two tunes are not found in any book on music. These two are Bengal's own tunes. Although these two tunes are beyond any treatise, Gurudev had shown equal honour for them like other *raaga-raagini-s* and did not at all ignore these.

Agamani

Andher kanther gaan agamani,
Sei gaan mile jaay dur hate dure
Sarater aakasete sona roddure.
[The song in the voice of the visually disadvantaged is *Agamani.*
From far to farther that song makes unison with the sky of the autumn, in the golden sun]

—*Sahaj-path* : Lesson XIII

This is the role of all *Agamani* songs. * * * * * * The lord of the mountain has been dreaming in the *raaginis* of *Lalit, Vibhas* and *Ramkeli* from the time of our grand-fathers and great grand-fathers. * * *

(Literature)

Gramyasahitya (Rural Literature)—*Loksahitya* (Folk)
Geyechhe agamani saratprate,
Geyechhe vijayar gaan –

[In the morning of autumn *agamani* has been sung.
The *vijaya* songs have been sung. *(Gaanbhanga-Kahini).*]

Amar raat pohalo saradaprate * * *
Viday-gatha agamani kata je.
[My night dawned in the autumn-morning. * * *
How strewn with the words of adieu is *Agamani.* (*Prakriti-Gitavitan*).]

Chhad go to tora chhad go. * * *
Vidayvelay eki hasi,
Dharli agamanir vanshi-
Jabar sure asar sure karli ekakar go.
[Leave, ye, leave * * * What a smile at the time for bidding adieu, Tuning *Agamani* on the flute—Making tunes of arrival and departure one in unison. (*Prakriti-Gitavitan*).]

Amar nayana-bhulano ele, * * *
* * * Sisir bheza ghase ghase
Arunranga charan phele. * * *
* * * Alochhayar aanchalkhani lutie pade vane vane, * * *
* * * Akashvinar tare tare jage tomar agamani.
[My eye-bewitching ye came * * ** * *
In dew-drenched grasses with steps adorned with sunshine. * * ** * *
The trails of light and shade tumble from forest to forest * * ** * *
With the strings of the *Akashvina* does awaken your invocation. (*Prakriti-Gitavitan*).]

"One day, in the morning of the autumn, a beggar songstress was singing the song of invocation."

(*"Galpaguchchha"—Rabindra Rachanavali,* Volume 18)

Saarigaan

Sukhe saarigaan gaay daandi
Kata kheya-tari dey paadi.
(Nadi)

Kata nadinade jaksha srater
Maajhkhane ek path dhari,
* * * * * * * * *
Kata saarigaan jagaye
[In happiness the oarsman sings *saarigaan-s.*
So many passenger-boats cross over. (The river)
In so many rivers amid a million trails of current.
An avenue is taken up * * * * * * * * *
By arousing so many *saarigaan-s. Utsarga (Dedication).*]

Je kheyar karnadhar tomake niyechhe sindhupare
* * * * * *
Katavar tari saarigaane
Nishanter nidra bhenge byethay bejechhe more prane
Ajana pather daak.
[The head oarsman of the boat who has taken you to the sea-shore * * * * * *
In so many times with his *saarigaan.*
Breaking the slumber of the end of night has tuned in my heart in pain.
The call of the way unknown. *Puravi* : "Satyendranath".]

Purnima-nishithe
Srote-bhasa eka tari jabe sakarun raaginite
[At full moon dead night when the lone boat floating on the current with melancholy raagini
(Mahua—"Kheyali").]

Parabasi chale eso ghare * * * *
Oi dekha katavar hala kheya parapar,
Saarigaan uthilo ambare.
[O foreigner, come to the room * * * *
You see how many times does the passenger boat cross,
Saarigaan overflowed in the cloud.
—Gitavitan.]

Aaz majhnadite saarigaan gaaiba jakhan
Tomar naam parbe bandha
Taar hathat tane.
[Today when I shall sing Saarigaan in the river-mid.

Thy name would be entwined. In its sudden *taan.*
—*Shyamali : "Milbhanga".*]

Jabe milan tarir saarigaan virahavanyar opar theke
Asuk sajal haoay.
[Then the saarigaan of the boat of union from the other end of the flood of anguish
In moistrous air let come (*Sravangatha).*]

Aazi sanjher yamunay go * * * *
Tarun chander kirantari kothay bhese jaay go
Tari sudur saari gaane * * * *
[Today in the Yamuna of the evening * * * *
Where does, the boat of light of the young moon float away. In his distant *Saarigaan* * * * * —*Gitavitan.*]

Ogo amar sravan megher kheya tarir majhi
* * * * * * * * * * * *
Tai tomari saarigaane. ** **
[O my boatman of the *kheya-tari* of the *Sravan* cloud
* * * * * * * * * * * *
So in your *saarigaan.* ** ** ** —*Gitavitan]*

Bhairavi

Ogo, ke tumi basia udas murati
Visad santa sobhate.
Oi bhairavi aar geyonako ei prabhate
[O, who thou art seated, a vacant image in beauty sad but quiet. Sing not this *bhairavi* in this moon.
(*Shyamali "Bhairavi* Gaan").]

Dur swarge baje jena nirav bhairavi.
Ushar karun chand shirna mukhachchhabi.
[In the distant heaven as if the silent *bhairavi* rings.
The melancholy moon at dawn as if is the ematiated picture of countenance. —*Chaitali : "Samapti".*]

Mukta nilamvare achchhay aloke gahe
Vairagyer sware je bhairavi gaan.

[In the open blue cloud in shadeless light does sing
In voice of renunciation the song of *Bhairavi.*
—*Naivedya.*]

Tai aaz utsaver bhorbela hate
Vaspakul aruner karun alote
Ullas kalloltale bhairavi raagini kende baje
Milan sukher vakshomajhe.
[So from the dawn of ceremony today.
In melancholy light of the vapourdrenched sun
Under the ripples of laughter ring a-crying the *bhairavi raagni. Puravi* —*"Utsaver Din".*]

Ei niravervakshe navachhande chhutave foara
Prabhati bhairavi
[In the breast of this silence in a new rhythm will make the fountain flow
The morning *bhairavi.* —*Puravi* : *"Ahavan".*]

Bhorer velay asrubhara adhir abhiman
Bhairavite jagiechhi gaan.
[At dawn the restless sentiment is filled in tears,
In *bhairavi* I have tuned up music.
—*Puravi* : "Aparichita".]

Jatin : On the day of your wedding from the dawn of the ceremony–
Himi : Please, elder brother, let it remain undisclosed.
Jatin : As if I'm hearing its tune in the flute in *Bhairavi.*
—*Grihapravesh.*

Sakalvelay viraher akashe
Sunya vasar gharer khola dware
Vhairavir tane lagao vairagyer murchhana.
[In the sky of separation in the morn.
In the unbarred door of the empty wedding room.
Begin the resonance of renunciation in the tune of *Bhairavi.* —*Sesh Saptak* : 28.]

Yet when the autumn sunshine slantingly falls on the corridor upstairs, the *natavat* of the pooja plays on in *bhairavi.* —*Lipika* : "Gali"

(He) hears that in the tune of *bhairavi* at dawn.–*Chhelevela*

Je atithi dehe bhorbelakar
Rup nila bhairavi,
[In that physique of the guest.
The appearance of dawn was taken by *bhairavi.*
—*Navajatak : "Seshdristi".*]

"When the turns of the *bhairavi* tune reach the ears, a typical idea dawns to the world. * * * * It seems as if a hand of rules is burning the handle of the organ ceaselessly, and with that pains of that rubbing a sombre, piteous, sad *raagini* is overflowing from the inner zone of the universe, all the light of the morning sun has become pale, the trees are as if hearing something silently, ** ** ** .

In the morning, today, a *bhairavi* was being played on in a *Sehnai.* It was appearing so exceedingly sweet that it was beyond any description.

—*Chhinnapatravali :* June 1889.

Sakalvelar aloy baje biday byethar bhairavi
[In the light of the morning, the *bhairavi* of the pain of farewell does ring. —*Gitavitan : "Prem".*]

Sarat sisire bhije bhairavi nirave baje.
[Drenching in the autumn-dews silently does the *Bhairavi* amuse. —*Gitavitan* : *"Prem".*]

Puravi

In the same way, to compose a song on the evening the composer might not sing *Puravi* by closing eyes and ears. *"Sangeet O Kabita"* (Music and Poetry) *Samalochana* (*Criticism*)

Snehamay chhayamay Sandhyasama aankhi meli
Ekbar bujhi hesecchile.
Swapnamay santimay puravi raagini-tane
Bandhiachha pran.
[Opening eyes affectionate, shadowy like the evening.
Smiled ye, as if once.

In the *puravi raagini-an* dreamy and peaceful.
Thou hast clasped my heart.
—*Sandhyasangeet,* "Upahar".]

Saanjher abha neme elo * * *
Puravi raaginiguli dur hate chale aase.
[The lustre of the evening loomed down * * *
The *Puravi raagini-s* come from the distance. *Chhabi Gaan* : *"Aachchhanna"*.]

Kave kon sandhevela ore tulechhile vala
Ori maajhe vaaje kon puravi raagini.
[When, in which evening did the dame lift him,
Which *Puravi raagini* does ring amid that.
—*Kadi O Kamal* : *"Bhavisyater Rangabhumi"*.]

Amid the golden darkness during sunset, the *Puravi* was to be played on in the *Nahvat.*
—*Panchbhut : "Apurva Ramayan"*

Astaravir sonar kirane
Nutan varana lekha
* * *
Hatas hridaye kandiya kandiya
Puravi raagini baaje.
[In the golden sunshine of the setting sun.
In new colour is written * * *
In the hopeless heart a-weeping.
The *Puravi raagini* does ring.
—*Sonar Tari : "Aakasher Chand"*.]

Oi suno baaje
Nihsabda gambhir mandre ananter maajhe
Sankha ghanta dhwani. Dhire namaiya aano
Vidroher uchcha kantha Puravir mlan-mandra sware!
[Listen
With sombre sound in the endless
The founds of conchshells and bells. Slowly bring down
The high voice of rebellion in that of the faded and sombre pitch of *Puravi.* —*Chitra : "Sandhya"*.]

Parpare surya gelo pate.
Puravite dhari tan ekmane rachi gaan
Gahite lagilo Ramdas.

[The sun set out in the other bank.
Tuning on Puravi and composing songs in rapt attention,
Ramdas began to sing. *Katha* : *"Pratinidhi"*.]

Sandhyavelar sonar abhay
Milie diye tan
Puravite sesh karechhi
Jakhan amar gaan.
[In the golden lustre of the evening.
Harmonizing the *tan* When in Puravi I have finished.
The song of mine. *—Gitanjali.*]

Yatra jakhan habe sara
Uthbe jwale sandhyatara,
Puravite karun banshari
Dware bajbe madhur swar.
[When the journey will end,
The evening stars will shine.
The sad flute in Puravi
Sonorous voice will ring in door! *—Geetamalya.*]

Baje Puravir chhande rabir
Sesh raaginir bin.
[In the rythm of *Puravi.*
The *veena* of the last *raagini* of the sun plays on.
—Puravi : "Sesh Raagini".]

Sanga sunya sayanher bairagya niswas
Swargasukhe klanta kon devatar baanshir puravi
Sunyatale dhare oi chhabi
[In the companionless evening hours the breath of renunciation falls. The *Puravi* emanating from the flute of which god tired of the happiness of heaven.
Holds up this picture on empty earth.
—Puravi : "Chhabi".]

Azike tara paduk dhara, miluk puravite.
Ekti sangeete.[Let them be trapped today, be in unison in *Puravi.*
In a single music *—Puravi* : *Abasaan.*]

Sayahner karun kirane
Puravite daak dao amar paoare ksane ksane
[In the sad light of the evening.
Beckon every moment in *Puravi* the prized myself
—*Puravi* : "*Na-Paoa*".]

Astaravi godhulite
Vale gelo *puravite*
Aar to adhik naai deri
[The setting sun in dusk
Said in *Puravi* :
No more delay is there. —*Puravi* : "*Vinahara*".]

Another would complete the day's work, sing in a vacant mood and would advance towards the human habitation * * * * Perhaps he would look at the stars in the sky, and would finish his *Puravi* song by going beside the doors of his house.

—*Galpaguchchha* : "*Raajpather Katha*"

Suryaster paar hate vajay Puravi
[Plays on *Puravi* from the shore of sun set.
—*Seshsaptak* : "*Smritipatheya*".]

Sandhyar alo sonay gala tare
Sakarun puravite.
[The light of evening in melted strings in gold.
In pensive *Puravi* —*Vithika : "Kaisorika*".]

Asta sindhukule ese ravi
Purav diganta pane
Pathaila antim puravi.
[Coming on the setting sea-shore.
The sun towards the eastern horizon.
The last *Puravi* did send. —*Bithika*.]

Er puravi or vibhaske asirvad kare chale jaak.
[Let its *Puravi* go away after blessing that's *vibhas*
—*Lipika : "Sandhya Prabhat*".]

Amar jabar velate .. .. ..
Yatra jakhan habe sara
Uthbe jwale sandhytara,
Puravite karun baansari
Dware bajbe madhur swar.
[At my time of departure .. .. ..
When the journey will come to an end
The evening star will shine out,
The pensive flute in *Puravi*.
The pleasant tune will play on at the door. –*Gitavitan*.]

Amar godhuli lagan ....
Ekhan ki suni puravir sure
Kon dure vaanshi baje.
[My moments of dust ....
What do I hear now in the tune of *Puravi*.
How far away theflute does play on. —*Gitavitan*.]

By the by, think why one recalls the evening in *Puravi* alone * * * Is there any excess of tender tunes in *Puravi* * * * ? As soon as I hear *Puravi* .. .. *raagini*, the image of evening becomes glowing in my mind. How far of it is due to total superstition and how far due to other reasons are subject to assessment.* * *

In sombreness, eccentricity, renunciation and tiredness, the evening is silent awaiting advent of the imminent dark night * * *.

It has been seen that in the *raagini-s* of the end of the day of ours the association of *Komal, Rekhav* and *Kadi-Komal* is a matter to be specially noticed * * *.

—*Pandulipi* : *"Sangeet O Bhav."*

To compose a song on the evening, the composer might not sing *Puravi* by closing eyes and ears. He might imagine the idea of evening. Then his tune will also come down automatically like the closing day, will wind up and will be exhausted.

—*Sangeet O Kabita*

Completing *Multan-Varoan, Puravi* began to play on in *Nahvat* amid golden darkness at the time of the setting sun.

—*Panchabhut* : *"Apurva Ramayan"*.

Sahana

Sundar sahana raage vangsir susware
Ki utsav hayechhilo amar jagate
[In beautiful *Sahana* raag in the pleasant tune of the flute
What a ceremony in my world was held!
—*Sonar Tari* : "*Manasundari*".]

Bibaha utsav rati * * *
* * * Dharechhe sahanar sur—
[The night of the marriage ceremony * * *
* * * Has played on the tune of *Sahana*
— *Kahini* : "*Gaan Bhanga*".]

It was I who made to agree to marry Damini. We did not make *Subhadristi* (exchange of auspicious look) between ourselves in the tune of *Sahana raagini* under the covering of any coloured *cheli* (Silken wedding piece of cloth). —*Chaturanga.*

Sahana raaginir rase jadita aazi e punyatithi.
[These auspicious hours of today is entangled with the *rasa* of *Sahana raagini,* —*Mahua* : "*Asirvaad*".]

Sediner sahanar sur
[The tune of *Sahana* that day —*Mahua : "Puratan"*.]

O je surabhavanaer ramar kamalavanavasi,
Marte neme vajailo sahanar nandaner baanshi,
[That she is a resident of the forest of lotus of Beauty's house of tunes.
The flute of Heaven in *Sahana* she played on descending on earth. —*Parishesh : "Parinay"*.]

Suryaster velay milaner digante ......
Subhadristir pradip tomar jwalo
[At the time of sunset in the horizon of union ......
Trim on your lamp of wedding glance.
In the tune of *Sahana.* —*Sesh Saptak* : 28.]

Siter sandhya sajaye vasar ghar.
*** *** ***
Sunitechhe ke se kar uddese
Sahanay vaanshi vaje.
[The winter evening decorates the wedding room.
*** *** ***
Who is listening to the flute.
Playing on and for whom in *Sahana!*
—*Vithika : "Aasannarati"*.]

...... Vasargharer navabadhu ......
Vatase, sahana raaginir karuna.
[...... the newly wedded bride in the wedding room ......
In the air is the sympathy of the *sahana raagini.*
—*Patraput* : 5.]

Ek sahanai baje tomar basite, o go shyamali,
Jedin aasi abar jedin jaai chale.
[O Shyamali, the same *sahana* plays on in your flute.
On the day of my arrival or that of return.
—*Shyamali : Shyamali.*]

In the wedding-assembly, the groom and the bride
Adorned with sandal paste and with wedding
Hats (*Topar*) on have sat on the wooden
Seat (*Pidi*) decorated with *alpana* ......
From the other side, the music of *Sehnai*
Is coming from thesky in *sahana raagini.*
Dharo sahanate Milaner pala,
Sajao jatane varaner dala.
[Muse on the episode of union in *Sahana.*
Decorate with care the welcome-tray. —*Geetavitan.*]

Amar malar phulerdale achhe lekha
Vasanter mantralipi.
** ** **
Sahana raagini er ranga range ranjita.

[In the cluster of flowers of my garden is written
The chanting letter of the Spring.
** ** **

The Sahana raagini is brightened with its colour.
—*Geetavitan : Chandalika.*]

Bibaher pratham batsare
Dike digantare
Sahanay bejechhila baanshi
[In the first year of wedding.
Everywhere.
The flute played on in Sahana
—*Sesh Lekha* : 8.]

The Achyarya sat with *Tomvura* to sing. The songs of *Dulha-dulhi* in the tune of *Sahana.*
—*Lipika* : *Upasanghar.*

Mane jani kare nagal pavona ......
Kono basa paay sei durashay gaanthi sahanar vani.
[Know I in mind that I shall not be able to get at anybody
With remote hope of an abode do I play on the message
of *Sahana.* —*Geetavitan : Prem.*]

Multani

Avasanna divaloke kotha hate dhire
Karun kapot kanthe gaao Multan.
[Where from in twice fatigued daylight slowly
Sing ye *Multan* in piteous voice of the dove.
—*Sonar Tari : "Manassundari".*]

Pathanera danday vane aasi,
Multanete tan dharechhe vaanshi-
Rabi takhan rakta-raage raanga
Sabe takhan jhikimiki vela.
[The Pathans stand in the forest,
The flute muses on in Multan,
With blood is the sun adorned
Sparkling out then, is the day, —*Katha : "Horikhela".*]

Gungunie savai mile
Katai je gaan kare

Dure laage multane tan,
Pade ase vela.
[Everyone hums together,
Sings so many songs
In the distances, the *taan* in *Multan* goes on
The day dies down.

—*Sishu : "Purano vat"*.]

[Know I not why the ceremonial flute in faded *Multan* has filled the fag end of the day.

—*Mahua : "Navavandhu"*.]

Takhan jhikimiki vela,
Karun klanti legechhe Multane.
[It was a sparkling day then
In *Multan* the piteous tiredness did persist

—*Patraput* : 12.]

Astarabir dehali duare
Vaanshite azike aankilo uhare
Multan raage surer pratima
Gerua ranger chhabi.
[In the doors of *Dehali* of the setting sun
In flute was the portrayed today
The image of tuning in the *Multan raag*
His picture in grey colour.

—*Navajatak : "Sesh Dristi"*.]

Amar diner sesh chhayatuku
Mishaile Multane
Gunjan tar rabe chiradin
Bhule jabe tar mane.
[The last shadow of my day, in Multan thou hast merged, Endless would be its resonance, And thou will forget its meaning. —*Rog Shajyay :* 10.]

Gaan dhare multan sure se
Vela seshe elo jabe basday ...
[In Multan he does attune his song. When at the day's end he comes to vasra ...... —*Chhada :* 10.]

Apni amar konkhane ***
* * * * *
Pather baanshi jaay ki kaye
Bikaal belaar Multane.
[My own self where * * *
* * * * * * * * The flute of the way does tell I know not in the *Multan* of the afternoon.

—*Geetavitan.*]

Mallar, Natmallar, Meghamallar, Suratmallar, Megh
Varsa elaechhe tar meghamayee veni.
Chahita pathik vadhu sunya pathapare.
* * * * *
Mallar gahita kara,
Jharita varasadhara,
Nitanta vajita gia katar parane.
[The rains have spread her tussle of clouds. The way farer bride would look at the vacant way. * * * * * *Who song, *Mallar ?* The fountain of rains would shower and would ring in poignance in the sad heart.

—*Manasi : "Ekaal O Sekaal".]*

Asad hatechhe sesh, mishay mallar desh
Rachi "bhara badarer" sur
[*Asad* is coming to an end, in unison of *Mallar* and *Desh*
I compose tunes for the rainful days.

—*Sonar Tari : "Varsayapan".*]

Bhurjapatay navageet kara rachana
Meghamallar raagini.
[Compose new songs on palm leaves in *Meghamallar raagini-Kalpana* : *"Varsamangal".*]

Mallarete mid milaye
Baje amar pran,
[In harmony of *mid* in *Mallar,*
My beart attunes, —*Utsarga* : *"Jhad".*]

Kakhano ba mallare tar asrudharar
Pagal-jhora jhare.

[Sometimes, agains, in mallar, with his tears the incessant fountain-shower falls. —*Palataka* : *"Mala"*.]

Sedin megher bhare
* * * *
Vakshe jege uthibe mallar
[With the burden of clouds *Mallar* would spring forth in the heart. —*Puravi* : *"Vinahara"*.]

Diganta asila purvadware,
Pathala nirghosh tar bazradhwani mandrita mallare
[The horizon came to the eastern wing and sent her message in the *mallar* through the resonance of echoes of lighting. —*Mahua* : *"Doot"*.]

Sedin bnisan bristi,
Rasta gali bhese jaay jale,
Eka janalar pase Sunit setare
Alaap karechhe suru surat-mallar ...
[That was a day of torrential rains the roads and the lanes were flooded alone in sitar, beside the window the *alaap* had been started by sunit with *surat-mallar...*
—*Punascha* : *"Bhiru"*]

Setarer jhankarer sathe
Sunit dharechhe gaan
Natmallarer sure–
Aaore piyaroa
Rimijhimi barakhana raage
[With the resonance of Sitar Sunit has started singing in the tune of *natmallar* : 'Aaore piyaroa' in *Rimijhimi barakhana raaga.* —*Punascha* : *"Bhiru"*]

Eso nipavane ....
Mallar gaane tava madhusware
[Come to the *kadamva* forest in songs with *mallar* and with your pleasing voice. —*Gitabitan* : *"Seshbarsan"*.]

Oi ase oi ati bhairava harase
* * * * * *
meghamallar raagini

Esechhe varasha, ogo nava-anuragini
[Yor come with boistrous laughter
* * * * * *
meghamallar raagini the rains have come, O newly devoted —*Gitabitan.*]

Gagane gagane apanar mane * * * *
* * * * * *
Meghamallare ki balo amare
Kemane kabo
[Throughout the sky in thy own mind * * * * * * * *
What ye tell me in *meghamallar*
How I can speak.
—*Gitabitan "Lila Nataraj".*]

Mallar raage garjiya othe gahi
[Roar a singing in the maller raaga
—*Varsamangal "Nataraj".*]

Jalbhara nayan pate
Bajichhe megharaagini
[In eyelids full of tears rings *Megharaagini*
—*Chhanda : "Chhander Artha".*]

Ami to diyechhi bhara sravaner
Meghamallar gaan
[I have already given with full *Sravan* the song of *Meghamallar* —*Sanai : "Deoa-Neoa".*]

Yantrata hate niye varsar gaane
Mallarer sur lagalem
[Taking the instrument on the hands and in the songs of rains
I tuned on *Mallar.* —*Sesh Lekha : "Ekti Din".*]

Visva-vanirave * * *
Pavan mallar geet gahichhe aandhar rate.
[With the sounds of the message of the universe * * *the wind is singing *Mallar* songs in the dark night.
—*Geetabitan.*]

Sravan varisan paar haye kee vani aase oi raye raye
*** *** *** *** *** ***
Vijane virahir kane kane sajal mallar gaane gaane
[What a message does in pause come crossing the *sravan* rains *** *** *** *** In the ears at the separatee in loneliness in tearful *mallar* songs.
—*Geetabitan.*]

Kon puratan praner tane * * *
Mallar gaan plavan jagay
Maner madhye sravan gaane
[Which old lure of heart * * * the *mallar* song awakens flood, in the mind with *stavan* songs. —*Geetabitan.*]

Eso eso ogo shyamachhaya ghana din
Ano ano tava mallar mandrita vin.
[Come, O, come the day with full of green shadow, bring, O, bring the veena resounding *mallar.* —*Geetabitan.*]

Azi pallibalika alakaguchchha sajalo
* * * * * *
Jena megharaaginirachita kee sur dulalo
Karnamule.
[The rural damsel adorned her tufts of hair today * * *
As if in ears what a tune she dangled with the composition of *megharaagini.* —*Geetabitan.*]

Azi jharo jharo mukhara badara dine
* * * * * *
Meghamallare sara dinamaan
Baje jharnar gaan,
[Today in dripping murmuring rainy day
* * * * * *
Throughout the day in *meghamallar*,
Echoes the song of the fountain. —*Geetabitan.*]

Amra na gaan gaoar dal je * * *
* * * * * *
Meghamallar dhari jadi ghate anabristi,

[We are the group of non-singers ** ** ** If drought prevails we tune on *Meghamallar*. —*Geetabitan*.]

In usage, we see that *Vasant* and *Vahar* are meant for the spring, and for rains, there are *megh, mallar, desh* and numerous others.

—*Galpaguchchha : "Ekti Ksudra Puratan Galpa* (A Little old Story)

Kanada

Jyotsnakashe chamke othe sashi, * * *
Sanai takhan dwarer kachhe basi
Gabhir sure dharlo kanada.
[In the moonlit sky the moon sparkles, sitting near the door the *sahnai* then tuned up the sombre *Kanada*.
—*Katha : "Horikhela"*.]

Kanadate Sahanate jagite habe je rate-
[In *Kanada* and *Sahara* we'll have to remain awake at night. —*Puravi, "Vinahara"*.]

How deep the call of darkness is
Yon rings *Kanada* in the *Veena* in
Unison with that unbloomed voice of the sky.
—*Shaapmochan*

Banshi baje Kanaday sugabhir tane
Saptarsir dhyaner ahavane
[The flute plays on in the sombre tune in *Kanada* at the call of meditation of the seven saints. —*Seshlekha*]

Vehag

Nidrahin rajanir paraje vehage
[At the sound of *vehag* of the sleepless night
—*Mahua : "Dina"*.]

The night awakened bird * * *
In the *Veena, Kedara* and *Vehag* ring, *Kalangda* does play on.
—*Shaapmochan]*

Hriday majhe lilar karnadhar
Ektarate vehag bajao
Bidhur sandhyay.
[O leader of actions, in the heart play on *Vehag* in *Ektara* in the mournful evening. —*Sanai : "Karanadhar"*.]

Uthichhe alaap mridu madhur vehag tane.
Chandrakare ullasita phullavane jhillirabe tandra ane re
[The slow but pleasant *alaap* is arising with the tune of *vehag* in the joyus forest filled with moonlight, drowsiness is beckoned with the sound of the crickets. -*Geetabitan : "Prakriti"*.]

Amavasyar ratre jemni vehag gaite vasa
Kokilgulor lage dasam dasa
[As soon as one sits in to sing *vehag* on the night before the new moon, the cuckoo is on her tantrums.
—*Geetabitan : "Vichitra"]*

Bhairon

The tune began *alaap* in the *bhairon raagini*—sombre, calm, pensive. It was just like the morning meditation of Mahadev when separation from *Sati* has made him restless.

—*Jogajog*

There is the tune of that peace in the *bhairon* of the the morning of today.

—*Jogajog*

Duar bahire tava asi jabe
Sur kare daki ami bhorer bhairave
[When I come out of your doors, I call attuning in the *bhairav* of dawn —*Navajatak : "Palatak"*.]

Our scholars attuned in *bhairon* and *todi* and said that it was a song for the morning. But is there any replica of the different sounds of the newly awakened world to be found in it ? Not even a little. Then what is the meaning of saying *bhairon* and *todi* as the *raaginis* of the morning? Its meaning is : the scholars have made us hear with all their heart the inherent music of all the sounds and silence of the morning. Any attempt to synchronize it with any external factor of the morning would end in vain.

—Pather Sanchay : "Antar-Bahir"

Moder bhairon raage prabhat rabi raage
Mukh-aadhar.
[In our *bhairon raag* does the morning sun shine,
Amid partial darkness. *—Geetabitan.*]

Lalit

Ratri prabhat hala
Suktara arun-aloy udasi
Toran dware bajilo baanshi vibhas-lalite
[The night dawned.
The morning star is eccentric in the light of the sun.
In the gateway the flute played on the *vibhas-lalit.*

—Punascha : "Mukti"]

Aalor amal kamal * * *
Saratranir veena baaja kamal dale
Lalit raager sur jhare ai
Sewli tale.
[The bright lotus of light * * * The veena of the Autumn Queen plays on amid the group of lotuses, the tune of *lalit raaga* falls at the feet of *Sewli*

—Geetabitan.]

Ogo sundar
Jakhan prabhate prakhar tarun alo
* * * * * *
Vibhase lalite naviner veena bejecche jale sthale
[O Beautiful, then the bright young lustre of the morning * * * * * * the veena of the young is playing on in land and in water in *Vibhas* and *Lalit*

—Geetabitan.]

Kata katha tare chhilo balite. * * *
Base base diba-rati bijane se katha ganthi
Kata je puravi raage kata lalite.
[I had so many words to tell her. * * * Sitting alone day and night I sew those words in so many *Puravi* and *lalit-raagas.* *—Geetabitan.*]

Usha asi mantra padi bajaila lalit raagini.
[The dawn came and chantingly played on the *lalit raagini.*
—*Kadi O Komal : "Ratri".*]

Jagia uthi vaitalik gahichhe joy gaan;
Prasaddware lalitasware baanshite uthe tan.
[Waking up, the morning prayer-singers are singing the song of victory; In the doors of the palace, the flute is attuned with the voice of *Lalit*
—*Sonar Tari : "Suptotthita".*]

This is the role of all songs of invocation. * * * The lord of the mountains has been listening to this dream in *Lalit, Vibhas* and *Ramkeli raaginis* from the time of our grand-fathers and great grand-fathers.

—*Lokasahitya : "Gramyasahitya"*
—Folk literature : "Rural literature".]

Pancham

Sadh jaay vasanter gaan gahibare * * *
Sahasa pancham raag apani se baje.
[There is the desire to sing songs of the spring. * * * The *Pancham raaga* alone tunes on all on a sudden.
—*Chaitali : "Samapti".*]

Tarunira mili tarani bahiya
Pancham sure dharila gaan-
[Plying a boat the youngsters together,
Tuned on songs in the *Pancham* —*Chaitali : "Patita".*]
Bajayechhi baansi pramatta pancham sure,
[The flute is playing on in the intoxicating *Pancham* tune,
—*Naivedya.*]

When the beautiful Radhika, being encircled with companions, came to sight, Govindadas has compared her with the charming *Pancham raagini.*

—Sanjibchandra : *Adhunik Sahitya* (*Modern Literature*)

We know what an indescribable restlessness of beauty the *raagini* instils into our mind. For this, as soon as the comparison between the

Pancham raagini and Radhika is made, an undirected but ever known pleasant idea that arises could not be made possible with any description.

—Sanjibchandra : *Adhunik Sahitya (Modern Literature)*

Where the flute will play on in *Pancham,* the dust of pollens of flowers will fly, shadows will embrace in moonlight-

—*Raja*

Tumi dak diyechho kon sakale ....
Beje othe panchame swar, kenpe othe bandha e ghar,
[You have called early in the morning ......The voice rings on in *Pancham,* this closed apartment trembles up
—*Geetabitan.*]

When the cuckoo began to proclaim the advent of the spring on earth in *Pancham* and *Shyama* became engaged in appreciating the new awakening of the morning in the forest * * *

—*Galpaguchchha : "Ekti khudra Puratan Galpa*" (A Bunch of stories : "A Short Old Story")

Bujhi bajao pancham raage
Dakhin haoar nava jouvaner bhatiali.
[As if you tune on in *Pancham raaga* the spree of the new youth of the southern wind. -*Patraput : "Baanshivallah".*]

In the splendour of colour of the *Asoka* forest the Sehnai was played on in the tuning of *Pancham raaga* along with the vibration of red colour today.

(Navin)

Vibhas

Bhorer akash dhwaniya dwaniya
Uthibe vibhas raagini
[Echoing the sky at dawn, the *Vibhas raagini* will arise
—*Prabhatsangeet : Ahavansangeet.*]

Hriday amar vibhas raage
Kee gaan dharechhe
[What a song my heart has attuned in the *Vibhas raaga*
—*Kheya : "Varshaprabhat".*]

Usharun hate ranga godhulir
Dur diganta pane
Vibhaser gaan hala avasan
Vidhur puravitane.
[From the sun of the dawn to the coloured dusk in the distant horizon the song of *Vibhas* came to a close in the pensive tune of *Puravi* —*Parishesh : 'Tumi'*.]

Roudre dey vairagir vibhaser tan.
[In the sun is offered the tune of *Vairagi's Vibhas-Vithika : "Vichchhed"*.]

Er puravi or vibhaske asirvad kare chale jaak.
Let its *Puravi* bless that *vibhas* and go away.
[—*Lipika : Sandhya O Prabhat*.]

Dakila more jagar sathi
Praner majhe vibhas baje,
Prabhat hala aandhar rati.
[The mate of awakening called me; in the heart does play on *vibhas,* the morning turned into the dark night.
—*Geetabitan*.]

Kedara, Kedari
[In the *veena, kedara* and *vehag* go on, and *kalangda* rings.
—*Shaapmochan]*

Ramkeli

This is the role of all songs of invocation. **** The lord of the mountains has been listening to this dream in *Lalit, Vibhas* and *Remkeli raagini* from the time of the grandfathers and great grand-fathers.
—*Lokasahitya*–"Gramyasahitya"
—(*Folk Literature* : "Rural Literature".)

Rising at dawn he has tuned on in *Ramkeli raagini.*
—*Jogajog.*

Iman Kalyan, Iman bhupali, Iman
Shuru hala horir matamati, Uditechhe faag ranga
Sandhyakase * * *
Dharia iman-bhupalite

Banshi beje uthla drut tale.
[The intoxicating game of 'holi' started. The 'faag' (Coloured dust) is spreading in the coloured evening sky. * * * Tuning on *Iman-Bhupali,* the flute played on in *drut taal. (Katha : "Horikhela"*.]

Imane aaz baanshi baje, man je keman kare
Akashe mor apan tarar tare
[The flute plays on in *Iman,* the mind aches, for the endearing star of mine in the sky —*Puravi* : *"Tara"*.]

Sandhya tarati * * *
Imane bajibe baksher shire shire
[The evening star * * * in *Iman* will play on in every reed of the chest. —*Vithika : Nimantran"*.]

Vasant, Vasant-Vahar, Vasanat pancham
Ami base apan veenate
Vaandhitechhilam sur gujaria vasant panchame.
[Seated with my own *veena* I was tuning with the resonance of *Vasant pancham* —*Mahua : "Pralayagata"*.]

In usage we come to see that for the spring *Vasant* is there.
—*Galpaguchchha :* "Ekti Puratan Galpa"
—(*A Bunch of Stories :* "An Old Story")
Vasant-vahar rings on in the Sitar of *Chaitra*
—*Chhanda : "Chhander Artha"*
—Rhythm : "The Meaning of Rhythm"
Puspita aranyatale prati padakshepe
Manjir vasantaraaag uthitechhe kenpe.
[Under the flowery forest air at every step,
The beautiful *vasantraag* trembles up. —*Sesh Lekha* : 8.]

Aadhkhana sur jemni lagai vasantavahare
Malayvayur dhat phire jaay, jaay, tatksanat ahare
Sei haaoate bichchhed taap palay Sri Radhar.
[When I join half the tune in *Vasantvahar*
O, the nature of the breezy wind instantly changes
In that wind Sri Radha's heat of separation flees away.
—*Geetabitan*.]

Jharo jharo * * jhare ranger jharana * *

* * * * * *

Vaner veenay veenay chhanda baje
Vasantapanchamer raage–
[The fountain of colours * * falls in showers
* * * * * * * *
In the *veenas* of the forest do play on rhythm
In the raaga of *Vasantpancham.* —*Geetabitan.*]

Mor sparshe baje
Je-tantrati tomar veenay,
Tahari pancham sware tomare ki nisheshe chinay
Tomar vasanta-raage.
[With my touch
The tune that plays on in your *Veena*
Does it make you known till the last with its *pancham* voice
In your *Vasant-raag?* —*Mahua : "Dina".*]

Ami tomar sange bendhechhi * * *
* * * * * *
Banshari bajai lalite-vasante
[I have stringed myself with you * * * * * * * * * *
I play on the flute in *Lalit* and *Vasant* —*Geetabitan.*]

Dipak

Aagoon lagalo kutire * * *
* * * * * * * * *
Pralaymatta ramanir kane
Bajila dipak raagini.
[Fire was set on in hutments * * * *
* * * * * *
In the ears of the lady intoxicated in destruction,
The *Dipak raagini* tuned on.
—*Katha : "Samanyakshati".*]

Lest he speaks any word without harmonizing the tune with the *Dipak* of his lecture of that day, * * *

—*Ghare Baire*

The tune of the *Dipak raagini* of the morning that was so

interesting as if somebody sprinkled water meant for washing utensils.

—*Ghare Baire*

Dipak tane uthuk dhwani
Dipta praner harsa.
[Let the echo arise in the tune of *Dipak*
The laughter of the illuminated heart. —*Valaka* : 4.]

Kakhano dipak raage chamak lage
Tara bristi jhare.
[Sometimes senssation spring forth in the *Dipak raaga*
The rains of stars shower. —*Palataka : "Mala".*]

Chhayanat

Kon gahan aranye * * *
Dhara-adharar majhe
Chhayanater raaginite amar banshi baje.
[In what a dense forest * * * Amid the touchable and the untouchable
My flute plays on in the *raagini* of *Chhayanat*
—*Geetabitan.*]

Kon khepa Sravan chhute elo Aswineri aanginay
* * * * * * * * *
Mathe mathe pulak lage chhayanater nrityaraage,
[Which eccentrie *Sravan* came running in the
Courtyard of Aswin * * * * * *
Joy spreads in every field in the dancing *raaga* of *chhayanat.* —*Geetabitan.*]

Je chhayare dharbe bale * * *
* * * * * * * * *
Aaz sarater chhayanate mor raaginir milan ghate
[The shadow to be caught * * * * * *
* * * * * *
In the *chhayanat* of today's autumn the union of my raagini takes place, —*Geetabitan.*]

Sohini raage milate meed
Chander Kshinaloke
[To synchronize *meed* in *sohini raaga*
In the faded light of the moon —*Parishesh : 'Vichitra'*.]

Sarang, Gourasarang

Dhusarvasan, he vaisakh, * * *
Trishnakarun sarang-tane.
[O Vaisakh with dresses of grey, * * *
In piteous thirst of *Sarang*-tune.
—*Nataraj : "Samvodhan"*.]

Amar tapta madhyanyer sunyata theke uchhvasita
Gour-saranger alaap
[Overflowing from the emptiness of my heated noon
The *alaap of Gour-sarang.* —*Patraput* : 12.]

Samasta e chhandabhanga asangati-majhe
Sanai lagay tar saranger taan,
[Amid all these break-away rhythmic inconsistencies
The tune of *sarang* does the *sehnai* play on.
—*Sanai : "Sanai"*.]

At least I do not feel the *Sarang raaga* as the tune of noontime in my heart.

—*Pather Sanchay : "Antar-Bahir"*.

E akashveenay goursaranger alaap–
Se alaap aschhe sarvakaler
Nepathya theke.
The alaap of *Gourasang* is in this *akashveena*
From the backdrop of all time is that
alaap coming.

Bhupali

Geyechhe gokuler goyal-gatha
Bhupal, Multani sure

[Has sung the songs of the dairy anecdotes of heaven in *Bhupali* and *Multani* tunes —*Kahini* : '*Gaanbhanga*'.]

Plays on the Esraz slowly on the roof-top that song of the *Bhupali* tune of his elder brother :

—*Jogajog*

Olo shefali, * * *
Amar sanjhe baje tomar karun bhupali
[Hello Shefali, * * *
In my evening your tragic bhupali rings. —*Geetabitan.]*

Varoa, Piloovaroan, Sindhuvaroan

Ekdin vajlo sanai varoan sure,
* * * * * *
Vadite elo natun bou
[One day the sehnai played on in the tune of *varoan*
* * * * * *
The bride in the house came.
—*Chhada : "Granthaparichay"*.]

Eman samay ekdin vajlo sanai varoan sure,
Vadite elo natun bou.
[At that time the sehnai once played on in the tune of varoan,
The bride in the house came. —*Chhelevela* : 7.]

Kakhano va vasanter sesh prahare klanta nahavater piloovaroan
Sometimes, again, in the last hours of the Spring, the *Piloovaroan* of tired *nahavat.*
—*Lipika : "Satero Vachhar".*

Hathat sandhyay
Sindhu-varoay lage taan
[Suddenly in the évening,
Tune embraces *Sindhu varoan*
—*Punascha : Vanshi.*]

An auspicious ceremony was held in the house, and so towards the afternoon the *nahavat* began to be played on in the *varoan raagini* from the top of the nearby state.

—*Panchabhut : Apurva Ramayana.*"

Finishing *Multan-varoan* the *Puravi* began to be played on in the *nahavat* amid the golden darkness of the sunset time.

—*Panchabhut : "Apurva Ramayana"*

Paraj, Paraj vasant

Nidrahin rajanir paraje vehage
[In *Paraj* and *vehag* of the sleepless night.-*Mahua : Dina*.]
[On that day the perplexed *meed* of *paraj* in the *veena*.
—*Shaapmochan*.]

The *Gandharva Ostads* with *Tamvura* on their shoulders, were very meticulously tuning on in *Paraj-Vasant*.

—*See* : 12.

Dhanasri Dhanasi

Setarer tare dhanasi
Meede meede unthe uthe bajiya
[The *Dhanasi* in the strings of the *sitar* plays on in every meed. —*Sfulinga* : 246.]

Dhanasrite sanai baje Kunjababur fatake
[In the gate of Kunjababu the *sehnai* in Dhanesri plays on. —*Granthaparichay : "Chhada"*.]

Upar talay haoar dolay navin dhane
Dhanasri sur murchhana dey sabuj gaane.
[With the swing of the wind above the new paddy
The tune of Dhanasri in green songs does resound.
—*Navajatak : "Bhumikampa"*.]

Todi

Our scholars attuned in *bhairon* and *todi* and said that it was a song for the morning. But is there any replica of the different sounds of the newly awakened world to be found in it? Not even a little. Then, what is the meaning of saying *bhairon* and *todi* as the *raagini-s* of the morning ? Its meaning is : the scholars have made us hear with all their hearts the inherent music of all the sounds and silence of the morning. Any attempt to synchronize it with any external factor of the morning would end in smoke.

—*Pather Sanchay : "Antar-Bahir"*

Khamvaz

I do not know in which house the wedding ceremony took place. The melanchely tune of *Khambaz* spread a scarf in the sky of the town.

—*Sahityer Pathey* : "*Sristi*"

Kalangda

Veenay vazte thake kedara, vehag
Vaje Kalangda.
[In the veena *Kedara* and *Vehag* go on
Plays on Kalangda. —*Shaapmochan*.]

Kafi Sindhukafi

Holir dine kata kafi
[So may *Kafi* on the day of 'holi'.
—*Kahini : "Gaanbhanga"*.]

Asavari

The day has grown old, the roof has been flooded with the scorching sun, * * * a song came to the mind : its tune is *asavari.* That song begins with, 'Vansari, hamari re' (O flute, thou art mine).

—*Jogajog*

Gouri

Moreover, that *yatra* performer, the eminent blind singer Srinivas who sat on its platform in the evening, played on the Violin and sang 'Gone, gone are the days, in the *Gouri raagini* ....

—*Vichitra Pravandha : 'Sarojini Prayan'*
(*Miscellaneous Essays* : "The Death of Sarojini").

Desh

And, for rains, *megh, mallar, desh* and numerous others.
-*Galpaguchchha : "Ekti kshudra Puratan Galpad"* (*A Bunch of Stories* : "A little Old Story").

Asad hatechhe sesh, mishay mallar desh
Rachi 'bhara badarer' sur.
[The *Asad* is coming to an end, uniting *mallar* and *desh,*
I compose the tune of full rainy season.
—*Sonar Tari : "Varsa Yapan".*]

Vahar

In usage we come to see that for the spring,
Vasant and *Vahar* are there * * *
—*Galpaguchchha : "Ekti Kshudra Puratan Galpa"* (*A Bunch of Stories* : "A little Old Story").

Yogia

Yogia raagini gaay ke re
Dhire dhire sur tar milaichhe charidhar
Achchhanna karichhe re prabhate re.
[Who sings the yogiya raagini,
Slowly its tune is in unison everywhere,
And is enchanting the morning.
—*Kadi O Komal : "Yogia".*]

Sindhu, Sindhu-Varoan, Sindhu Kafi

Hathat sandhyay
Sindhu-varoayay lage tan,
Samasta akase baje
Anadikaler virahavedana.
[Suddenly in the evening
Tune embraces sindhu-varoan
In the whole sky rings
The pangs of saparation of time *sans* beginning.
—*Punascha : "Vaanshi".*]

The quotations in connection with the usage of *raaga-raagini*-s in accordance with the time of day and night that I have referred to from the few books on music from the ancient time upto the twentieth century, bear references to three words such as *'prahar'*, *'yam'* and *'danda'*. Thinking over expositions of the true meanings of these three words to the readers of this era, what has been written by Haricharan Bandyopadhyay in his *Bangla Bhasar Abhidhan (Dictionary of the Bengali language)* is quoted below :

"Prahar	—	The eighth part of the day, three hours.
Yam	—	The eighth part of day and night, three hours.
Danda	—	Twenty-four minutes."

Of the tunes that we have come to learn from Gurudev's poems, songs and other writings, I think there is need for some discussions on *Vijoya* and *Aagamani* songs.

In this country of ours, numerous *aagamani* and *vijoya* songs were composed and sung in the morning centering the ceremony of the *Durga Pooja* in the nineteenth century. Only the learned Bangalee singers would sing these songs. In this matter, the statements of Gurudev's two elder brothers are remarkable. In his memoirs Satyendranath Tagore wrote :

> "On the day of *Vijoya,* Vishnu (Chakraborty), our house musician would come to sing *aagamani* and *Vijoya* at dawn. Just as the songs of the *yatra* are original, so was Vishnu's song classical. How marvallous it appeared! Hearing him, the audience were charmed."
>
> Jyotirindranath Tagore informs : "On the day of *Vijoya* the songs of the singer, Vishnu, would be held in our house in the morning."

As the singers of *Ostadi* (classical) songs would sing the songs in the morning, evidence from Gurudev's writings that those were sung in the *raaga-raaginis* of those days, are found. He informs that these songs have been heard "from the time of our grandfathers and great grand-fathers in *Lalit, Vibhas* and *Ramkeli raaginis-s*." These three are known as the *raagini-s* of the morning.

Although there is a reference to the *sahana raagini,* Gurudev used it in most cases by assimilating it with the joyous fastivals of the Bengalees that is centering it around the various functions like weddings, unions, auspicious days.

In ancient books on music, we do not come across such directions. The only reference to this is to be found in the book *Sangeet Saar* by Kshetramohan Goswamy, the court-singer of Jatindramohan and Sourindramohan Tagore, and published in the nineteenth century. In that book, the reference to a few *raagini-s* that he has made as "should be sung in festivals and auspicious activities" also includes the *sahana*. Obviously, as this *raagini* was used on the day of the festival or at the time of auspicious functions in songs and music, Kshetramohan informed this in his book. Gurudev also supported this view and expressed his attitude in his songs, poetry and writings.

The songs that Gurudev composed from his early youth to the second decade of the twentieth century and those were gradually printed in different books, there, the names of many *raaga-raagini-s* and *taal-s* were mentioned. It is seen that nearly all the *raaga-raaginis* pure and mixed of current Hindi songs in Bengali in the nineteenth century are there. In comparison, the numbers of Bengal's own tunes, other provincial tunes and foreign tunes are very few.

In the second half of his life, Gurudev stopped mentioning the names of *raaga-raagini-s* and *taal-s* in his songs. This was due to the fact that as there were complexities related to mixing of tunes in the songs of those days, it was very difficult for him to analyse them. But if correct knowledge is achieved about the pure and the mixed *raaga-raagini-s* used by Gurudev in the first half of his life, I believe it would be easy to expose the mystery of the mixing of tunes of the songs with nameless *raaga-raagani-s* composed by him towards the latter half of his life. If at any time there is any correct evaluation and analysis of the use of *raaga-raagini-s* in the songs of the second era of Rabindrasangeet, attention must be given to this long list of *raaga-raagini-s* of the first half. Hence, thinking over the above, the following list of the names of *raaga-raagini-s* used in Gurudev's books of songs :

1. *Ahang,*
2. *Asavari, Asavari Todi,*
3. *Alaiya,*
4. *Iman, Iman Kalyan, Iman Bhupali,*
5. *Kalyan,*
6. *Kafi, Kafi Kanada, Kafi Misra,*

7. *Kamod,*
8. *Kanada, Suha-kanada, Nayeki-Kanada, Kanada-Misra, Kanada-Sindhu,*
9. *Kalangda, Kalangda Misra,*
10. *Kedara, Kedara Misra,*
11. *Kukubh,*
12. *Khat, Khat Lalit, Khat Misra,*
13. *Khamtvaz, Khambaz Jhinjhit, Mysore Khamvaz, Khamvaz Misra,*
14. *Khamvar,*
15. *Gara, Gara Bhairavi,*
16. *Gor,*
17. *Goursarang, Goudmallar, Goursarang Misra,*
18. *Gouri,*
19. *Chhayanat, Chhayanat Misra,*
20. *Jangla,*
21. *Jayjayanti, Misra Jayjayanti,*
22. *Jilaf,*
23. *Jhinjhit, Jhinjhit Khamvaz, Karnatik Jhinjhit, Jhinjhit Misra,*
24. *Tori, Desi Tori, Durvari Tori, Nachari Tori, Gujari Tori, Tori Bhariavi,*
25. *Deogiri,*
26. *Desh, Desh Khambaz, Desh Vehag, Desh Sindhu, Desh Misra,*
27. *Deshkar,*
28. *Tilak Kamod,*
29. *Dhun,*
30. *Nat, Natakendra,*
31. *Piloo, Piloo Varoan, Piloo Misra,*
32. *Paraz,*
33. *Puravi,*
34. *Purnasadaz,*
35. *Prabhati,*
36. *Vadabhangsa Sarang,*
37. *Vasant, Vasant Vahar, Vasant Misra,*
38. *Vahar, Vahar Misra,*
39. *Varoan, Misra Varoan,*
40. *Vangali,*
41. *Vibhas, Vibhas Misra,*
42. *Valaveli, Devagiri Velaval, Velavali Misra,*
43. *Velavati,*

44. *Vehag, Vehag Khamvaz, Misra, Vehag,*
45. *Vehagara,*
46. *Vagesri, Vagesri Misra,*
47. *Veloar,*
48. *Bhairon, Bhairon Misra,*
49. *Bhairavi, Asha Bhairavi, Sindhu Bhairavi, Ananda Bhairavi, Bhairavi Misra.*
50. *Bhatiari,*
51. *Bhupali, Jangla Bhupali, Bhapali Misra,*
52. *Mallar, Mallar Misra,*
53. *Majh,*
54. *Maru Kedara,*
55. *Multan, Multani, Multan Misra,*
56. *Misra,*
57. *Yogiya, Yogiya Vibhas,*
58. *Raj Vijoy,*
59. *Ramkeli, Ramkeli Misra,*
60. *Lalit, Lalit Vasant, Lalit Kalangda, Lalit Misra,*
61. *Lalitagouri,*
62. *Sankara, Sankarabharan,*
63. *Safarda,*
64. *Sahana,*
65. *Sindhu, Sindhu Kafi, Sindhu Jhinjhit, Sindhu Khamvaz, Desi Sindhu, Sindhu Misra,*
66. *Sindhura,*
67. *Surat, Misra Surat,*
68. *Sohini,*
69. *Hamvir, Hamvir Kedara, Hamvir Vehag.*
70. *Hemakhem,*
71. *Sugrahi Misra.*

After the above, the names of the tunes outside the books on music that we come across are :

1. The tune of *kirtan,* or *kirtan,*
2. The tune of *Baul,* or *Baul, Baul Kirtan,*
3. Foreign tunes,
4. *Bhajan,*
5. Mysore *Bhajan,*
6. *Ramprasadi,*
7. Scotch *Kedara,*

8. The tune of *Saari Gaan.*

From this list it is being seen that the numbers of mixed *raaga-raagini-s* are more than those of pure ones. But it is not that he composed all the mixed tunes. He collected most of these from classical Hindi songs.

In course of discussions on the *raaga-raagini-s* used in Rabindrasangeet we generally say that Gurudev introduced numerous mixed tunes by breaking the rules of the *raaga-raagini-s* of the classical music. How far it is true necessitates calm thinking.

During the whole of the nineteenth century, there was a natural tendency among the composers of Bengali songs, who were educated in the classical Hindi songs to compose songs in the mixed *raaga-raaginis.* A remarkable example of this is to be found in the songs of the eminent signers and lyricists like Ramnidhi Gutpa or Nidhubabu. The names of mixed *raaga-raagini-s* that we find in his book in the printed songs are the following :

1. *Pahadi-Jhinjhit,*
2. *Soghrai Vahar,*
3. *Gara Jhinjhit,*
4. *Adana Vahar,*
5. *Kamod Goud,*
6. *Paraz Kalangda,*
7. *Vehag Jhinjhit,*
8. *Iman Puria,*
9. *Vageswari Kanada,*
10. *Multani Vahar,*
11. *Lalit Bhairav,*
12. *Iman Jhinjhit,*
13. *Bhimpalasi Vahar,*
14. *Bhumpali Kalyan,*
15. *Sindhu Khamvaz,*
16. *Asha Bhairavi,*
17. *Iman Bhupali,*
18. *Elaiya Jhinjhit,*
19. *Kamod Khamvaz,*
20. *Kafi Joyjayanti,*
21. *Kafi Palash,*
22. *Kedara Khamvaz,*

23. *Gada Kafi,*
24. *Jyoyet Jhinjhit,*
25. *Vageswari Adana,*
26. *Vageswari Vahar,*
27. *Vihanga Vihag,*
28. *Bhupali Jhinjhit,*
29. *Malkosh Vasant,*
30. *Malkosh Vahar,*
31. *Multani Palash,*
32. *Yogia Gandhar,*
33. *Ramkeli Lalit,*
34. *Shyam Puravi,*
35. *Mohini Malkosh,*
36. *Sahana Adana*

Dasu Roy or Dasarathi Roy, a Panchali writer achieved great fame in the middle of this century. He was properly educated in classical Hindi songs. His songs were only very popular as lyrical poems in the world of poetry. He was born in 1212 B.E. (1805) and died in 1264 B.E. (1957). In his early youth, he took up the work of composing songs in the Bengali language. The total number of songs he composed till the end of his life is about 840. In those days, those who achieved fame in composing songs by following Dasarathi Roy were Krishnakamal Goswami, Rasikchandra Roy, Gopal Ude, Monomohan Basu, Rajkrishna Roy, Matilal Roy, Brajamohan Roy etc. The only mixed *raaga-raagini-s,* besides pure ones, that Dasarathi Roy used in his songs are :

1. *Ahang Sindhu, Ahang Vinbhas.*
2. *Adana Vahar, Adana Vagesri.*
3. *Alia Vibhas, Alia Misra,*
4. *Kanada Vahar, Kanada Vagesri, Kanada Vasant, Multan Kanada.*
5. *Kalangda Vahar, Kalangda Paraz,*
6. *Khat Bhairavi,*
7. *Jhinjhit Khamvaz, Khamvaz Joyjayanti, Sindhu Khamvaz, Surat Khamvaz,*
8. *Gara Bhairavi, Sindhu Bhairavi, Lalit Bhairavi,*
9. *Misra Chhayanat,*
10. *Joyjayanti Misra, Joyjayanti, Mallar,*

11. *Jhinjhit Ahang, Jhinjhit Ramprasadi, Lum Jhinjhit,*
12. *Misra Tori,*
13. *Paraz Vahar,*
14. *Piloo Khamvaz, Piloo Vavongda,*
15. *Vasant Vahar, Vahar Jangla, Vahar Vagesri, Sahana Vahar,*
16. *Vibhas Misra, Vibhas Ramprasadi,*
17. *Vehag Jangla,*
18. *Bhairon Lalit, Bhairon Ramkeli,*
19. *Mangal Vibhas,*
20. *Misra Ramkeli,*
21. *Yogia Lalit, Lalit Vasant,*
22. *Desh Sindhu,*
23. *Surat Adana, Surat Khamvaz, Surat Joyjayanti,*
24. *Suhini Vahar.*

A few words on the mixed *raaga-raagini-s* of Gurudev's songs, I think, necessitate discussion. We generally think that the *raaga-raagini-s* of classical music are enclosed with strict rules. As Gurudev was against these rigorous principles, he had launched his programmes of the mixing of tunes like an iconoclast. But the fact is different.

In the world of songs of the nineteenth century, there was a natural and forceful atmosphere to compose Bengali songs in the mixed *raaga-raagini-s*. We have got direct evidence to this from the aforementioned lists of mixed *raaga-raagini-s* of the songs of Ramnidhi Gupta or Nidhibabu and Dasarathi Roy. The main reason for providing lists from the songs of these two persons was that both of them were the composers of various Bengali songs of the last century and were also appropriately educated in *Ostadi* music and qualified. It was due to their influence that the world of the Bengali songs of the previous era was directed. Gurudev attained from his very period of birth such a natural atmosphere of mixed *raaga-raagini-s*. He had heard this type of songs many times, knew many songs, and a definite idea about real procedure of mixing tunes also grew in his mind. For this reason, whenever he set tunes on his own songs, then the fusion did not pose difficulty to him. He could easily do that. This means that he never made any endeavour at mixing like an iconoclast. He did so being influenced by the natural fusion of *raagas* of the nineteenth century out of his own. Of course, one must admit that Gurudev had advanced towards the finer method of fusion than the one to be found in the composers of songs of the last era.

Appendix

SONAR BANGLA
RABINDRANATH TAGORE

My *Sonar Bangla,* I love you
Ever your skies, your breeze
Play the flute in my heart.
In *Falgun,* in your mango-grove
The perfume makes me wild with joy.
ah, me.
In *Aghran,* in your fields full of grain
what sweet smile have I seen.
What beauty, what shade, what tenderness, what enchantment
With your *anchal* have you spread
at the root of the bunyan tree
and at the shores of your rivers.
Your voice is like bliss to my ears,
ah, me.
When your face is pale with sadness
my eyes fill with tears.
In this playground of yours mother,
My childhood have I passed;
My life, I know, is blessed
by your dust on my limbs,
At day's end, in the evening
When you light the lamp,
ah me,
Leaving all my play
I come running to you, my mother.
In your fields where cattle graze
and at your ferry-ghat for crossing over to the other shore,
all day in your shadow-covered village lanes where birds
sing in your courtyard filled with grain,

my days then pass away
ah, me,
They are my brothers all, your shepherds and your peasants
At your feet, mother, I make obeisance,
the sacred dust with the crown of my head
Whatever wealth I have in my poverty
I shall lay before you;
ah me;
Never shall I again buy from the outsider
the fatal noose
as garland for my neck.

–Translated by
Amiya Chakraborty
Courtesy :

The Visva-Bharati Quarterly, Vol. VIII, Part III, New Series, Nov. 1942-Jan. 1943, pp. 1-2.

INDEX